PHILIPPIANS
and
PHILEMON

BELIEF

A Theological Commentary
on the Bible

GENERAL EDITORS

Amy Plantinga Pauw
William C. Placher†

PHILIPPIANS
and
PHILEMON

DANIEL L. MIGLIORE

WJK WESTMINSTER
JOHN KNOX PRESS
LOUISVILLE · KENTUCKY

© 2014 Daniel L. Migliore

First edition
Published by Westminster John Knox Press
Louisville, Kentucky

14 15 16 17 18 19 20 21 22 23—10 9 8 7 6 5 4 3 2 1

Scripture quotations from the New Revised Standard Version of the Bible are copyright © 1989 by
the Division of Christian Education of the National Council of the Churches of Christ in the U.S.A.
and are used by permission. Scripture quotations marked RSV are from the Revised Standard Version of the Bible, copyright © 1946, 1952, 1971, and 1973 by the Division of Christian Education
of the National Council of the Churches of Christ in the U.S.A., and are used by permission.

Book design by Drew Stevens
Cover design by Lisa Buckley
Cover illustration: © David Chapman/Design Pics/Corbis

Library of Congress Cataloging-in-Publication Data

Migliore, Daniel L., 1935-
Philippians and Philemon / Daniel L. Migliore. -- First edition.
pages cm. -- (Belief: a theological commentary on the Bible)
Includes bibliographical references and index.
ISBN 978-0-664-23263-4 (hardcover : alk. paper) — ISBN 978-0-664-26012-5 (pbk. : alk. paper)
1. Bible. Philippians--Commentaries. 2. Bible. Philemon--Commentaries. I. Title.
BS2705.53.M54 2014
227'.607--dc23

2013049522

It is not abstract argument, but example
that gives [the church's] word emphasis and power.

DIETRICH BONHOEFFER,
Letters and Papers from Prison

Contents

PHILEMON

Publisher's Note

William C. Placher worked with Amy Plantinga Pauw as a general editor for this series until his untimely death in November 2008. Bill brought great energy and vision to the series, and was instrumental in defining and articulating its distinctive approach and in securing theologians to write for it. Bill's own commentary for the series was the last thing he wrote, and Westminster John Knox Press dedicates the entire series to his memory with affection and gratitude.

William C. Placher, LaFollette Distinguished Professor in Humanities at Wabash College, spent thirty-four years as one of Wabash College's most popular teachers. A summa cum laude graduate of Wabash in 1970, he earned his master's degree in philosophy in 1974 and his PhD in 1975, both from Yale University. In 2002 the American Academy of Religion honored him with the Excellence in Teaching Award. Placher was also the author of thirteen books, including *A History of Christian Theology, The Triune God, The Domestication of Transcendence, Jesus the Savior, Narratives of a Vulnerable God,* and *Unapologetic Theology.* He also edited the volume *Essentials of Christian Theology,* which was named as one of 2004's most outstanding books by both *The Christian Century* and *Christianity Today* magazines.

Series Introduction

Belief: A Theological Commentary on the Bible is a series from Westminster John Knox Press featuring biblical commentaries written by theologians. The writers of this series share Karl Barth's concern that, insofar as their usefulness to pastors goes, most modern commentaries are "no commentary at all, but merely the first step toward a commentary." Historical-critical approaches to Scripture rule out some readings and commend others, but such methods only begin to help theological reflection and the preaching of the Word. By themselves, they do not convey the powerful sense of God's merciful presence that calls Christians to repentance and praise; they do not bring the church fully forward in the life of discipleship. It is to such tasks that theologians are called.

For several generations, however, professional theologians in North America and Europe have not been writing commentaries on the Christian Scriptures. The specialization of professional disciplines and the expectations of theological academies about the kind of writing that theologians should do, as well as many of the directions in which contemporary theology itself has gone, have contributed to this dearth of theological commentaries. This is a relatively new phenomenon; until the last century or two, the church's great theologians also routinely saw themselves as biblical interpreters. The gap between the fields is a loss for both the church and the discipline of theology itself. By inviting forty contemporary theologians to wrestle deeply with particular texts of Scripture, the editors of this series hope not only to provide new theological resources for the church but also to encourage all theologians to pay more attention to Scripture and the life of the church in their writings.

We are grateful to the Louisville Institute, which provided funding for a consultation in June 2007. We invited theologians, pastors, and biblical scholars to join us in a conversation about what this series could contribute to the life of the church. The time was provocative and the results were rich. Much of the series' shape owes to the insights of these skilled and faithful interpreters, who sought to describe a way to write a commentary that served the theological needs of the church and its pastors with relevance, historical accuracy, and theological depth. The passion of these participants guided us in creating this series and lives on in the volumes.

As theologians, the authors will be interested much less in the matters of form, authorship, historical setting, social context, and philology—the very issues that are often of primary concern to critical biblical scholars. Instead, this series' authors will seek to explain the theological importance of the texts for the church today, using biblical scholarship as needed for such explication but without any attempt to cover all of the topics of the usual modern biblical commentary. This thirty-six-volume series will provide passage-by-passage commentary on all the books of the Protestant biblical canon, with more extensive attention given to passages of particular theological significance.

The authors' chief dialogue will be with the church's creeds, practices, and hymns; with the history of faithful interpretation and use of the Scriptures; with the categories and concepts of theology; and with contemporary culture in both "high" and popular forms. Each volume will begin with a discussion of *why* the church needs this book and why we need it *now*, in order to ground all of the commentary in contemporary relevance. Throughout each volume, text boxes will highlight the voices of ancient and modern interpreters from the global communities of faith, and occasional essays will allow deeper reflection on the key theological concepts of these biblical books.

The authors of this commentary series are theologians of the church who embrace a variety of confessional and theological perspectives. The group of authors assembled for this series represents more diversity of race, ethnicity, and gender than any other commentary series. They approach the larger Christian tradition with a critical respect, seeking to reclaim its riches and at the same time to acknowledge its shortcomings. The authors also aim to make available to readers a wide range of contemporary theological voices from many parts of the world. While it does recover an older genre of writing, this series is not an attempt to retrieve some idealized past. These commentaries have learned from tradition, but they are most importantly commentaries for today. The authors share the conviction that their work will be more contemporary, more faithful, and more radical, to the extent that it is more biblical, honestly wrestling with the texts of the Scriptures.

William C. Placher
Amy Plantinga Pauw

Preface

When asked to write this commentary on two of the apostle Paul's letters, I was delighted to accept the invitation. I began my academic career in the area of New Testament studies, having been persuaded by James I. McCord, then president of Princeton Theological Seminary, to interrupt my graduate studies in systematic theology for a brief period to teach New Testament courses at the seminary. I took up the challenge and have never regretted my decision. For three happy years, I taught exegesis courses on the Gospels of Mark and Matthew, theological themes in the New Testament, and various courses on the history of New Testament interpretation. When I returned to the area of systematic theology, I did so with a lasting appreciation of the mutually enriching bond between biblical studies and systematic theological work. It is, of course, no accident that Martin Luther and John Calvin, the magisterial reformers of the sixteenth century, were at the same time theologians of the first rank and superb biblical commentators. It is also no accident that the theology of Karl Barth, the premier Protestant theologian of the twentieth century, has proved to have remarkable staying power in no small part because of his many close, and often provocative, readings of Scripture.

Systematic theology is always in need of careful and fresh study of the biblical texts to free its own work from philosophical straitjackets and hardened orthodoxies and to keep it faithful to its task of reclaiming the gospel for ever-new times and places. Similarly, biblical studies are in constant need of the reminder that these texts are not merely of historical and literary interest but are the Scriptures of a community of faith that returns to these texts again and again for theological and spiritual sustenance and direction. John Calvin, it should be recalled, wrote his *Institutes of the Christian Religion* as a guide to the study of Scripture, and Karl Barth intended his multivolume *Church Dogmatics* as a work of sustained attentiveness to the scriptural witness as living word of God, an attentiveness necessarily incomplete and always subject to correction by new and better understandings of Scripture.

As will become apparent, in the commentaries in this volume I am indebted to and in conversation with the work of many biblical scholars and theologians past and present. I have learned much about Pauline theology from Paul Meyer, J. Christiaan Beker, J. Louis Martyn, Richard B. Hays, Ernst Käsemann, and, of course, from Martin Luther, John Calvin, and Karl Barth. As helpful resources on Philippians, I would mention especially the commentaries of Markus Bockmuehl, Gordon Fee, Peter O'Brien, and Stephen Fowl; and on Philemon, the commentaries of Markus Barth and Helmut Blanke, Joseph Fitzmyer, Ben Witherington III, Cain Hope Felder, Douglas J. Moo, and John Nordling. I am grateful to C. Clifton Black, who read a draft of my commentary on Philemon and made helpful suggestions, and to the anonymous New Testament scholar who read a draft of my Philippians commentary and offered good advice. Many thanks also to the members of adult study groups at the Lawrenceville Presbyterian Church, New Jersey; at the United Presbyterian Church of West Orange, New Jersey; and at a gathering of pastors in the Near East School of Theology in Beirut, Lebanon, all of whom patiently worked through various sections of this volume with me and offered lively responses and wise comments. A special thanks to Amy Plantinga Pauw for inviting me to contribute to the Belief series, and to Don McKim and Julie Tonini for their invaluable editorial guidance. Thanks also to Kate Skrebutenas, reference librarian at Princeton Theological Seminary, for her expert and cheerful assistance on many occasions, and to Teresa Reed, faculty secretary, who greatly lightened the mechanical burdens of readying a manuscript for publication. Finally, I want to thank my wife, Margaret, for encouraging me to take on this assignment and for helping me in so many ways to bring it to completion. All remaining flaws, minor or major, are my own.

Abbreviations

ACCS   Ancient Christian Commentary on Scripture
ANF   *Ante-Nicene Fathers*
CD   Karl Barth, *Church Dogmatics*
CNTC   Calvin's New Testament Commentaries
KJV   King James Version
LCC   Library of Christian Classics
LW   Luther's Works
NPNF[1]   *Nicene and Post-Nicene Fathers,* Series 1
NRSV   New Revised Standard Version
RSV   Revised Standard Version
WJE   Works of Jonathan Edwards

PHILIPPIANS

Introduction:
Why Philippians? Why Now?

In addition to being the preeminent missionary of the early Christian movement, the apostle Paul is one of the truly great letter writers of all time. Although each of his letters has a distinctive appeal, Philippians is a special favorite of many Christians. Relatively brief, it is pastoral, joyful, and theologically rich. Most important, it contains a message that speaks powerfully to the church in every age.

Throughout our study we should keep in mind that we are reading a letter. We will no doubt recognize in it some familiar features of personal letters. With their direct address to their readers (who are often family or friends), their identifiable hand script, and their candid sharing of experiences, concerns, and hopes, personal letters perhaps come closest of all written forms of communication to face-to-face meetings.

The Letter to the Philippians, however, is much more than a personal letter conveying greetings and news to friends. It is primarily a pastoral letter from an apostle to one of the congregations he has founded. Although Paul does not make a point of calling himself an apostle in his Letter to the Philippians, as is his custom in most of his letters, it is clear that he writes as the spiritual leader of his readers and that they acknowledge his leadership. Indeed, the exquisite combination of tender affection and pastoral instruction exhibited in this letter helps to account for its wide appeal.

Even compared with other literary forms in the Bible, Paul's letters stand out as a distinctive form of communication. We will be disappointed if we expect them to read like Gospel narratives that recount the many things that Jesus taught and did and that describe in some detail the events surrounding his arrest, crucifixion, and resurrection. We will also be disappointed if we look in Paul's letters for a running account of the expansion of the early Christian church, such as we have in the book of Acts, or for dramatic visions of the final events of human history, like the ones in the book of Revelation. Philippians and the other letters of Paul are written to particular congregations in particular contexts to address the challenges they face and to offer pastoral instruction and encouragement.

Frequently on the road, moving from one city to another in his missionary journeys, Paul wrote letters to keep in touch with the members of congregations he had founded. Return visits to share their common life in Christ, however desirable, were infrequent or impossible. It was only by letter writing that he could offer, in his own words, the encouragement, warning, and instruction that his young Christian communities needed and that he was so eager to provide.

Since we have a number of letters from Paul, it is fair to ask, Why study Paul's Letter to the Philippians in particular, and why study it now? I offer a fourfold answer to these questions. First, because, the imprisoned apostle offers in this text one of his most eloquent and joyful witnesses to the "surpassing value" (3:8) of knowing and following Jesus Christ as Lord and Savior. Second, because the congregation to whom Paul writes is in many respects like many congregations in our own time, struggling to be faithful, worried about the future, and in need of guidance as they deal with potentially damaging disagreements among themselves. Third, because the church in Philippi finds itself in the complex and diverse religious, social, and political environment of the Roman Empire, where, as in the post-Christendom world of today, the questions of who is really Lord of the world and who deserves our ultimate allegiance and honor are unavoidable and urgent. Finally, because the theology of this letter holds together aspects of the gospel, like belief and practice—"talking the talk and walking the walk," as the familiar contemporary phrase puts it—that are often separated in the lives of many Christians today.

Paul's Letter to the Philippians has found and continues to find many appreciative readers because of its Christ-centered

understanding of Christian faith and life, its summons to joyful confidence in God in the midst of suffering, its moving expressions of
Christian friendship, the literary beauty of many of its passages, and
the window it opens, however briefly, into Paul's own faith journey.
In this letter, the church of Philippi—but also the church of every
time and place—is called to live in "a manner worthy of the gospel of
Christ" (1:27) by sharing in the life of humility and self-giving love
of its crucified and risen Lord.

Paul in Prison

The Letter to the Philippians was written by Paul from prison (1:13,
14, 17). Scholars debate whether this imprisonment was in Rome,
Ephesus, or Caesarea.[1] The resolution of this question, however, is
not of decisive importance for interpreting the letter or discerning
its significance for readers today. Far more important is the simple
fact that Philippians is a letter written from prison by an apostle of
Jesus Christ.

In a memorable painting, Rembrandt depicts Paul in his prison
cell. Having paused for a moment from writing to one of his congregations, the apostle is in deep meditation. He has removed one of
his sandals and his bare foot rests on it, perhaps the artist's reminder
of Paul's many physically demanding missionary journeys. A bright
field of light surrounds the writer, possibly suggesting the presence
of the Spirit of God. Next to Paul's many manuscripts stands a large
sword, symbol of the power of the Word of God but also an omen of
the apostle's coming martyrdom. The crossbars in the window not
only define the place of writing as a prison cell but also remind us of
the crucified and risen Christ who is at the heart of Paul's gospel and
of his own suffering in his apostolic vocation.[2]

The imprisoned author of the Letter to the Philippians was born a
Jew in the city of Tarsus in Asia Minor (Acts 21:39). This city was a

1. A good summary of the arguments is provided by Markus Bockmuehl, *The Epistle to the
Philippians* (London: A & C Black, 1998), 26–32.
2. This painting, *Saint Paul in Prison,* is one of many depictions of Paul by Rembrandt, who was
obviously deeply moved by the life and witness of the apostle.

meeting place of east and west, a center not only of lively commerce but also of renowned academies. The initial schooling and experience Paul acquired in Tarsus would have given him early exposure to the culture of the larger Greco-Roman world and its mélange of religious beliefs and practices. We do not know whether it was in Tarsus that Paul acquired his Roman citizenship, but we do know that this status would eventually provide important legal advantages in his later missionary journeys.

Paul's education continued in Jerusalem, where he was trained in the strict teachings of the Pharisaic school of Jewish law. As a young man, he was, in his own words, "more zealous" for the traditions of his people than many of his peers (Gal. 1:14). Indeed, his zeal would lead him to become a violent persecutor of the church (Gal. 1:13).

Whether as persecutor of the church or as one of its apostolic leaders, Paul would continue to describe himself without hesitation as a person of Jewish descent, "a Hebrew born of Hebrews" (Phil. 3:5), "an Israelite, a descendant of Abraham" (Rom. 11:1).

The most important fact about Paul, however, is neither his Pharisaic training nor his Roman citizenship but instead his personal encounter with Jesus Christ. His persecution of the church came to an abrupt end when he received a revelation of the risen Jesus on the road to Damascus and was given a commission to "proclaim him among the Gentiles" (Gal. 1:15–17). While there are three dramatic descriptions of this event in the book of Acts (9:1–19; 22:6–16; 26:12–18), Paul's own letters provide only sparse details (Gal. 1:15–17; Phil. 3:4–11). Looking back from this meeting with Christ, Paul could say that even before he was born, God had set him apart for his special mission (Gal. 1:15). Convinced of his calling, he endured numerous dangers, deprivations, beatings, and imprisonments as he fearlessly proclaimed the crucified and risen Jesus as Lord in the complex and cosmopolitan world of the Roman Empire (2 Cor. 11:23–28).

To use his own preferred self-designation, Paul was "a slave [or servant] of Jesus Christ" (Phil. 1:1). Still more intimately, he called himself "a person in Christ" (2 Cor. 12:2). His life was centered on love of Christ and the vocation Christ had given him. As evident in the Letter to the Philippians and in his other letters, Paul did not simply preach the gospel to others; he was personally and deeply committed to it. While he understood the purposes of God as profoundly communal in nature, this did not prevent him from calling God "my God" (Phil. 4:19) and Jesus Christ "my Lord" (3:8). The depth of his personal faith shines through the many memorable declarations found in the letter: "For to me, living is Christ and dying is gain" (1:21); "I want to know Christ and the power of his resurrection and the sharing of his sufferings" (3:10); "I can do all things through him [Christ] who strengthens me" (4:13).

Ascribing all that he had accomplished as an apostle to the grace of God (1 Cor. 15:10), Paul considered himself "the least of the apostles" because he had previously persecuted the church (1 Cor. 15:9). As ambassador for Christ, he felt miserable if he did not have the opportunity to preach the good news (1 Cor. 9:16). Every waking moment was devoted to what he describes in the Letter to the Philippians as proclaiming the gospel with "all boldness" (1:20) and straining forward to "the heavenly call of God in Christ Jesus" (3:14).

That Paul's Letter to the Philippians was written from prison augments the power of its message for Christians of every time and place. In our own time, we have learned to respect and even honor letters from prison. During his incarceration prior to his martyrdom under the Nazi regime in Germany, Dietrich Bonhoeffer wrote letters from prison that posed deep questions about the meaning of faith in Christ in the modern world after the collapse of Christendom. "What is bothering me incessantly is the question . . . who Christ really is, for us today." "What do we really believe? I mean, believe in such a way that we stake our lives on it?"[3] Many Christians today continue to find both inspiration and challenge in the strong affirmations and unsettling questions found in Bonhoeffer's prison letters. We might also recall the memorable letter from a Birmingham jail written by Martin Luther King Jr. during the early days of the civil rights movement. King pointedly defended his civil disobedience of unjust laws to fellow pastors who questioned his nonviolent protest

3. Dietrich Bonhoeffer, *Letters and Papers from Prison* (New York: Macmillan, 1971), 279, 382.

tactics as reckless and counterproductive.[4] King's Birmingham letter is a reminder of the opposition that is encountered and the price that often has to be paid by those who dare to speak up for truth and justice. Or think of how the letters of Nelson Mandela from prison in South Africa during the apartheid era have stirred many of their readers to take action in their own country on behalf of the dignity and freedom of all people.[5] As these few examples show, a letter from prison, where the author faces not only serious deprivations but also the possibility of execution, often rings with a credibility that cannot be matched by the supposedly authoritative declarations of secular magistrates or church leaders written in the comfort of their governmental or ecclesiastical offices.

The witness of Paul's Letter to the Philippians, written from prison with faith, courage, and not least with sparkling joy, has compelling and abiding power. In this letter an apostle proclaims the lordship of Christ, and the church of every age—if it has not become complacent, forgetful, or fearful—takes notice.

A Church Troubled by Internal Disagreements

One of the distinctive features of Paul's Letter to the Philippians is the evidence of his very close friendship with members of this congregation. More than any other congregation Paul founded, the church in Philippi faithfully supported his missionary work by providing him with helpers and sending him financial gifts on a number of occasions (Phil. 1:5; 4:15).

In Acts 16:11–40, Luke recounts the story of the travel of Paul and Silas to Philippi and the founding there of a Christian community. Written a number of years after Paul's Letter to the Philippians, the Lukan account is likely a dramatized rendering of the event. In any case, we are told that it all began with the preaching of the Word of God to a group of God-fearing women who had gathered for prayer

---

4. Martin Luther King Jr., *Letter from Birmingham City Jail* (Philadelphia: American Friends Service Committee, 1963).
5. Nelson Mandela, *Let Freedom Reign: The Words of Nelson Mandela*, ed. Henry Russell (Northampton, MA: Interlink, 2010).

by the river on the Sabbath. After one of the women, named Lydia, was baptized along with her family, she opened her home to Paul and Silas. Described as "a dealer in purple cloth" (Acts 16:14), Lydia was evidently a well-to-do merchant of Philippi. From this account, one of the things we learn is that from the beginning women played an important role in the Christian community in Philippi.

According to the story in Acts, during their stay in the city, Paul and Silas were arrested and imprisoned after Paul created a stir by healing a disturbed slave girl who had made a lot of money for her owners by fortune-telling. Her owners were angry because "their hope of making money was gone" (Acts 16:19). In Philippi as elsewhere, the proclamation of the gospel placed Christians at risk in part because it not only challenged the prevailing religious practices but also unsettled the social and economic status quo. The account in Acts further reports that after an earthquake sprung open the doors of the prison, the frightened jailer became a believer and was baptized. Later, when it was discovered that Paul and Silas were entitled to the legal rights of Roman citizens, the magistrates publicly apologized to the two evangelists before they left the city. We do not know how many other visits Paul paid to Philippi, but he fondly remembered his friends in Christ there, and they continued to support him.

Scholars tell us that the city of Philippi was religiously, socially, and economically diverse. In its mixed population were Greeks, Romans, Thracians, and other ethnic groups. Inhabitants of the city "were organized in *collegia,* usually of a religious nature."[6] There were worshipers of "classic Greco-Roman gods and goddesses, Thracian deities, and Oriental cults (Isis)."[7] In addition to its religious diversity, Philippi had different social and economic classes. Some residents of the city were landowners, others farmers or shopkeepers, and many others slaves.[8] No doubt something of this social and economic diversity was also present in the Philippian church. If so, we cannot discount the

6. Chaido Koukouli-Chrysantaki, "Colonia Iulia Augusta Philippensis," in *Philippi at the Time of Paul and after His Death,* ed. Charalambos Bakirtzis and Helmut Koester (Harrisburg, PA: Trinity, 1998), 23.

7. John Reumann, *Philippians* (New Haven, CT: Yale University Press, 2008), 3.

8. See Peter Oakes, *Philippians from People to Letter* (Cambridge: Cambridge University Press, 2001).

possibility that these social and economic disparities were factors in the tensions and quarrels that Paul addresses in his letter. We know that differences in social and economic backgrounds contributed to friction and disagreement among members of other churches that Paul founded (1 Cor. 11:17–22). We are also aware that these factors remain very real challenges in the life of many churches today.

It seems likely, then, that Paul's call to the Philippians to take part in the sufferings of Christ would have had in mind not only social harassment and imperial persecution but also possible clashes between weaker and poorer members of the congregation and those with greater means. As Peter Oakes argues, the situation in Philippi is likely to have had "a strong economic component."[9] This is not to say that economic differences were the only source of tensions in Philippi. Other factors were doubtlessly involved in the disputes that had arisen. As every contemporary pastor and congregation knows, the call to discipleship and unity in Christ has many dimensions—responsible witness to the gospel, the strengthening of faith, concern for social and economic justice, and not least the healing of frayed personal relationships among church members for any number of reasons. Challenges to the church usually come in clusters rather than in the form of one issue alone.

As we shall see, a variety of concerns lie behind Paul's many exhortations in the letter. He pleads with his readers to avoid arguing with each other, to give up feelings of superiority and looking down on others, and to consider the rights and needs of others more than their own. He calls them to live in unity and to help and support each other. A very specific case in point is a disagreement between two women in the church, Euodia and Syntyche (4:2). We do not know the particular nature of their disagreement, but it is obviously part of the larger context of tensions within the church that Paul is addressing in his letter that calls repeatedly for unity in Christ.

While quarrels and conflicts in Philippi were clearly not as severe as those of the church in Corinth, Paul nevertheless takes them seriously. That is because he knows that conflicts in the church often undermine the reality of new life in Christ and the effectiveness of

---

9. Ibid., 99.

its witness. If being in Christ were merely a private affair, divisions in the church would pose no serious threat. For Paul, however, to be in Christ is to take part in a new community—indeed, a "new creation" (2 Cor. 5:17)—called to bear witness to the gospel not only in word but in the manner of its common life and service.

As most Christians today would readily agree, the signs of disharmony in the churches that Paul addresses, whether comparatively minor as in Philippi or full-blown as in Corinth, are far from absent in contemporary church life. Is there a church today that does not experience disagreements and divisions both small and large: minor quibbles over matters like whether to use wine or grape juice in the Eucharist or whether the Sunday worship service should begin at 10:00 or 11:00 a.m.; and major debates over the congregation's core convictions, its mission statement, or the percentage of its budget that should go to mission rather than building improvements, not to mention heated controversies about ministry to undocumented immigrants, peace advocacy, or the marriage of same-sex couples? Today as ever, Christian communities need to hear and heed Paul's bracing challenge to be of one accord in faith and service and to live together "in a manner worthy of the gospel of Christ" (1:27).

A Church Located in a Roman Colony

The church in Philippi faced serious threats from outside as well as potentially demoralizing divisions within. Named after Philip, the king of Macedonia who ruled the area some four hundred years before Paul's missionary journeys, Philippi had become by the first century CE a Roman colony and "a leading city" (Acts 16:12) of the area. Its laws, ethos, and other cultural institutions were modeled after the great capital of the Roman Empire. Some veterans of the Roman army had settled there, and its free residents were considered citizens of Rome. Indeed, "Philippi was almost unique among cities Paul addressed in his letters; it differed from other places he evangelized because of its 'Roman-ness.'"[10] An important dimension of its Roman character was the preoccupation of its residents with

10. Reumann, *Philippians*, 3.

honor and social status. According to Joseph Hellerman, Philippi was "arguably the most status-conscious city in the Roman East, a colony stamped, moreover, with a military mentality sharply attuned (a) to the social stigma of slavery and (b) to the contrasting honor associated with the patriline of an esteemed citizen soldier."[11] Paul is clearly aware of this social and political context of the church in Philippi, and not surprisingly both the language and content of his letter reflects this fact.

It is important to remember that the missionary journeys of Paul represented "the transition of the early Christian movement from the Palestinian farmlands and fishing villages to the mainstream of life and the norms of Roman imperial culture."[12] His proclamation of the lordship of Christ was necessarily a disturbing and even subversive factor in this context. We misread Paul if we view him through the lens of later doctrines of the separation of church and state. We also misread him if we isolate his counsel to Christians to be "subject to the governing authorities" (Rom. 13:1) from his summons to resist intimidation by or accommodation to all opponents of the gospel (Phil. 1:28; Rom. 12:2). What is missing in both cases is awareness of the extent to which Paul's gospel of the lordship of Jesus Christ challenged the ideologies and practices embodied in imperial Rome. The same gospel, rightly preached and heard, continues to challenge the idolatrous claims of empires of our own time.

The ideology of empire was inescapable in a colony of Rome like Philippi. As Peter Oakes writes, "Imperial ideology was all around: on coins, in statues, in processions, games, and feasts, in pictures and inscriptions."[13] Not least, the claims of empire were present in the cult of the emperor. Caesar Augustus was praised as "savior," "lord," the ruler who had established the Pax Romana throughout the known world. N. T. Wright notes that especially in the eastern part of the empire, there was "strong pressure to establish the emperor-cult, not least because special rewards were available for cities that

---

11. Joseph Hellerman, *Reconstructing Honor in Roman Philippi* (New York: Cambridge University Press, 2005), 142.
12. Allen Dwight Callahan, "Dead Paul: The Apostle as Martyr in Philippi," in *Philippi*, ed. Bakirtzis and Koester, 72.
13. Oakes, *Philippians*, 174.

did so."[14] While there is no mention in Paul's letter of any members of the Philippian church being imprisoned or executed for their confession of Christ, these possibilities must have been on the mind of Paul and the readers of his letter, especially in view of his own imprisonment and impending trial.

All this suggests that in our effort to understand the letter of Philippians and its significance for the church today, it would be a serious mistake to overlook or downplay the demands of the imperial cult and the ethos of empire surrounding the church in ancient Philippi. The audacity of Paul's proclamation in Philippians and his other letters immediately stands out in the simple fact that Jesus Christ is confessed not simply as "*our* Lord" (a confession that might readily be tolerated in religiously pluralistic Philippi) but "*the* Lord" (a claim that directly challenged not only the multitude of lords and gods but also the lordship of Caesar and the entire imperial cult). If the good news of the lordship of Christ proclaimed by Paul was unsettling to the dominant powers in the first century, it continues to be disturbing to the reigning powers of our world today. To be sure, the claims of empire that press on the church may be less blatant than they were in the Roman Empire or in Nazi Germany. Still, in often subtle and easily ignored ways, the church today has to contend with idols in many spheres of life: political, economic, cultural, technological, and religious. Who is the Lord worthy of our unconditional trust, and with what kind of power does this Lord rule? Paul's affirmation of Jesus as *the* Lord, in all its personal and political ramifications, is assuredly one important answer to the questions, Why Philippians? Why now?

Central Themes of the Letter

If readers of this commentary were asked what they knew about Paul's teaching, probably a good number would say that he is the apostle who emphasizes the doctrine of justification. According

---

14. N. T. Wright, *Paul: In Fresh Perspective* (Minneapolis: Fortress, 2005), 65. See further: N. T. Wright, "Paul's Gospel and Caesar's Empire," in *Paul and Politics*, ed. R. Horsley (Philadelphia: Trinity, 2000), 173–81.

to this doctrine, being accounted right or made right with God is not something that we achieve. Rather, it is the gracious gift of God given through Jesus Christ and received by faith alone in him. Faith in Christ is not without works, but the works, far from being the cause of a new relationship with God through Christ, are its fruit.

Pauline scholars continue to engage in a vigorous debate about how best to interpret his doctrine of "justification by faith" and "righteousness from God."[15] Some defend the classical Reformation understanding of justification as the new relationship with God based not on our works but solely on the gift of God's forgiveness of our sins in the sacrificial death and resurrection of Jesus Christ.[16] While agreeing in some respects with this understanding, other scholars have offered a "new perspective" on Paul that criticizes introspective and individualistic readings of his theology, reappraises his understanding of Jewish law, and underscores his corporate emphasis.[17] Still other scholars stress an "apocalyptic" reading of Paul's theology that sees the work of Christ as the inaugural event of the cosmic victory of God's righteousness and reign throughout the entire creation.[18]

As I hope to show, all three of these perspectives on Paul's theology have some purchase on his Letter to the Philippians. We will find the theme of God's righteousness as coming from God rather than from ourselves. In addition, we will find an emphasis on not only believing in Christ but also living as a new people in Christ who are

15. For a helpful survey of past and present interpretations of Paul's theology, see Stephen Westerholm, *Perspectives Old and New on Paul: The "Lutheran" Paul and His Critics* (Grand Rapids: Eerdmans, 2004).

16. Martin Luther, "Two Types of Righteousness," in *Career of the Reformer*, LW 31, ed. Harold J. Grimm (Philadelphia: Muhlenberg, 1967), 297–306; see also Mark C. Mattes, *The Role of Justification in Contemporary Theology* (Grand Rapids: Eerdmans, 2004); Mark Husbands and Daniel J. Treier, eds., *Justification: What's at Stake in the Current Debates* (Downers Grove, IL: InterVarsity, 2004); John Piper, *The Future of Justification: A Response to N. T. Wright* (Wheaton, IL: Crossway Books, 2007).

17. N. T. Wright, *Justification: God's Plan and Paul's Vision* (London: SPCK, 2009); James D. G. Dunn, *The Theology of Paul the Apostle* (Grand Rapids: Eerdmans, 1998); Krister Stendahl, "The Apostle Paul and the Introspective Conscience of the West," *Harvard Theological Review* 56 (1963): 199–215.

18. Ernst Käsemann, "'The Righteousness of God' in Paul," in *New Testament Questions for Today* (Philadelphia: Fortress, 1962), 168–82; J. Christiaan Beker, *Paul the Apostle* (Grand Rapids: Eerdmans, 1998); J. Louis Martyn, *Theological Issues in the Letters of Paul* (Edinburgh: T. & T. Clark, 1997).

called to bear witness to his lordship whatever the circumstances. Then, too, we will find Paul's robust hope in the coming completion of all of God's purposes and his expectation of the full participation of the faithful in the glory of God. In brief, this commentary will attempt a reading of Paul's Letter to the Philippians that avoids a reduction of the gospel to a single doctrine or a single aspect of Christian life. For the writer of this letter, the gospel encompasses the righteousness from God that comes through the faithfulness of Christ; the new corporate life in Christ that includes our sharing in his sufferings and in his resurrection power under the direction of his Spirit; and the confident hope that looks to the imminent coming of Christ the Savior and the consummation of life in him to the glory of God.

As is true of all of Paul's letters, many themes are present in his Letter to the Philippians. The more prominent themes can be identified in summary fashion.

First, by means of the celebrated Christ hymn of 2:5–11 that constitutes the centerpiece of the letter, Paul affirms that *Christ Jesus is both Lord of all and the supreme model of Christian life.* Reminding the Philippians that though Christ was equal with God, he humbled himself, taking on the condition of a slave and becoming obedient even to death on a cross, Paul urges his readers to abide in Christ and let their lives be conformed to his way of humility and self-giving love. He calls them to resist the surrounding ethos of power and honor and indeed every self-centered way of thinking and living that sets one's own safety, security, and social status over the needs of others. "Let the same mind be in you that was in Christ Jesus" (2:5) is Paul's central exhortation. Throughout the letter Paul insists that when Christians confess Jesus as Lord, this is every bit a matter of practice as it is of belief.

Second, Paul exhorts the Philippians to put an end to their internal disputes and not give in to the temptations of bickering and quarreling. He appeals to them to *reclaim the unity in Christ that is threatened by signs of disunity among them:* "Stand firm in one Spirit" (1:27); "Be of the same mind" (2:2; 4:2); "Have the same love" (2:2). Paul summons all members of the church to take seriously their unity in Christ, their crucified and risen Lord, and to follow his way of costly regard for others. In our time of polarization, not only in the politics of the wider society but also in the life of the church, it is hard to imagine a word more relevant than Paul's appeal to the church to manifest a new life together of peace, harmony, and mutual helpfulness as a sign of what God in Christ purposes for the whole creation.

Third, the theme of *joy and hope in the midst of suffering* pervades this letter. Paul wants to assure the Philippians that, far from obstructing the spread of the gospel, his own imprisonment and whatever might follow from it, including his possible execution, actually serves to further the gospel. Closely related to this, he offers encouragement to the Philippians who are also suffering on behalf of the gospel. He knows that they live in an environment that is at best precarious and that might become even more hostile. He summons them to rejoice with him as together they stand firm in the faith. This summons speaks as well to Christians today, urging them to live out their discipleship, whatever the circumstances, not in a morose spirit but with abundant joy and confident hope. How could Christians not rejoice and how could their hope not be strong if, as Paul firmly believes, Christ the Lord reigns?

Fourth, Paul gives a personal account of how Christ has turned upside down his understanding of righteousness *from "a righteousness of my own" to "the righteousness from God"* (3:9). As we shall see, his account of his own relinquishment of everything he once considered valuable in order to gain Christ is clearly shaped by the earlier description of the self-emptying and humility of Christ in the Christ hymn and, like that hymn, serves the purpose of urging members of the church in Philippi to join him in making the mind of Christ their own as well.

Finally, we find the theme of *thanksgiving both in giving and in receiving* in a letter written to thank his friends for their generous support of his labors on behalf of the gospel. As already noted, this support took the form of financial aid, but it also included sending personal assistants who sometimes risked their lives in helping Paul in his work. Paul wants to acknowledge these gifts and express his deep gratitude for them. He thus commends the Philippians for their excelling "in the matter of giving and receiving" (4:15). His commendation reminds the church today that life in Christ will express itself in many concrete practices, not least of which is mutual giving and receiving with thanksgiving and prayer to God.

In summary, running through Paul's Letter to the Philippians are the themes of Christ as at once humble Lord and supreme paradigm of Christian life; of unity in Christ that overcomes the forces of dissension; of a readiness to suffer for the sake of the gospel that does not rob us of joy in Christ; of the radical difference between a righteousness of our own and a righteousness from God; and of a life of thanksgiving in mutual giving and receiving.

A Theological Reading of Philippians

Interpretations of texts differ in part because we read them in different contexts, with different questions, and for different purposes. This is true of biblical interpretation, as it is of every interpretive act. Every author of a biblical commentary brings certain assumptions, questions, and objectives to the task. At the outset, it may be helpful for me to say a few words about mine.

First, I approach the text of Philippians as a literary unity even though this remains an open issue among Pauline scholars. An early Christian writer, Polycarp, speaks of several letters of Paul to the Philippians. We do not know whether he was referring to letters other than our text of Philippians that are now lost or to fragments of letters that were later compiled into the single letter known to us. On the basis of careful literary and historical study, a number of modern scholars argue that the present canonical Letter to the Philippians is actually a composite of two or three letters pieced together by the early church. Roughly summarized, these scholars contend that 4:10–20 is an initial letter of thanks for the gift brought by Epaphroditus from Philippi. A second letter, comprising 1:1–3:1a (perhaps also including 4:2–9 and 4:21–23), was written to accompany the return of Epaphroditus to Philippi after he had recovered from a serious illness. Finally, 3:1b–4:1 is a separate letter in which Paul attacks those who teach and live in ways contrary to the gospel he proclaims.

The possibility that the Letter to the Philippians is actually a composite of letters certainly cannot be discounted. Nevertheless, while there are rough edges and some abrupt transitions in the letter in its present canonical form, I think it holds together and makes sense when read as a single, integral writing.[19] After all, Paul is writing a letter that speaks from the heart to one of his congregations who face particular challenges in their own context. He is not engaged in writing in the classical style of a systematic theological monograph where everything fits in its place and the transitions from one topic to another are carefully crafted.

Second, I assume that in this as well as in his other letters, Paul has a clear message and a coherent theology. This is not to say, however, that I work under the supposition that there is a single *doctrine* that forms the core of all of Paul's letters. Rather, I hold that Paul's theology has a *central focus*: the history of Jesus Christ in whose crucifixion and resurrection the God of Israel has performed a new and definitive act of free grace for the salvation of the world. The fullness of this history, however, cannot be reduced to a single doctrine. Moreover, my assumption of the coherence of Paul's theology does not mean that every aspect of his theology is explicitly deployed in each letter. As Gordon Fee and others have noted, if we had only the Letter to the Philippians, it would be impossible to derive from it all that we know of Paul's theology.[20] Nevertheless, it makes little sense to try to read the Letter to the Philippians in a vacuum, as though Paul had never written any other letters. Hence I will not hesitate to make reference where appropriate to Paul's other letters under the assumption that he does have a coherent theology even though not all of it is recoverable from the Letter to the Philippians or any other single letter of his.

Third, I am in agreement with contemporary Pauline scholars who emphasize the crucial role of narratives in his ethical instruction and guidance of the church.[21] The prominent role of narrative

---

19. This is the view of the majority of contemporary Pauline scholars, including Bockmuehl, *Philippians*, 20–25; Peter T. O'Brien, *The Epistle to the Philippians* (Grand Rapids: Eerdmans, 1991), 10–18; Gordon D. Fee, *Paul's Letter to the Philippians* (Grand Rapids: Eerdmans, 1995), 21–23.

20. Fee, *Philippians*, 20.

21. Especially helpful in this regard are the writings of Stephen E. Fowl, *Philippians* (Grand Rapids: Eerdmans, 2005); and Richard B. Hays, "The Role of Scripture in Paul's Ethics," in *Theology and Ethics in Paul and His Interpreters* (Nashville: Abingdon, 1996), 30–47.

in the Letter to the Philippians is preeminently seen in his use of the Christ hymn in chapter 2. Paul urges his readers to conform their thinking and practice to the cruciform way of Christ described in this hymn. The brief narratives of Timothy and Epaphroditus and Paul's more extensive story of his own faith journey serve as additional though clearly secondary examples in Paul's call to Christian life and service. All this means that for Paul, Christian life is not a matter of being obedient to a set of abstract moral principles but of learning to discern in particular situations what is conformable to the story of the crucified and risen Christ and what builds up the faith, love, and hope of the people of God.

Finally, in correspondence with the goal of the commentary series of which this volume is a part, I will offer a "theological reading" of Philippians. The desirability and the danger of a theological reading of Scripture is a matter of considerable discussion today. The danger involved in this undertaking is that of trying to read more out of the text than is actually in it or finding in it what we want to find in it. The technical way of describing this danger is doing *eis*egesis rather than *ex*egesis. We must respect the fact that this letter was written to a particular congregation in a colony of the Roman Empire in the first century. This means that the feet of every serious commentator must be planted on the solid ground of the text. I happily express my gratitude for all that I have learned from New Testament scholars who have devoted their lives to careful literary-historical readings of the text of Philippians and to their ventures of theological reflection based on these readings.[22]

The approach taken here, however, will be to privilege reflection on the theological content of this letter as a canonical document of the church that lives by the message of its Scriptures.[23] Accordingly, my task as author of this commentary and my invitation to its readers is to explore not only what Paul's letter says to the Philippians but also, and of equal importance, what it says to us. Although sections of the commentary titled "Further Reflections" are especially dedicated to theological meditations on themes of the letter, I have

---

22. For authors of commentaries especially helpful to me, see the preface to this volume.
23. John Calvin and Karl Barth are magisterial theological readers of Scripture, and I gratefully acknowledge my debt to both.

tried to lift up the theological and pastoral dimensions of the material throughout.

In spite of the ever-present danger of overinterpretation, the effort to read Philippians and other scriptural books theologically is both necessary and desirable. For most of its history, the church has read Scripture this way, asking whether there is a Word of God for us today in these texts and how Christian life in our own time and place should be guided and governed by these texts. Just as Christians in times past were convinced that Scripture bears witness in the power of the Holy Spirit to the living Word of God, we too are invited to approach the text with that faith, memory, and hope. For the study of Philippians offered here, this means reading the letter in a way that, while honoring literary-historical concerns, persistently wrestles with the theological subject matter of the text and dares to listen for a message directed to the church today. In other words, we undertake to read Philippians as people of faith who are eager to learn what it means to confess Jesus Christ as Lord and become faithful and responsible Christian witnesses here and now. Like the Philippians, we too are in need of the apostle's encouragement, warning, and counsel. Even if we do not live in a Roman colony of the first century, the gospel of Jesus Christ to which Paul bears witness contains the word of life for every time and place. It is in this spirit that we turn to a detailed study of the Letter to the Philippians.

1:1–1:2

Greetings

The opening of Paul's Letter to the Philippians is similar in form to the customary greetings with which letter writers in the Greco-Roman world of the first century began their message: first, the identification of the writer; next, the name of the person or persons to whom the letter is being written; and finally, a brief word of greeting.

1:1a
The Author

While his greetings generally follow this conventional pattern, what a difference faith and life in Christ makes in the opening words of a letter from Paul. As in all his letters, he wants to identify himself, and those to whom he is writing, primarily in relation to Jesus Christ. This is no mere literary convention for Paul. As he writes in another letter, "If anyone is in Christ, there is a new creation: everything old has passed away; see, everything has become new!" (2 Cor. 5:17). Christ has changed everything in Paul's life: how he thinks and speaks of God, how he understands his vocation, how he makes decisions and relates to others, even how he begins (1:1–2) and ends (4:23) his letters. Note how often the name of Jesus Christ appears already in these opening two verses. Paul calls Timothy and himself "slaves" or "servants" (*douloi*) of Christ Jesus, writing to "all the saints in Christ Jesus who are in Philippi," with a blessing of "grace to you and peace from God our Father and the Lord Jesus Christ." *Of* Christ Jesus, *in* Christ Jesus, *from* the Lord Jesus Christ, and as we shall hear later, *for*

Christ, *with* Christ, and *to* Christ. If the philosopher Spinoza is often called the God-intoxicated philosopher, Paul of Tarsus may aptly be called the Christ-consumed apostle.

Several features of Paul's salutation in this letter are worth noting. For one thing, he places alongside his own name the name of his fellow worker Timothy. Not Paul alone, but "Paul and Timothy" together send greetings to the Philippians. While there is no reason to believe that this means that Timothy has coauthored the letter with Paul, Timothy's value as a pastor was well known to the Philippians (2:22), and Paul is happy to set his name alongside his own. This gracious gesture already tells us something about Paul's understanding of Christian life and ministry, as well as signaling an important part of the message he wants to communicate. The Christian is not a Robinson Crusoe or a Lone Ranger. Not even an apostle goes it alone.

> A hero, a genius, a "religious personality" stands alone; an apostle has others beside him like himself and sets them on his own level.
>
> Karl Barth, *Epistle to the Philippians*, 9.

Paul needs and wants the help of others in the ministry of the gospel. By placing the name of Timothy next to his own, Paul implies that, just as Christian life and service flourish only in community, so true leadership in this community is not a solo performance but a shared responsibility. Paul wants it to be known that he is the leader of a missionary team just as he writes not to a collection of isolated individuals but to a community of believers who are one in Christ and who together share in the service of the gospel. As we shall soon see, the call to unity, solidarity, and cooperation in Christ is one of this letter's themes, making it entirely appropriate that in the very first words we read not just the name Paul, but "Paul and Timothy."

Another notable feature of the salutation is the term Paul uses to describe himself. In the opening of his other letters, Paul regularly identifies himself as an "apostle" of Jesus Christ (e.g., Gal. 1:1; 1 Cor. 1:1; 2 Cor. 1:1; Rom. 1:1). Here in Philippians, Paul describes himself, not by his apostolic office, but simply as one of the "slaves" or "servants" of Christ. For Paul, the title "slave of Christ Jesus" is not ornamental speech or a mere rhetorical flourish; neither is it a demeaning or degrading title. On the contrary, it summarizes what Christian faith and life are all about. As Paul will affirm in the central passage of the letter, "slave" is precisely what Christ chose to become for

> I am among you as one who serves.
>
> (Luke 22:27)

our sake, and in doing so, he radically transformed the meaning of the word. If God has come to the world humbly in the form of a "slave" (2:7), what greater dignity could one have than to be a faithful servant of the servant Lord?

So much is Paul's sense of his own personal identity tied to Christ that he can say not only that he is one of the slaves of Jesus Christ, but also that, as he will soon put it, "to me, living is Christ" (1:21). We will have to return to this mind-stretching statement later. For now, it is sufficient to say that the author of our letter knows himself and his purpose in life as fully and irrevocably defined by his relationship to Christ. His entire being is given over in love, dedication, and service to his living Lord. Such an understanding of identity is not easy for many readers today to grasp. Many think of their personal identity as something given by their DNA, or perhaps by family or ethnic or national history, or perhaps by their own decisions, experiences, and achievements. Paul does not identify himself in these ways. For him, identity is not something he gives to himself, or something given to him by inheritance or the surrounding culture, or even something he has by virtue of his relationship to those whom he addresses in this letter. His identity is given to him by Christ whom he serves. He is who he is by the grace of his Lord and by his calling and service to the gospel.

The absence of the term "apostle" at the very beginning of the letter, frequently found at the beginning of Paul's other letters, signals a "relationship of extraordinary trust" between this author and his readers.[1] Paul unquestionably feels at home with this congregation, more so than with any of his other congregations. He does not start off by playing his apostolic card. He does not have to defend his apostleship as being on a level with that of Peter, as in, for example,

---

1. Karl Barth, *The Epistle to the Philippians* (Louisville, KY: Westminster John Knox Press, 2002), 10.

the Letter to the Galatians. Of course, both Paul and the Philippians know that he has apostolic authority, as the content of the letter clearly demonstrates. But with this particular community of Christians he does not have to make a special point of it. So he begins his letter by identifying himself simply as someone in the service of his and their Lord. In much the same way, a pastor who has blessed and been blessed by a congregation for many years might comfortably omit all the fancy titles—Rev., DMin, PhD—from her newsletter to her parishioners and simply say, "From pastor Jane, in the service of Christ."

1:1b

The Readers

Paul's salutation identifies not only himself but his readers as well in relationship to Christ Jesus. He writes "to all the saints in Christ Jesus who are in Philippi" (1:1b). It is important not to miss the little word *all* in this salutation and in the verses immediately following (1:4; 1:7; 1:8). Paul writes not just to the wealthier members of the congregation in Philippi, or to its charter members, or to some special clique, or to those who might like to think of themselves as special favorites of Paul. He writes to all the saints who are in Philippi. This little word *all,* like the word *servant* and like the inclusion of Timothy as fellow servant, again announces what will become a major theme of the letter. In the repetition of this single word *all,* Paul underscores the importance of unity, solidarity, inclusivity, and communion in Christ in contrast to the infighting, quarreling, and attitude of "us" versus "them" that is always a threat in the life of the church just as it is in every other form of human society. While there may be nothing in Philippi like the severe infighting present in the church in Corinth, there are nevertheless both external conditions and internal disagreements that threaten the unity even of this most beloved of Paul's churches. Paul is sensitive to this threat and wants his letter from the start to be understood as personally addressed to all the saints.

Note, too, that Paul sends his letter to all "the saints" in Christ Jesus who are in Philippi. The word *saints* here and elsewhere in Paul's letters does not refer to people who live especially holy lives. Rather, it designates people elected by God in Jesus Christ and called to be his disciples and servants. True saints do not look to themselves for evidence of their holiness and certainly do not strut before others as "holier than thou." They recognize that they have no holiness apart from Christ. It is not something they have earned and can claim as their possession. Confessing Jesus as Lord, the saints find their holiness in what their Lord has done for them and what he enables them to become and do in the service of the gospel. Note further that these saints to whom the letter is written do not hover somewhere in the clouds, above every particular time and place, like phantasms or ghosts. Their feet are on the ground here in this world. They live "in Philippi," a colony of the Roman Empire in the first century, just as other saints to whom Paul writes dwell not in some never-never land but in places like Rome, Corinth, and Galatia, and in our own time, too, in particular places like Copenhagen, London, Seoul, New York, San Francisco, and Peoria.

Somewhat surprisingly, the "all" to whom Paul writes explicitly includes "the bishops and deacons." I say surprisingly because Paul does not mention bishops (he does once mention a "deacon," Rom. 16:1) in the other letters generally acknowledged by NT scholars as having been authored by him. Although there has been a good bit of speculation on the part of commentators, we do not know for sure the precise duties of these leaders. We can say with some confidence, however, that we are not to understand "bishops and deacons" in just the same sense these positions will come to have in later centuries of Christian history. While the terms indicate that there are leaders ("overseers" and "helpers") of the congregation, this does not mean there is an established ecclesiastical hierarchy in Philippi, or for that matter in any other of the Pauline communities. Certainly we are not to think of the sharp dividing line between clergy and laity that developed in later centuries and that continues to characterize the life of many churches today. Paul addresses all the saints, all who, like him, are recipients of the grace of Christ and are called to holy life and faithful service in him. Whatever particular responsibilities members of the community may have in their common life, all who are in Christ are of equal dignity.

Whatever their duties, why does Paul single out these leaders of the Philippian community in his salutation? Some commentators think it shows "a nascent concern for church government" on Paul's part.[2] After all, capable leadership and a division of responsibilities are important factors in Christian community, as they are in all forms of social life. In his letter to the church at Corinth, Paul elaborates on the importance of distinctions of gifts within the community (1 Cor. 12:4–11). By making special reference to "the bishops and deacons" in his salutation, Paul may simply want to recognize the valuable service these leaders are providing in the ongoing life of the community. Other commentators suggest that Paul may mention these leaders at the very beginning of his letter to enlist their help in addressing the discord that threatens the church's unity in Christ and the strength and solidarity of its witness.

There is, however, another possibility. As Joseph Hellerman has shown, Philippi was a colony "preoccupied with social status."[3] By calling himself a "slave of Jesus Christ" rather than using the honorific title of apostle, and by singling out the leaders of the congregation for special mention, Paul may be addressing "the special temptation to privilege positions of honor and status" that marked the social environment of Philippi.[4] In his opening words, Paul is already beginning to sound a major theme of the letter: the greatest honor is not to rule but to serve.

> **He calls himself a slave and not an apostle. This is a great honor, to be a slave of Christ.**
>
> John Chrysostom, *Homily on Philippians,* cited in *Galatians, Ephesians, Philippians,* ed. Mark J. Edwards, ACCS 8 (Downers Grove, IL: InterVarsity, 1999), 217.

2. Markus Bockmuehl, *The Epistle to the Philippians* (London: Hendrickson, 1998), 54.
3. Joseph H. Hellerman, *Reconstructing Honor in Roman Philippi: Carmen Christi as Cursus Pudorum* (New York: Cambridge University Press, 2005), 199 n. 35.
4. Ibid., 162.

1:2

The Blessing

The last clause of the salutation is Paul's blessing: "grace to you and peace from God our Father and the Lord Jesus Christ" (1:2). Grace and peace—there is a world of meaning in each of these words, and together they may be said to comprise a brief description of the whole of life in Christ. In these two words we have a "compact expression of [Paul's] whole message."[5] *Grace* (in Greek, *charis;* cf. Hebrew *hesed,* "steadfast love") is Paul's word for the free gift of God's love, forgiveness, and new life embodied in the ministry, death, and resurrection of the Lord Jesus Christ. Paul is the apostle of God's free grace par excellence. Indeed, *grace* is Paul's signature word; it stands at the beginning and end of this and his other letters like bookends that hold in place everything else on the shelf.

Some readers today may be surprised to know how important grace is for Paul. After all, is *love* not the key word in the vocabulary of Christian faith and life? Paul would not disagree. Indeed, he himself gives support to this view (most famously in 1 Cor. 13). Love, however, needs to be carefully defined, especially when we speak of the love of God. Because *love* is a word used in so many different ways, the word *grace* guards the distinctive biblical meaning of the love of God. Grace underscores the very special and costly love of God for the world. God's love for us is unfathomably gracious; it is faithful, steadfast, freely given, altogether undeserved love. Grace is the name of the incomparable generosity of God who brings us into being, sustains us, and redeems us. That we creatures receive the gift of life from our Creator is already a matter of grace. We do not exist necessarily. Save for the grace of God, we would not exist at all. Even more astonishing, by grace alone God has given the gift of forgiveness and new life to creatures who have strayed from their true destiny and who would be lost apart from the redemptive work of God in Jesus Christ.

If we are not awestruck by God's grace—God's wondrous and unmerited love and forgiveness—we have not yet fathomed the meaning of the word *grace* as Paul uses it. Paul begins his letter to

---

5. Barth, *Philippians,* 11–12.

> Amazing grace, how sweet the sound . . .
>
> John Newton, "Amazing Grace"

the church in Philippi, as he did to the churches in Rome, Ephesus, Corinth, and elsewhere, by commending his hearers to the astonishing and joyful message of the grace of God in Jesus Christ whereby sins are forgiven, a new creation dawns, hope beyond hope arises, and the seed of peace with God and our fellow creatures takes root.

Peace (in Greek, *eirene;* in Hebrew, *shalom*) like grace is one of the great words of the Bible. The Hebrew word *shalom* means much more than simply the absence of conflict and chaos. It has a rich, positive meaning—the fullness of life in community, the flourishing of human life in relationship to God and others. As Paul uses the word, it refers to the fullness and harmony of new life in Christ. The peace of Christ is a peace that "surpasses all understanding" (4:7), a peace far transcending the provisional conflict resolutions and fragile personal and international treaties and armistices that we so often equate with true peace.

Grace and peace—these are the blessings with which Paul begins his letter to his friends in Philippi. To repeat: he does not refer to grace and peace in general, not as these words may be used in everyday discourse, and certainly not when defined in any way we please. Paul passes the grace and peace *of Jesus Christ* to all the saints in Philippi and to all who dwell in a thousand other places in countless other times. Paul's blessing, like his message, is always relentlessly particular. He does not engage in generalities, which are always perilous for Christian faith and life. Not God in general but God the Father of Jesus Christ and our Father. Not any Lord but "the Lord Jesus Christ." Not spirituality in general but "the Spirit of Christ" at work in us. Paul's is a particular gospel of a particular Lord. To be sure, this gospel and this Lord, and the grace and peace that he offers, are of universal significance. Yet as Paul understands them, they are specific in source, in content, and in promise. They come from God our Father and the Lord Jesus Christ and are born in us by his Spirit.

We follow in Paul's footsteps when, in our services of worship, and perhaps even in our chance meetings, we pass this very particular grace and peace of Christ to one another. Not just "Hi" or "Good morning," but "The peace of Christ be with you." Not just "How are you?" or "Be well," but "May you receive the grace and peace that comes from God our Father and the Lord Jesus Christ." That is what the saints in Chicago or Beijing or Mexico City are at least implicitly saying when they greet each other with, "Peace" or "Shalom." That is, if they are greeting each other in the Spirit of new community in Christ as Paul greets the saints in Philippi.

1:3–11

Thanksgiving and Prayer

As in most of his letters, Paul's greetings are followed by words of thanksgiving. He tells the Philippians that he joyfully remembers them in his prayers, thanking God for their sharing in the gospel "from the first day until now" (1:5). After expressing his love and longing for them (vv. 6–8), he offers a prayer on their behalf (vv. 9–11).

1:3–8

Thanksgiving for Sharing in the Gospel

One of the reasons for Paul's letter is to express his gratitude to the Philippians for the gifts they have sent him (4:10, 14–16). But note that his thanks are directed first and foremost to God in prayer: "I thank my God" (1:3). Far from being an empty formula, this phrase, appearing in other Letters of Paul as well (Rom. 1:8; 7:25; 1 Cor. 1:4; Phlm. 4), points to the fact that all of Paul's thinking, acting, and dealings with others are set in the context of prayer and thanksgiving to God.

We do not know the precise nature of the gifts Paul received or, if money, the precise amount. We can assume, however, that when Paul offers joyful prayers of thanksgiving on account of the Philippians' "sharing in the gospel from the first day until now" (1:5), he is referring, at least in part, to the material support that the church in Philippi has often given him. Whether in the first or the twenty-first century, the gospel ministry requires material support. There is need for a place to worship, for the resources to support the proclamation of the gospel, the educational responsibilities of the church, and the concrete efforts to help the sick and the poor near and far. When material provisions are joyfully offered and gratefully received, they become tangible expressions of a common sharing in God's grace and in the common ministry of the gospel. Paul is thankful for the material support of his Philippian friends and partners in ministry.

Yet while he is appreciative of such support, it is neither the primary reason for Paul's thanksgiving nor the deepest cause of his joy. Karl Barth helpfully offers the image of three concentric circles of meaning that are present in Paul's prayers of thanksgiving for the Philippians' "sharing in the gospel."[1] In the outermost circle, the phrase refers to the material gifts Paul has received from the saints in Philippi from the very beginning of their relationship. As already mentioned, this support is indispensable and deserves recognition. But in a second circle of meaning we are taken to a deeper level. Paul is thankful for the Philippians' reception of the gospel and their continuing participation in its proclamation and service by their worship, confession, and witness in their own particular context as well as in their support of Paul's ministry elsewhere. Then finally, there is the innermost circle of meaning in Paul's thanksgiving to God. Above all, Paul is thankful that the Philippians "share in God's grace" with him (1:7), that they too are recipients of the grace of God in Jesus Christ that binds all believers together in a new community of faith, love, and service. Christians are what they are by the grace of God, and their service is given out of gratitude for what they have received. It is above all this common "sharing in God's grace" and common participation in the new life in Christ that motivates Paul's thanksgiving and gives him great joy.[2]

1:6–8 *A Special Friendship*

Paul's warm words of thanksgiving at the beginning of his letter are evidence of his intimate bond with the Philippians. He freely expresses his love for them and tells them he knows that they love him too. Just as they "hold him in [their] heart" (1:7), he "longs" for

---

1. See Karl Barth, *The Epistle to the Philippians* (Louisville, KY: Westminster John Knox Press, 2002), 16.
2. Ibid., 16.

all of them "with the compassion of Christ Jesus" (1:8). Later in the letter Paul addresses them as "my brothers and sisters, whom I love and long for, my joy and crown" (4:1). To be sure, Paul addresses the recipients of his other letters too as "brothers and sisters" and "beloved." But the words of affection used here and the overall tone of Philippians make it special among Paul's letters. Nowhere in this letter do we find anything close to his words of rebuke to the Galatians: "I am astonished that you are so quickly deserting the one who called you in the grace of Christ and are turning to a different gospel" (Gal. 1:6). Even compared with his Letter to the Romans, Paul's expressions of affection for the Philippians stand out. True, he gives thanks for the church in Rome because their faith "is proclaimed throughout the world," and he expresses a "longing" to see them that they may be mutually encouraged by one another's faith (Rom. 1:8, 12). These are indeed very positive words, but not quite what we hear in Philippians: "my joy and crown."

In noting the special relationship of Paul and the Philippians evident throughout the letter, many commentators explore whether it is apt to describe this relationship as one of friendship.[3] The question turns in large part on how we define friendship. Is the understanding of friendship that prevailed in the ancient world adequate to grasp Paul's view of belonging to the new community in Christ? Are some uses of "friend" in modern society (think of the members of Facebook,

> **Christ lives and acts as a friend and creates friendship.**
>
> Jürgen Moltmann, *The Church in the Power of the Spirit* (New York: Harper & Row, 1977), 119.

with their scores, hundreds, or even thousands of virtual "friends") anywhere near what Paul had in mind in speaking of the Philippians as his "beloved"? In fact, Paul does not use "friends" in this passage or elsewhere in the letter. Instead, he regularly calls the Philippians "brothers and sisters" and "beloved." This suggests that if we are inclined to characterize the relationship of Paul and the Philippians in terms of friendship, it would be more precise to speak of it as a

---

3. Markus Bockmuehl, *The Epistle to the Philippians* (London: Hendrickson, 1998), 34–38; Gordon D. Fee, *Paul's Letter to the Philippians* (Grand Rapids: Eerdmans, 1995), 2–7; and most extensively, Stephen E. Fowl, *Philippians* (Grand Rapids: Eerdmans, 2005), 205–35.

friendship in Christ or as a Christian brotherhood and sisterhood, grounded in the grace and friendship of God embodied in Christ.

In the spirit of what Paul says here about his special bond with the Philippians, several salient features of Christian friendship may be identified. First, as seen in Paul's relationship with the Philippians, friendship in Christ is not so much a matter of persons choosing to enter into relationship with one another as their being brought into relationship by their common calling in Christ. Friends in Christ are aware that their friendship has its deepest basis not in themselves but in something—or more accurately, Someone—beyond themselves who has brought them together, sustains their love, and gives them a common vocation. Their friendship is based on "sharing in the gospel" (1:5), sharing "in God's grace" (1:7), and sharing in "the privilege not only of believing in Christ, but of suffering for him" (1:29). Christian friends are bound together in Christ. Their friendship cannot be sustained apart from the grace and vocation they have received from him.

Second, friendship in Christ as represented in Paul's letter is not something fickle or episodic; it is not simply a matter of warm feelings that might quickly come and just as quickly go. It is characterized by an abiding mutual faithfulness. Note that Paul gives thanks that the Philippians have shared in the gospel with him "from the first day until now" (1:5). This phrase speaks of the constancy and persistence of their relationship of mutual love over a significant stretch of time. Such constancy and perseverance are not grounded in the inherent capacities of the friends themselves but in the grace of God and in the service of the gospel that they share. Then, too, among the many ways Christian friends show their faithfulness to one another is in their prayers. Paul prays for the Philippians (1:3), and as we will see, they also pray for him (1:19).

Third, Christian friendship as Paul speaks of it in this letter is fired by "the compassion of Christ" (1:8). The word translated here as "compassion" (*splanchna*) literally refers to a person's inward parts or bowels. It is often used in Scripture to mean an intense affection or heartfelt love. Paul's description of his longing for the Philippians "with the compassion of Christ" explodes the myth that the Christian gospel ignores or demeans the affective and emotional side of human existence. Just as Paul's love for Christ is wholehearted and knows no reservations, so his love for the Philippians is deeply felt and given freely and fully. Indeed, he describes it as a participation in the full-bodied love of Christ who, as the Gospels tell us, had "compassion" on the crowds who followed him and sought his help (cf. Mark 6:34). Christian friendship is a participation in the compassionate love of God in Christ even to death on a cross. Christians are called to love God and neighbor not halfheartedly, or on certain occasions, or with a thousand reservations, but as God loves the world and as Paul says he loves the Philippians—"with the compassion of Christ."

That the strong and lasting bond between Christian friends has its basis in the God of the gospel is evident in Paul's striking word of assurance: "I am confident . . . that the one [God] who began a good work among you will bring it to completion" (1:6). No doubt all true friends want only what is good for one another, and no doubt this mutual goodwill includes a hope for the fulfillment and completion of one another's lives. But Paul's word of assurance goes considerably beyond this. He finds the basis of firm hope for his friends not in what he can do for them or in what they can do for themselves, but solely in the promise of God given in Jesus Christ. For Paul, God is the power of good beginnings and good endings in all things, not least in our relationships with one another. The work that God has begun in us will be completed by God. It is the faithfulness of God, not our own or our friends' faithfulness, that is the source of the unwavering confidence that the goal of our life and that of our friends in Christ will be reached. God begins every good work, God sustains it, and God will complete it: this is Paul's confidence. The God made known in Jesus Christ never tires of befriending us. God is faithful, and a shared knowledge of this fact anchors and empowers our mutual faithfulness in Christian friendship.

Commenting on Paul's assurance to the Philippians that God will complete the good work he has begun among them, Calvin offers a qualification. He questions whether we can ever be sure of the standing of others before God equivalent to the assurance that we have of our own salvation. "There is," he says, "a great difference, because the assurance of faith remains shut up within, and does not spread to others."[4] In other words, the best we can do, Calvin thinks, is to be charitable in our judgment of others and hope for their inclusion among God's elect. I take issue with Calvin on this point. He introduces a distinction between the confidence one has in God's gracious purposes for oneself and the confidence one has in God's purposes for one's brothers and sisters. There is no basis for this distinction in the text. Paul says he is confident that God will complete the work he has begun in his friends in Christ, and we have no basis for thinking that Paul's confidence in this regard is of a lower grade than the confidence he has in his own standing before God. Paul's confidence rests neither on the faith of the Philippians nor on his own faith but solely on the grace and faithfulness of God.

With these brief comments in mind, we will want to be careful not to simply equate the mutual love of Paul and the Philippians with our everyday experiences of friendship. While an analogy may well be discerned between friendship in Christ and other forms of friendship, in the use of analogy in theology there are both important similarities and even greater differences. The inhabitants of Philippi no doubt had multiple friendship ties. They had their *collegia*, or associations. They belonged to various religious groups. They probably exchanged gifts. Moreover, many Philippians were Roman citizens, and those who claimed this honor considered themselves "friends of Caesar." The friendship of Paul and the Philippians, however, was of a different order. It was rooted in the shared gift of God's grace in Christ, formed in the fellowship of his followers, and outwardly expressed in their partnership of service in his name.

> **Professing commitment to Jesus as Lord connects us not only to Jesus but to one another in a new way.**
>
> Rowan Williams, *On Christian Theology* (Oxford: Blackwell, 2001), 172.

On the side of the Philippians, the great gift they received from their friend Paul was the proclamation of the gospel of God's fathomless grace, and it is primarily for this reason that they held Paul dear to their heart. On Paul's side, the great gift he had received and continued to receive from the Philippians was not primarily their

4. John Calvin, *Galatians, Ephesians, Philippians and Colossians*, CNTC, ed. David Torrance and Thomas F. Torrance (1965; repr., Grand Rapids: Eerdmans, 1979), 229.

money. It was their "sharing in the gospel," their sharing with him in the grace of God, and their sharing with him not only in the privilege of "believing in Christ" but also in "suffering for him as well" (1:29). The very special friendship of Paul and the Philippians is based in the love of God in Christ. Their friendship is a "cruciform friendship";[5] they are friends of one another because they are one in the crucified and risen Christ.

We should not overlook the final phrase in Paul's assurance that God will complete the good work he has begun among his brothers and sisters in Philippi. Paul adds: "by the day of Jesus Christ" (1:6). A similar reference to "the day of Christ" is also found in Paul's prayer for the Philippians (1:10). These are the initial but not the only indicators in this letter that Paul's thinking is profoundly *eschatological*, that is, driven by the conviction that God's kingdom has been inaugurated with power in Jesus Christ and that the consummation of God's purposes for humanity and the world is near. Paul's confidence, thanksgiving, and joy are ignited and sustained by what God has done and is doing among God's people. At the same time, Paul also has an indomitable confidence in what God will yet do. His reference to "the day of Jesus Christ" indicates clearly that he looks to the future coming of Christ and the universal recognition of his lordship. He eagerly hopes for that day when God will complete God's purposes in Christ for the Philippians and for the whole world. As Charles Cousar suggests, the phrases "from the first day" (i.e., when the gospel of salvation accomplished in Christ was first preached to and received by the Philippians) and "the day of Jesus Christ" (i.e., the day when Christ will return and God's purposes will be completed) constitute the points of departure and destination of the life and witness of the church.[6] The church exists between these two "days," "between the times," as the dialectical theologians of the early twentieth century famously put it. It exists between the day remembered and the day hoped for, between the day of the ministry, death, and resurrection of Christ in which we now participate by faith and the day for which we ardently hope, the day of his coming again in glory to judge and to save.

5. Fowl, *Philippians*, 220.
6. Charles B. Cousar, *Philippians and Philemon*, New Testament Library (Louisville, KY: Westminster John Knox Press, 2009), 30.

This eschatological dimension of Paul's thinking is important for a proper understanding of the letter as a whole. As Paul understands the gospel of God's grace in Jesus Christ, it produces the very opposite of hopelessness and resignation to the way things are in the present. The gospel is profoundly hopeful. Jesus Christ is coming again to complete and manifest his lordship over all creation. God has begun a good work in you, Paul says, and God will bring it to completion. In the meantime, Christians are called to responsible living and faithful service.

All these words of thanksgiving, joy, and confidence with which Paul's Letter to the Philippians begins should not be confused with a pious romanticism. As the Philippians are told, and as Paul experiences firsthand, he is writing from prison (1:7). Paul does not have to be informed that Christian life and service is no bed of roses. He knows this not only from his present situation but also from many past experiences as ambassador of Christ. While he speaks joyfully and confidently of God's grace to the Philippians, his imprisonment is a reminder to all that following Christ may exact a high price. Grace is costly; it is costly for God in Jesus Christ, and it is also costly for every disciple and servant of Christ. While "sharing in the gospel" brings thanksgiving and joy, Christians are not immune from conflict, rejection, and suffering. So Paul is thankful that the Philippians share in the grace of God, and this includes a share both in Paul's "imprisonment and in the defense and confirmation of the gospel" (1:7). This theme of suffering for Christ as part of Christian life is prominent in Philippians, and we will have much more to say about it in due course.

However important the theme of suffering in Paul's letter, neither his message nor his situation leads him to think of his ministry as oppressive. In these early verses and throughout the letter, he writes not as one carrying a heavy burden but as one who rejoices. He prays for the Philippians "with joy" (1:4) and says he is able to "rejoice" that the gospel is widely proclaimed, even if sometimes out of questionable motives (1:18). He further insists that he will "continue to rejoice" because he knows the Philippians are praying for him (1:18). As we shall see, in the final section of the letter, Paul composes a veritable symphony of joy (4:4–7). Paul can offer his thanksgiving prayer with joy because he is convinced that the grace of God in Jesus Christ will triumph over all its opponents, because God is faithful, because the sufferings that Paul is now experiencing and that the Philippians either are beginning to experience or may soon experience are nothing in comparison with the sure victory of the love of God in Christ.[7] In his letter to the Christians in Rome, Paul declares: "I am convinced that neither death, nor life, nor angels, nor rulers, nor things present, nor things to come, nor powers, nor height, nor depth, nor anything else in all creation, will be able to separate us from the love of God in Christ Jesus our Lord" (8:38–39). Although the word "joy" does not appear in this familiar passage, it captures well the joyful tone that, despite present conflict and struggle, permeates the Letter to the Philippians. Already evident in his opening prayer of thanksgiving and intercession, Paul's call to rejoice grows stronger as the letter proceeds.

1:9–11
A Prayer for the Philippians

After Paul gives thanks for the Philippians' sharing in the grace of God and in the gospel, he offers a prayer on their behalf. He prays that their love may increase more and more (not quantitatively but in breadth and depth); that it will be yoked with knowledge and insight which will enable the Philippians to discern "what is best" (that is, what really matters in the light of Jesus Christ, in contrast to what is far less important); that in the day of Christ they will be pure and blameless (which does not mean perfect moral rectitude but a simplicity of faith in Christ and a life that depends on his righteousness); and that they will have produced by the grace of God through

> [Prayer is] the chief exercise of faith. . . . Words fail to explain how necessary prayer is, and in how many ways the exercise of prayer is profitable.
>
> John Calvin, *Institutes of the Christian Religion* 3.20.1.

---

7. As J. Lewis Martyn states, "In Paul's letters there is never a hint that God will ultimately lose." *Theological Issues in the Letters of Paul* (Edinburgh: T. & T. Clark, 1997), 283.

Christ a "harvest of righteousness" to the glory and praise of God (1:9–11). This is among the loveliest of Pauline prayers, similar in passion and content to a prayer found in Ephesians, a letter that Paul may also have written: "I pray that, according to the riches of his glory, [God] may grant that you may be strengthened in your inner being with power through his Spirit, and that Christ may dwell in your hearts through faith, as you are being rooted and grounded in love. I pray that you may have the power to comprehend, with all the saints, what is the breadth and length and height and depth, and to know the love of Christ that surpasses knowledge, so that you may be filled with all the fullness of God" (Eph. 3:16–19).

Note first that Paul prays that the love of the Philippians might "abound" (1:9 RSV), that it might "overflow" more and more (NRSV). The image here of overflowing or abounding love is reminiscent of Paul's description in Romans 5:20 of the extravagant grace of God that "abounded all the more" when sin increased. In both passages, the image of "overflowing" love, of grace that "abounds all the more," expresses surfeit and inexhaustibility. For Paul, the love that superabounds and overflows is not love in general but the love whose source is the God of the gospel. God's love overflows freely in the world's creation; overflows freely in God's providential care of the world; overflows freely in the reconciling action of God in the life, death, and resurrection of Jesus Christ; and is poured freely into our hearts by the Holy Spirit (Rom. 5:5).

Theologians will later speak of the eternal life of God as a boundless fountain of overflowing love, overflowing from the eternally shared love of Father, Son, and Holy Spirit. Paul says nothing directly in this passage about the triune life of love. Even so, his prayer that the love of the Philippians might "overflow more and more" presupposes and anticipates what he will say about the self-giving love of God in the great Christ hymn of chapter 2. It is because of the grace of God in Christ that Paul confidently prays that the love of the Philippians may grow ever stronger as their lives are conformed to Christ and they participate ever more fully in the overflowing love of God in him. This participation of the Philippians and of all Christians in God's love in Christ by the Spirit is, of course, always partial and broken, for only God's love overflows in perfect freedom and unbroken constancy. Still, Paul's prayer is that their love—and by extension the love of readers of his letter today—will "overflow more and more."

Note, second, that Paul prays that as the love of the Philippians overflows it may show increasing "knowledge and full insight" (1:9). The Greek word *aisthesei*, translated "insight" (NRSV) or "discernment" (RSV), suggests the "capacity for practical concrete judgment."[8] The importance of Paul's linking of love, knowledge, and discernment in this prayer cannot be overstated. He does not pray for an unknowing love or a loveless knowledge. What good would be a love that lacks wisdom and sound judgment, and what good would be a merely cerebral knowledge that is separated from love? Over the centuries, Christian theologies and movements within the church have often impoverished their witness or have even fallen into serious errors because they have severed love and practical wisdom. On the one hand, we have had impressive intellectual renditions of Christian faith disconnected from a passionate love of God and neighbor. But what value would all our orthodox Christologies have—a Calvin might well ask in the spirit of Paul's prayer—if Christ were only a grand idea for us and our hearts remained like ice rather than being set on fire by the love of God embodied in Christ for us?[9] On the other hand, we have also had many zealous ethical versions of Christian faith whose calls to action have gradually weakened, become confused, and even collapsed in exhaustion because of the lack of strong theological foundations or the absence of clear standards to determine the best course of action and the appropriate means to accomplish the hoped-for ends. Just as Paul prays that the knowledge of the Philippians will be joined to love and not become mere information or freewheeling speculation, he also prays that their love will be yoked to knowledge and discernment and not decline into mere sentimentality or simply feeling warm inside. Knowledge without love, Paul says in another letter, is like the noise of "a clanging cymbal" (1 Cor. 13:1). Equally true, Paul would surely add, is that what passes for love but lacks the wisdom

8. Peter O'Brien, *The Epistle to the Philippians* (Grand Rapids: Eerdmans, 1991), 77.
9. John Calvin, *Institutes of the Christian Religion* 3.1.1; ed. John T. McNeill, trans. Ford Lewis Battles, LCC (Philadelphia: Westminster, 1960).

of Christ crucified (1 Cor. 1:22–25) easily declines into patronizing "charity" or soon just runs out of breath.

For Paul, the test of whether our love is wise and our wisdom joined to love takes place when we are called "to determine what is best" (1:10), what is truly important, "what really matters."[10] Already in this prayer it is clear that for Paul, Christian life is not simply a matter of following a set of rules; it involves the creative act of discernment in concrete situations of "what is best" among a multitude of possible options. At this point, Paul does not yet specify in what way Christians are to go about determining what is best in any given situation. That specificity will soon be given by Paul in his recounting of the way of Christ (2:5–11). Already here, however, even if only implicitly, Paul is praying that the Philippians will be given the ability to make practical, concrete decisions and judgments that are guided by what God has revealed of the character and redemptive purpose of God and of our true humanity in Jesus Christ. Our decisions, Paul's prayer implies, will manifest both love and wisdom when they are made in conformity to the love and wisdom of God revealed in the incarnate Lord.

Paul's concern that Christians learn to discern "what is best"— what really matters—underscores the fact that not every issue or every question that confronts a Christian congregation or the Christian church as a whole falls into the category of the truly important. The church has often been guilty of what Jesus described as straining at a gnat and swallowing a camel (Matt. 23:24). In other words, what is really important may be overshadowed by small and relatively unimportant matters. Calvin called these matters *adiaphora* or secondary things, and he counseled the church not to allow its unity to be threatened or its mission undermined by making a big deal about lesser things while the really important matters go unattended.[11]

Then Paul prays that the Philippians will be "pure and blameless" in the day of Jesus Christ (1:10). This cannot possibly mean that Paul is praying that they will be found blameless as measured by whether they have successfully observed every "jot and tittle" of

10. See J. Ross Wagner, "Philippians," in *The New Interpreter's Bible One-Volume Commentary*, ed. Beverly Roberts Gaventa and David Peterson (Nashville: Abingdon, 2010), 843.
11. Calvin, *Institutes* 4.17.43.

the law (Matt. 5:18 KJV). As Paul will later explain, it is precisely this sort of supposedly blameless adherence to the letter of the law that often leads to a spirit of self-righteousness that causes one to look down on others. Such a spirit was at work in Paul's early life as a fiercely devout Pharisee. In the light of Christ, however, he came to view this sort of self-achieved righteousness as altogether different from the righteousness that comes from God. The purity and blamelessness of life that Paul speaks of in his prayer for the Philippians refer to the integrity and steadfastness of a life of faith and love that is entirely dependent on the grace of God, that is formed by the way of Christ, that stands in contrast to a life centered on oneself, and that rejoices in the new community that God is building beyond the high walls we erect to separate ourselves from others.

In the final petition of the prayer, Paul employs the beautiful image of a "harvest of righteousness" (1:11). He is confident that if Christian love truly overflows among the Philippians; if their love is joined with wisdom and the ability to discern what really matters; if their life formed by such love leads to a spirit of humility, integrity, and steadfastness in their relationship to God and neighbors; they will produce a "harvest" of righteousness that "comes through Jesus Christ for the glory and praise of God." This verse can be read in two ways. On the one hand, the emphasis can be placed on Christ as the source of the harvest of righteousness with which the saints will be "filled" (RSV). On the other hand, the emphasis can be placed on the saints "having produced" the harvest of righteousness that comes through Jesus Christ (NRSV). Although I think the priority should be given to the first reading, the second reading has its proper place in the context of the first. Paul will later have much more to say about the meaning of the "righteousness from God," but already here he makes it clear that righteousness is not our own achievement but "comes through Jesus Christ." At the same time, the content of his prayer implies that the righteousness of which he speaks here as well as later in the letter is more than an orthodox doctrine to be believed. It is also a new way of life that is lived out in everyday Christian practice. It is the fruit of a new humanity, the blessings of God's new world in Christ, far richer and far more abundant than the most plentiful of fall harvests.

Note, finally, that Paul concludes his prayer with a doxology: "for the glory and praise of God." Similar doxologies are found at the end of the Christ hymn, "to the glory of God the Father" (2:11), and in the concluding lines of the letter, "to our God and Father be glory forever and ever" (4:20). Paul's letter and indeed his entire theology are enveloped in doxology, in praise and thanksgiving to the God of grace made known in Jesus Christ.

FURTHER REFLECTIONS
Prayer

Paul is a man of prayer. He does not pray because he feels obligated to do so; he does not pray because he is a religious show-off; he does not pray because he is a foxhole Christian. He prays because as an heir of the faith of Israel in the living God and as an apostle of the risen Lord Jesus Christ, prayer is as natural to him as breathing in and breathing out. Fred Craddock has it just right: "All reconstructions of Pauline theology that omit his prayers, eulogies, benedictions, and doxologies are incomplete and misrepresent the apostle whose talk *to* God was integral to his talk *about* God."[12]

For many churchgoers today, prayer can be deeply problematic. This may be due to widespread views that modern science rules out the activity of God in the natural order or in human affairs. Or it may be due to questions about the efficacy of prayer in the face of overwhelming experiences of evil like the Holocaust or catastrophic natural events like hurricanes, earthquakes, and tsunamis. Whatever difficulties we may have in praying, however, it is clear that the firm theological convictions, strong ethical exhortations, and sensitive pastoral advice found in Paul's Letter to the Philippians are inseparable from his practice of prayer.

All of the great theologians of the church have been people of prayer. According to Origen, life is "a single great prayer."[13] For Augustine, prayer arises from the longing of our restless hearts

12. Fred B. Craddock, *Philippians,* Interpretation (Atlanta: John Knox, 1985), 79.
13. *Origen: An Exhortation to Martyrdom, Prayer, and Selected Works,* trans. Rowan A. Greer (New York: Paulist, 1979), 104.

for God.[14] Thomas Aquinas says that in prayer we honor God and place our lives in God's hands.[15] For John Calvin, prayer is "the chief exercise of faith."[16] For Martin Luther it is "speaking to God in words and thoughts."[17] For Dietrich Bonhoeffer, it is "the heart of Christian life."[18] Karl Barth writes that in prayer we enjoy "a genuine and actual share" in the lordship of God.[19] When Barth wanted to describe in detail the shape and dynamics of Christian life, he chose "invocation" as his overall theme, organizing his entire presentation around the petitions of the Lord's Prayer.[20]

We can learn much from Paul's life of prayer. He knows that prayer has many forms and accents. While he prays "constantly with joy" for the Philippians (1:4), there are also times when he prays in distress, as when he pleads for God to remove his "thorn in the flesh" (2 Cor. 12:7-9). Paul unquestionably prays with confidence (Phil. 1:6), but his confidence is not in himself, or in his own power of prayer, but in God's faithfulness. Nor are we to think of Paul as a person whose prayers are always eloquent or free-flowing. He acknowledges that we do not know how to pray, but that nevertheless the Spirit of God intercedes for us with sighs "too deep for words" (Rom. 8:26).

> **"We do not know how to pray."**
> **True, but fortunately the Spirit**
> **does, and will make us saints if**
> **we dare...**
>
> Sarah Coakley, "Ordinary within the Extraordinary," *Harvard Divinity Bulletin* 33, no. 1 (Spring, 2005): 17.

Notable, too, is that Paul prays first of all for others and not primarily for himself. He prays that love will increase among his brothers and sisters and that they will receive the wisdom to approve and choose what is best (1:9–10). Moreover, Paul finds encouragement

---

14. Augustine, *Confessions and Enchiridion*, LCC VI, ed. Albert C. Outler (Philadelphia: Westminster, 1955), 1.1.1.
15. Thomas Aquinas, *Summa theologiae*, trans. Fathers of the English Dominican Province (New York: Benziger, 1947), 2-2, Q. 83, art. 3.
16. Calvin, *Institutes* 3.20.
17. Martin Luther, *Luther's Small Catechism with Explanation* (St. Louis: Concordia, 1986), 169.
18. *Dietrich Bonhoeffer Works*, vol. 10, *Barcelona, Bern, New York: 1928–1931* (Minneapolis: Fortress, 2008), 577.
19. Karl Barth, *CD* III/3 (Edinburgh: T. & T. Clark, 1960), 285. (Hereafter cited as CD followed by volume and page.)
20. Karl Barth, *The Christian Life: Church Dogmatics IV, 4; Lecture Fragments* (Grand Rapids: Eerdmans, 1981), 36–44.

in knowing that his friends are praying for him and that through their prayers the Spirit of God is graciously at work for his deliverance. For Paul, we do not pray alone; we pray in and with the support of a community of prayer.

There are still other benefits to gain from attending to Paul's exhortations to pray and his own practice of prayer. They may help us to understand the indispensability of prayer in our worship services and in our service to others. Is a sermon divorced from prayer anything other than an interesting (or perhaps not so interesting) lecture on religion or morality? Would a celebration of the Lord's Supper from which the Great Thanksgiving Prayer was omitted be a genuine Eucharist? Can our actions on behalf of others be responsibly undertaken apart from a spirit of humility and repentance that is inseparable from genuine prayer?

The importance of prayer in Paul's letters may also prompt us to reflect more deeply on the central affirmations of Christian faith. Who is the God to whom we pray? Paul's prayers, doxologies, and benedictions are addressed to the God of unfathomable love and grace revealed in Jesus Christ. When closely examined, Paul's language and practice of prayer are implicitly Trinitarian. Not, of course, Trinitarian in the sense of the later conceptuality of the Council of Nicaea (325 CE). Still, in the Letter to the Philippians Paul speaks of God "the Father" (1:2; 2:11; 4:20); of "the Lord Jesus Christ" as equal with God (2:6); and of "sharing in the Spirit" (2:1) and worshiping "in the Spirit of God" (3:3). Paul's prayer is Trinitarian-shaped prayer that corresponds to a Trinitarian apprehension of God as "our Father," as "our Lord Jesus Christ," and as "the Spirit" at work among us and in our worship and service.[21]

Finally, we might ask: Is there any connection between Paul's practice of prayer and the prayers of Jesus? The Gospels not only tell us that Jesus taught his disciples to pray; they also tell us that prayer pervaded his entire ministry, including his time of agony in the garden and on the cross. Did Paul know the Lord's Prayer? Whether he did or not, Paul's practice of prayer is strikingly congruent with

21. See Sarah Coakley, "Why Three? Some Further Reflections on the Origins of the Doctrine of the Trinity," in *The Making and Remaking of Christian Doctrine: Essays in Honour of Maurice Wiles*, ed. Sarah Coakley and David A. Pailin (Oxford: Clarendon, 1993), 29–56.

the prayer Jesus taught his disciples. In the Letter to the Philippians, Paul addresses God as "Father" (1:2), just as Jesus instructed his disciples to address their prayer to "Our Father." Furthermore, Paul prays that the lives of the Philippians will render "glory and praise of God" (1:11; cf. "Hallowed be your name"). In his prayer Paul looks forward eagerly to the "day of Christ" (1:10; cf. "Thy kingdom come"). He prays that the lives of the Philippians may be "pure and blameless" (1:10; cf. "Thy will be done, on earth as it is in heaven"). He knows the secret of being content whether well fed or hungry (4:12; cf. "Give us this day our daily bread"). He prays that the love of the Philippians for each other will overflow more and more (1:9), no doubt with the immeasurable love of Christ for us all in mind (2:5–8; cf. "Forgive us our debts, as we forgive our debtors"). He wants them to avoid selfishness and pride (2:3; cf. "Lead us not into temptation, but deliver us from evil").

John Calvin makes the point that recognition of the Lord's Prayer as the model prayer for Christians does not necessarily involve exact repetition of its words. Agreement in substance is what matters.[22] Paul may not have used the exact words of Jesus, but the Spirit of Jesus, the "mind of Christ," is fully evident in his prayers and should also be in ours.

22. Calvin, *Institutes* 3.20.49.

1:12–26

Paul's Imprisonment

Paul now turns to the matter of his present imprisonment and the concerns this raises for the Philippians and for him. He explains that his imprisonment has actually helped to spread the gospel (1:12–14), even if some preachers have used it as an occasion to advance themselves (1:15–18a). Fully aware of the peril he faces, Paul remains confident and joyful. Although he would gladly die and be with Christ, he considers it necessary that he survive the present danger for the sake of the Philippians and their progress and joy in the life of faith (1:18b–26).

1:12–14
Imprisonment for Christ

That Paul addresses the matter of his imprisonment so early in his letter indicates he is aware his situation deeply troubles his brothers and sisters. They are naturally concerned for his safety and indeed for his very life. Paul wants to give his friends assurance and reason to be confident. Notably, he now no longer addresses them by the rather formal name of "saints," as in the salutation, but employs the far more intimate and pastoral designations "brothers and sisters" (1:14) and "beloved" (2:12). These are Paul's favorite ways of speaking of fellow Christians, whether in Philippi (1:12; 1:14; 2:12; 3:1; 3:17; 4:1; 4:8) or elsewhere (e.g., Rom. 1:7; 12:19; 1 Cor. 4:14; 2 Cor. 7:1; Phlm. 1). For Paul, Christians are "beloved" in the first place by God (Rom. 1:7), and for that reason above all they are also

Paul's own "beloved" (Phil. 4:1; Rom. 12:19). He also addresses them as "brothers and sisters" because they are all children of one God, "our Father" (Phil. 1:2), and all are bound to one another in Christ even more closely than members of a biological family.

Beyond their understandable concern for the personal health and safety of their leader, there is no doubt another anxiety troubling the Philippians. They may wonder whether the indefinite incarceration and possible execution of Paul could mean the beginning of the end of the young Christian movement. Might they be hearing catcalls and "we told you so" from detractors of the faith who point to Paul's imprisonment as an empirical disqualification both of his ministry and of the gospel he had preached to the Philippians, the one they had adopted at some risk?

Paul hastens to assure his friends that what has happened to him has actually served "to spread the gospel" rather than forecasting its demise (1:12). Indeed, the good news proclaimed by Paul has become something of a public topic, even being widely known among members of the "imperial guard" (*praetorium*), a phrase likely referring to some of the Roman soldiers who were assigned to the place where Paul was imprisoned.[1] Besides this, Paul says his being a prisoner "for Christ" (1:13) has actually bolstered the confidence of most of the other brothers and sisters in the city who are now proclaiming the word of God "with greater boldness and without fear" (1:14). Paul's point is that his imprisonment, far from leading to a retreat of the gospel to the confinement of a prison cell, has resulted in an increasingly bold extension of the gospel into the public domain.

What Paul says here goes against the grain not only of the Philippians' assumptions but of ours as well. We often suppose, as did they, that the spread of the gospel is most likely to occur when it meets with no obstacles like harassment or persecution from its enemies. The gospel is bound to flourish, we think, where there is freedom of religion, tolerance of different faiths, and a strict separation of church and state. Likewise, it must necessarily languish where these factors are absent. This assumption may have a measure of truth,

---

1. Markus Bockmuehl, *Philippians* (London: Hendrickson, 1998), 75.

but it is far from being universally valid. The vitality of Christian house churches under repressive social and political regimes, as in Mao Tse-tung's communist China or in the base communities of Latin America during the era of mid-twentieth-century military juntas, are but a few examples to the contrary.[2] Indeed, we might well ask whether the Christian gospel is especially vulnerable to cultural accommodation and even to being trivialized in situations where the designation "Christian" becomes a cultural or national matter of course, where it is, so to speak, as American as apple pie. Søren Kierkegaard railed against this sort of Christian existence: devoid of any muscle tone, knowing nothing of conflict with the forces of evil in the world, and so comfortable with its social environment that it no longer knows what being a Christian disciple means and the costs it entails. In a post-Christendom era, with its striking religious and moral pluralism, the significance of Paul's reminder that the spread of the gospel can and does occur even under the most unlikely circumstances should not be forgotten.

> As soon as the opposition is taken away, the thing of being a Christian is twaddle.
>
> Søren Kierkegaard, *Attack on "Christendom,"* trans. Walter Lowrie (Boston: Beacon, 1944), 127.

1:15–18a

Opportunistic Preachers

Paul frankly acknowledges that there is a downside to his imprisonment. Seeking to take advantage of his situation to advance their own interests, some are proclaiming Christ from "envy and rivalry" (1:15), others out of "selfish ambition" (1:17). We may wonder who these people are and just what they are saying. Commentators offer a number of theories. The general consensus is that these disreputable

---

2. In his seminal work on Latin American liberation theology, Gustavo Gutiérrez speaks of the base communities as "a major source of vitality within the larger Christian community" bringing "the gospel closer to the poor and the poor closer to the gospel." *A Theology of Liberation* (Maryknoll, NY: Orbis, 1988), xli.

preachers do not offer a gospel that flat-out contradicts Paul's; their opposition to him is probably best described as "personal rivalry."[3] Are they preachers who want to make hay out of Paul's imprisonment and advance their own leadership credentials? Are they trying to place themselves in the limelight and climb the ladder of success in the fledgling Christian movement? Are they spreading rumors that Paul is a has-been and that Christians must now look to others for new and more responsible leadership? Are they evangelists who have long doubted Paul's apostleship and now claim that his imprisonment is confirmation of their doubts? Are these preachers insinuating that by his reckless style of proclamation Paul not only bears some responsibility for his imprisonment but also unnecessarily brings disrepute on the young community of believers, placing them all in danger?

We just do not know who Paul has in mind when he says that some are proclaiming Christ out of envy and rivalry, that they have selfish motives, and that they could not care less if their innuendoes and rumors make Paul all the more miserable in his confinement. What we do know is that Paul rises above these efforts of his rivals to disqualify him. Whatever their motives, Paul rejoices that they nevertheless proclaim Christ (1:18b).

Perhaps we should not be surprised that Paul had detractors even among those who might otherwise be considered fellow preachers of the gospel. After all, Paul may not have been a particularly attractive "personality," whether in physical appearance, in his public speaking ability, or in his skill in smoothing over his differences with others. He may have been rather argumentative by nature, and he certainly proclaimed a controversial gospel.[4] In any case, the sort of rivalry among church leaders briefly registered in this passage certainly did not end after the first century. As in other professions, personal rivalries and unfounded innuendoes and charges to further one's own career are not unheard of in the ministry. If there are cases of zealous entrepreneurs or ambitious politicians climbing the ladder of success by planting seeds of suspicion about the competence or integrity of their competitors, there are unfortunately also instances of

---

3. Peter T. O'Brien, *Philippians* (Grand Rapids: Eerdmans, 1991), 105.
4. Karl Barth, *The Epistle to the Philippians* (Louisville, KY: Westminster John Knox Press, 2002), 29.

church leaders engaging in similar practices either from resentment or to secure a popular following or a higher ecclesiastical position for themselves. Now as in the first century, however, such unsavory motives and practices have a damaging effect on the church and its mission.

Paul evidently knows that reports of his competitors for leadership of the church have gotten back to Christians in Philippi. He cannot avoid the issue; he has to address it. But note that he does not do this in a way that would inevitably lead to a rift in the church. Even though he labels his detractors envious and selfish, he does not on that account rule them out of the church. He does not simply brand them heretics or apostates. He graciously acknowledges that, even if their motives are shoddy, insofar as they are proclaiming Christ, they are part of the ministry in which Paul shares.

But just how convincing is Paul's "What does it matter?" (1:18a)? Can we easily separate true preaching of the gospel from the personal motives and life practices of the preachers? If preachers proclaim the gospel only because it proves to be a lucrative business, or because they think that by doing so they will augment the power and reputation of their congregation, denomination, nation, or culture, does the truth of the proclamation remain unaffected? Can Christ ever be truly "exalted" (1:20) by people with base motives? Cannot our motives and actions invalidate the gospel we proclaim? These are more difficult questions than they appear on the surface.

No doubt sinful motives and life practices of all Christians, preachers and lay folk alike, do bring discredit on the gospel. Such attitudes and practices should be exposed and placed under judgment. Nevertheless, we must ask: Is the truth of the gospel entirely dependent on the absolute purity of our motives and behavior in sharing the gospel with others? Are any of us entirely free of envy, rivalry, and selfishness in our proclamation of the gospel? If our honest answer to this question must be no, then we should be wary of suggesting that unless someone's life is in perfect correspondence to the gospel they proclaim, the content of their proclamation is falsified. Selfish motives and immoral behavior can certainly *betray* the truth of the gospel. They can make it all the more difficult for hearers to receive and believe the gospel that is proclaimed. But from this it does not follow that the message itself is falsified by the flaws of its messengers. While it is certainly the case that "truth is in order to goodness,"[5] the truth is not helpless unless the character of its bearer is blameless. Were it otherwise, we would have to say that the gospel is true only if the purity of our motives and the impeccability of our behavior provide it with the necessary confirmation. Paul's response to such a view would surely be that it is God and not we who confirms the power and truth of the gospel. Preachers are "earthen vessels" of the gospel (2 Cor. 4:7 RSV). All is grace.

Another way of saying this is that the truth of the gospel ultimately speaks for itself. The Word of the living God shines in its own right. God's Word is the "word of life" (Phil. 2:16); it is bright, luminous, and radiant.[6] The effectiveness of the Word proclaimed does not depend on the preacher's eloquence or the saint's moral perfection. We cannot take credit if the gospel meets with a positive response among its hearers. Paul certainly did not: "I planted, Apollos watered, but God gave the growth. So neither the one who plants nor the one who waters is anything, but only God who gives the growth" (1 Cor. 3:6–7).

Once it is acknowledged that it is God and not our eloquence or moral perfection that confirms the truth of the gospel, it is helpful to underscore again that our flawed motives and devious practices can get in the way of the grace of God, can bring damage and discredit to the message that is proclaimed, can bring ridicule and disparagement to the mission of the church. So when Paul says, "What does it matter?" (1:18), he does not mean that our motives and practices are a matter of indifference. That would be tantamount to saying that we are free to sin with abandon, or at least to take lightly our responsibilities as Christ's disciples, since the grace of God accomplishes its purposes regardless of what we do. As Paul makes clear elsewhere, he will have none of that sort of talk: "Should we continue in sin in order that grace may abound? By no means! How can we who died to sin go on living in it?" (Rom. 6:1–2).

---

5. *The Constitution of the Presbyterian Church (U.S.A.)*, Part II, *Book of Order* (Louisville, KY: Office of the General Assembly, 1999), G-1.0304.
6. See Barth, *CD* IV/3.1:38–165.

A cavalier attitude about the integrity of our Christian witness would fly in the face of all that Paul wants to say in the Letter to the Philippians. As we shall soon see, this letter finds its center in the call to imitate Christ and to live a life worthy of the gospel. Assuredly, then, Paul's "What does it matter?" is not a flippant response to a serious issue in Christian ministry. It simply means that it is not we but the Spirit of God who is the effective power of every witness to the gospel and who alone ultimately confirms its truth. For this reason, Paul rejoices when the gospel of God is preached, "whether out of false motives or true" (1:18b).

1:18b–20
Speaking with All Boldness

As already noted, in addition to their concern about whether Paul's imprisonment could have adverse effects on the advance of the gospel, the Philippians are also worried about Paul himself. What are his prospects for timely release from captivity? Will he survive his present ordeal, or is he marked for execution? Will there be a trial, and how will Paul acquit himself? While Paul does not describe the details of his imprisonment or whether a trial is pending, his situation is clearly serious. But he is not discouraged. Indeed, he "will continue to rejoice" (1:18c). He rejoices because he knows that the Philippians are praying for him, and he is confident that through their prayers and with "the help of the Spirit of Jesus Christ," the present ordeal will "turn out for my deliverance" (1:19). It is not clear whether by "deliverance" Paul is here referring to his release from prison or to deliverance from his mortal existence that will bring him closer to Christ. The question is not easily answered. Perhaps the best answer is both. Paul does hope to see the Philippians again; in fact, he seems to be counting on it, as indicated by his hopeful words "when I come to you again" (1:26). At the same time, he is confident that if he should not survive this imprisonment, an even greater "deliverance" will be his.

Whatever happens—whether he is in or out of prison, whether he lives or dies—Paul is ready to proclaim the gospel "with all boldness" so that "Christ will be exalted" (1:20). Just as it does not matter to him whether some preachers proclaim Christ out of love and others out of selfish ambition, so long as "Christ is proclaimed in every way" (1:18), so the most important thing for Paul is not whether he lives or dies but only that Christ be honored and glorified. This is what Paul desires above all: to proclaim the gospel boldly so that Christ will be "exalted" ("magnified," as Calvin, Barth, and KJV translate the Greek verb *megalyno*).[7] Magnifying Christ is the signature goal of Paul's life and theology. For this reason he will not knuckle under to pressure. He will continue to speak boldly.

Paul's description of witness to the gospel as calling for boldness and fearlessness (1:14, 20) is also an implicit summons to his brothers and sisters in Philippi to be bold and to stand firm in face of whatever pressures they may be experiencing. Do not be "intimidated" by your opponents, he says a few verses later (1:28). It is not difficult to imagine the considerable risk taking and exceptional boldness required to bear witness to the crucified Christ as Lord in a city where the splendor and power of Rome is everywhere visible and celebrated and where Caesar is praised as lord and savior.

"Boldness" (in Greek, *parresia*) in the midst of danger is a characteristic of the biblical witness and a marker of the true Christian disciple.[8] The OT prophets spoke boldly. Indeed, one of the distinguishing marks of the true prophet in contrast to the false is that the former speaks truth to power whatever the consequences, whereas the latter says only what those in power want to hear. After King David has Uriah, the husband of Bathsheba, killed and then takes her as his own wife, the prophet Nathan confronts him. He tells the king a parable about a rich thug who seizes the small belongings of a poor man. David is outraged at the injustice and demands to know who engaged in such treachery. Nathan boldly charges: "You are the man!" (2 Sam. 12:7). Similarly, Peter and the other apostles speak with Christian boldness when, in response to the demand that they

---

7. John Calvin, *Galatians, Ephesians, Philippians and Colossians,* CNTC, ed. David W. Torrance and Thomas F. Torrance (1965; repr., Grand Rapids: Eerdmans, 1979), 236; Barth, *Philippians,* 35.

8. As used in Scripture, the word *boldness* suggests public speech and action free from fear. See *The New Interpreter's Dictionary of the Bible* (Nashville: Abingdon, 2006), 1:486.

desist from their preaching, they declare, "We must obey God rather than men" (Acts 5:29).

> **In life and in death we belong to God.**
>
> A Brief Statement of Faith, Presbyterian Church (U.S.A.) *Book of Confessions*, 10.1

The Reformers of the sixteenth century also showed boldness in their proclamation of the gospel. When Luther stood before the Diet of Worms in 1521 with his life on the line, he refused to compromise his commitment to the word of God attested in Scripture, famously stating: "Here I stand, I can do no other. God help me! Amen."[9] No less courage was required when the confessors at the Synod of Barmen in 1934 opposed the effort of the Nazis to bring the Evangelical Church in Germany under the control of the state. They boldly declared: "Jesus Christ, as he is attested for us in Holy Scripture, is the one word of God which we have to hear and which we have to trust and obey in life and in death."[10]

Boldness or courage is not often included in conventional lists of Christian virtues, or if mentioned, it is not very high on the list. We are more likely to recognize virtues like kindness and compassion as belonging to Christian character. It is easy to forget that when Jesus blesses the meek, or when Jesus and Paul describe themselves as servants, this does not mean lack of courage in face of efforts to twist the truth, or to truncate the gospel to make it less offensive, or to abuse the helpless. While Jesus calls love of God and neighbor the greatest of the commandments, and Paul declares love to be the greatest of God's gifts (1 Cor. 13:13), the love of which both Jesus and Paul speak is a tough love, and this love of God casts out all fear (1 John 4:18). When faithful witness to the gospel is at issue, Paul knows that all fear must be replaced by boldness. The boldness of which Paul speaks is not mere bravado or swagger. Nor is it an expression of bitterness and anger toward one's opponents. As the larger context of Paul's talk of boldness makes clear, his boldness is linked to his joyous confidence in the love of God made known in Jesus Christ.

9. See James M. Kittelson, *Luther the Reformer* (Minneapolis: Augsburg, 1986), 161.
10. The Theological Declaration of Barmen, in *The Constitution of the Presbyterian Church (U.S.A)*, Part I, *Book of Confessions* (Louisville, KY: Office of the General Assembly, 1999), 8.11.

Note that Paul gives two reasons why, although he is in prison, he expects things "to turn out for my deliverance." He expects release "through your prayers" and with "the help of the Spirit of Jesus Christ" (1:19). Earlier we considered how important prayer is in Paul's life and ministry. In the opening prayer of the letter he expresses confidence that the God of sovereign grace to whom he prays with joy will complete the good work begun in them (1:6). Now he continues to rejoice, knowing that his friends in Philippi are praying for him and that, whatever trials he faces, he will find deliverance and will not be put to shame (1:20).

Some attention must also be given, however, to the second reason for Paul's confidence that things will turn out for his deliverance—"the help of the Spirit of Jesus Christ." What is Paul's understanding of the Holy Spirit and the Spirit's relationship to Christ and God the Father? In part, this question arises because the Holy Spirit does not play as explicit a role in Philippians as in other letters of Paul. For example, while he refers to the Spirit as many as eighteen times in chapter 8 of Romans alone, and numerous times in the Corinthian letters, the word *Spirit* appears only four times in Philippians where it either refers or may refer to the Spirit of God or Christ(1:19; 1:27; 2:1; 3:3) On the basis of statistics like these, one might conclude that Paul's theology in this letter is more binitarian (God is only Father and Son) than Trinitarian (God is Father, Son, and Spirit). Such a conclusion may seem to find support from the fact that the Spirit is missing in the opening blessing of the letter, "Grace to you and peace from God our Father and the Lord Jesus Christ" (1:2), as well as in Paul's concluding reference to the riches of God's glory in Jesus Christ and the ascription of glory to God the Father (4:19–20). However, judging that Paul's understanding of God in Philippians ignores the Spirit and is properly described as binitarian would be a serious mistake.

It would be a mistake, first, for the obvious reason that the judgment would be anachronistic. As previously noted in our reflections on prayer, the doctrine of the Trinity is nowhere explicitly formulated in Paul's letters, as it would be in later centuries and particularly at the Council of Nicaea in 325 and the Council of Constantinople in 381. In repeating the Nicene-Constantinopolitan

Creed, Christians confess their faith in one God, Father, Son, and Holy Spirit. They confess that the Son is "of one substance" with God the Father, and that the Spirit is "the Lord and Giver of life" and is "worthy to be worshiped and glorified" together with the Father and the Son. Such formulations are still many years away from Paul's writings, either here in Philippians or in his other letters. Nevertheless, just because Paul does not use the precise words of Nicaea does not mean that we cannot discern a proto-Trinitarian way of thinking and speaking about God in his letters, including the Letter to the Philippians.

Second, faulting Paul as more binitarian than Trinitarian in this letter fails to take into account some important evidence to the contrary. In addition to the passage in which he expresses confidence of deliverance because of the help of the Spirit of Jesus Christ, he will later refer to the Spirit as a reality in whom he and the Philippians "share" just as they share the new life "in Christ" (2:1). Still later he will describe Christian worship as taking place "in the Spirit of God" (3:3). Moreover, even when Paul does not explicitly use the word *Spirit* in the letter, he surely assumes the Spirit's presence and work, as evident in his multiple references to the Spirit in his other letters. For example, who if not the Spirit is the ultimate source of the knowledge and insight to help the Philippians "to determine what is best" (1:10)? Who empowers them to bring forth the "harvest of righteousness" (1:9–11), if not the Spirit who is active in their lives? When Paul assures the Philippians that "God is at work" in them "both to will and to work for his good pleasure" (2:13), is this not an indirect reference to the presence and activity of the Spirit? If Paul in Romans declares that "the Spirit helps us in our weakness" (8:26), where else would the imprisoned Paul of the Letter to the Philippians find the strength to speak "with all boldness" (1:20) save in the help of "the Spirit of Jesus Christ"?

A fair parsing of all these explicit references and indirect allusions to the Spirit in Philippians would be that for Paul the Spirit is the power of God at work in the worship and service of the believing community, even as the crucified and risen Christ is the embodied focus of this worship and service, and God the Father is the one to whom all glory is given. Thus, despite the infrequency of explicit references to the Spirit in Philippians, for Paul, in this letter as else-where, the risen Christ is present and active to the glory of God in the power of the Spirit. Paul's God language is admittedly complex; nevertheless, it points in the direction of what can be called a proto-Trinitarian way of speaking about and praying to God.

To summarize: Encouraged by the prayers of his friends and con-fident in the help of the Spirit of Jesus Christ, Paul is prepared for whatever may come. However risky it may be, he will speak boldly. He is not arrogant about this determination. He does not say that the ordeal he faces is a piece of cake. He says that his "expectation and hope" is that he will "not be put to shame in any way" (1:20). His declaration is not, "Whatever comes will be easy to endure" but, to paraphrase, "No matter what, I will rejoice, for my hope is in God." In other words, Paul's confidence is based not in himself but in the grace of God in Jesus Christ at work through the Spirit. This is what helps him to remain steadfast and not falter under pressure or show any shame in his witness to the gospel. We are again reminded of his words to the church in Rome that nothing can "separate us from the love of God in Christ Jesus our Lord" (Rom. 8:38–39). Whether facing life or death, Paul rejoices and speaks "with all bold-ness," confident that "Christ will be exalted" (1:20).

1:21–26

Living Is Christ, Dying Is Gain

The Philippians' concern about Paul's imprisonment and his own future prompts his memorable declaration: "For to me, living is Christ and dying is gain" (1:21). The centrality of Christ for Paul is summed up in this "intensely personal confession."[11] Paul's con-fession is that his life is entirely consumed by dedication to Christ, that in all that he says and does his

---

> **Living or dying (Rom. 14:8), waking or sleeping (1 Thess. 5:10), Paul belongs to Christ.**
>
> Fred Craddock, *Philippians* (Atlanta: John Knox, 1985), 28.

---

11. O'Brien, *Philippians*, 120.

goal is to exalt Christ and to serve as his apostle to the Gentiles. He is declaring that he lives in, with, for, and on account of Christ, that he has no autonomous identity, no meaningful existence apart from Christ. As he states elsewhere: "I have been crucified with Christ; and it is no longer I who live, but it is Christ who lives in me. And the life I now live in the flesh I live by faith in the Son of God, who loved me and gave himself for me" (Gal. 2:19–20).

On the basis of passages like these, Albert Schweitzer and some other Pauline scholars have spoken of the "mystical" side of Paul's faith. Whether *mystical* is the best word to describe the matter is debatable. The word often suggests an ethereal and private experience, and this is certainly not what Paul means by saying that for him, "living is Christ and dying is gain." Not debatable, however, is that Paul's relationship with Christ is far more than merely notional or theoretical. It is at once deeply personal and eminently practical. Of course, Paul's affirmation "For to me, living is Christ" should not be interpreted to mean that Paul thinks he *is* Christ, or conversely, that Christ has *become* Paul. What it does mean is that Paul is convinced he has no reason for living apart from Christ. Paul's new and true identity is found only "in Christ."

Clarification of what Paul means by saying "For to me, living is Christ" is not aided by searching for analogies in the experience of people who invest themselves totally in particular activities or vocations. We might think of a Lou Gehrig saying, "For me, living is baseball," or a NASA astronaut, "For me, living is space exploration," or a Picasso, "For me, living is painting," or a Lyndon Johnson, "For me, living is politics." True, each of these affirmations may express a more or less free and joyful commitment to what is considered an exciting and worthwhile activity or vocation. While such analogies may bear a superficial resemblance to Paul's free and joyful "to me, living is Christ," in the final analysis they fall short of illuminating the depths of Paul's affirmation. His life is freely and totally dedicated to and claimed by a living Lord who is his Savior and the Savior of the world and who has claimed him for the service of the gospel. "I live to worship Christ; I live to serve Christ; I live to share Christ with others"—this paraphrase of Paul's "for to me, living is Christ" says far more than simply declaring that one's life is caught up in what is considered an exciting activity like baseball, space exploration, painting, or politics.

Coupled with Paul's affirmation that "living is Christ" is his affirmation that "dying is gain." This second of the two affirmations has generated at least as much comment as the first. Scholars tell us there is abundant evidence in the literature of Paul's time—and both earlier and later—that death was viewed as "gain" by those who looked for an escape from the troubles of life. Recall how Plato has Socrates, with cup of hemlock in hand, contemplate his death with great serenity. If death is no more than a dreamless sleep, Socrates says, it will be an "unspeakable gain."[12] This view of death, however, is not even close to Paul's meaning in speaking of death as "gain." He is not thinking of death as oblivion or a long and blissful slumber. Nor is "dying is gain" a way of saying he is overwhelmed by his missionary labors and wants to throw in the towel. Paul is not weary of life, burned out, and ready to end it all as soon as possible. Death for Paul is gain because it will bring still deeper union with Christ than he enjoys at present. Although he already lives "in Christ," Paul sees death as making possible "an enlargement of the experience of Christ."[13]

In brief, Paul is affirming that whether he lives or dies, he belongs to Christ, and Christ transforms death even as he transforms life. As Paul will later say, Christ is the Savior who will one day "transform the body of our humiliation that it may be conformed to the body of his glory" (3:20–21). Paul expresses the same conviction in another letter: "We do not live to ourselves, and we do not die to ourselves. If we live, we live to the Lord, and if we die, we die to the Lord; so then, whether we live or whether we die, we are the Lord's" (Rom. 14:7–8).

Some commentators wonder whether Paul may actually be contemplating suicide in this passage. Is he, like Shakespeare's Hamlet, setting for himself two final options: "To be or not to be?" According to this view, Paul is trying to decide whether to continue to live or to bring about his own death. In his dire straits Paul assesses his remaining options, and one of them is to commit suicide. This line

---

12. Plato, *Apology,* 40.
13. Charles B. Cousar, *Philippians and Philemon,* New Testament Library (Louisville, KY: Westminster John Knox, 2009), 39.

of thought, however, is not at all the direction of Paul's thinking here. Note that he states the issue in terms of what he prefers, not in terms of what he has the power to choose. Expressing a preference and making a choice are two different things. It is hard to imagine Paul thinking of himself here or elsewhere as one who has mastery over his life and death, as one who possesses the freedom to be the final arbiter of his destiny. For Paul, it is his Lord who ultimately makes the decision as to what his calling will be. Although he might for a moment "prefer" to die at this juncture of his missionary work, he realizes that his communities still need him. He is therefore willing to "remain and continue with all of you for your progress and joy in faith" (1:25).

Paul's meditation on his living or dying bears comparison with the prayer of Christ in Gethsemane: "Not what I want, but what you want," Christ prays (Mark 14:36). In both cases, the human will is being conformed to the will of God. In his prayer in Gethsemane, Christ asks that the cup of suffering be allowed to pass, but then affirms at once his unconditional willingness to obey the will of the Father. Paul, for his part, seems for a moment to prefer dying in order to be united more fully with Christ, only quickly to recognize that he is being called to continue to serve the young churches even if it means further labor and further suffering. In the one case, Christ, facing the terrible prospect of crucifixion and separation from the Father, fleetingly asks if there might be an alternative way to fulfill his mission but then immediately, freely, and unconditionally affirms the will of his Father. In the other case, Paul momentarily expresses a preference to be more closely united with Christ in death only soon to relinquish this thought for the sake of continued service of Christ by assisting the Philippians in their progress and joy in faith.

How should we describe Paul in light of his brief but gripping meditation on living and dying in Christ? Kierkegaard famously wrote that Paul is an apostle, not a genius.[14] He is no philosophical genius like Plato, and he is no poetic genius like Shakespeare. We might add that he is also no tragic hero like Shakespeare's Hamlet

---

14. *The Essential Kierkegaard*, ed. Howard V. Hong and Edna H. Hong (Princeton, NJ: Princeton University Press, 2000), 339–41.

pondering whether "to be or not to be." That is *not* Paul's question. There is no evidence here of a martyr complex in Paul. He has no interest in going out in a blaze of glory. Neither a genius, nor a hero, nor someone in search of martyrdom, Paul wants only to be a faithful witness to Jesus Christ, one who obediently follows the calling of his Lord in life and in death.[15]

For many commentators, Paul's meditation on life and death in this section has raised the question of a significant change or development in Paul's thinking about the end of his life and the final consummation of God's purposes. Did Paul in his early writings assume that he would be alive when Christ returned (1 Thess. 4:15); later come to hold that believers who died would "sleep" until the return of Christ (a view supported by Oscar Cullmann[16] but rejected by most other NT scholars[17]); and then finally arrive at the conviction that even if he died before Christ returned, his death would nevertheless be "gain" because he would be immediately "with Christ" (1:21, 23)? No doubt underlying this question is the desire, even anxiety, to know what the condition of those who die before the return of Christ will be.

A fair reading of the Letter to the Philippians, however, would confirm that Paul has no anxiety about the well-being of those in Christ who die before the glorious coming of the Savior. They will be safe with Christ, in still deeper communion with him, awaiting the denouement of God's redemptive purposes in Christ: the resurrection of the dead and the subjection of all things to himself (3:21). In other words, Paul has no difficulty holding together, on the one hand, the conviction that his death will be "gain" because he will be "with Christ" in even closer communion; with the confident expectation, on the other hand, that beyond his death a future "day of Christ" will come (1:6, 10), a new arrival of the Savior who will conform our body of humiliation to "the body of his glory" and

---

15. Karl Rahner offers the following definition of martyrdom: "A martyr is one who freely accepting his death in faith, is killed by powers inimical to Christ, and bears a noble testimony as a 'witness' to faith in Jesus Christ." *On the Theology of Death* (New York: Herder & Herder, 1969), 82.

16. Oscar Cullmann, *Immortality of the Soul or Resurrection of the Dead?* (New York: Macmillan), 48–57.

17. See D. E. H. Whitely, *The Theology of Paul* (Philadelphia: Fortress, 1964), 262–69.

will consummate God's work of redemption throughout creation (3:20–21; cf. Rom. 8:31–39). In brief, "life with Christ at death is no problem for the apostle."[18]

Paul does not provide us with a lot of particulars about the end time, any more than Jesus did (cf. Mark 13:32). For Paul as for Jesus, getting the chronology of the end of all things just right is not the important thing; faithfulness is. Unmistakable, however, is Paul's conviction that God's redemptive work accomplished in Christ and moving relentlessly toward consummation is not merely "soul saving" but death conquering and cosmos renewing. That is all we know and all we need to know about how our personal end will be related to the still outstanding consummation of God's purposes when the lordship of Christ will be revealed to all (2:11).

FURTHER REFLECTIONS
In Christ

The phrase "in Christ" or its equivalents like "in the Lord" occur frequently in all of Paul's letters and, according to Gordon Fee, no fewer than twenty times in the Letter to the Philippians.[19] At the beginning and end of the letter Paul sends greetings to all the saints "in Christ Jesus" (1:1; 4:21); in the passage that constitutes the centerpiece of the letter, Paul urges the Philippians to have the mind that is "in Christ Jesus" (2:5); later, he assures his friends that the peace of God that passes all understanding will keep their hearts and minds "in Christ Jesus" (4:7). How should we understand this unique marker of Paul's understanding of the gospel, and what significance does it have for Christian life and service today?

For Paul, being "in Christ" expresses a *new personal identity* that comes as a gift of new life by virtue of Christ and his saving work on our behalf. As Paul explains more fully in 1 Cor. 15:22, just as our old sinful identity was "in Adam," so our new identity is found "in Christ." In him we are new persons, a "new creation" (2 Cor. 5:17). Christ has made our humanity his own, and by faith we are given a

18. O'Brien, *Philippians*, 137.
19. Gordon D. Fee, *Paul's Letter to the Philippians* (Grand Rapids: Eerdmans, 1995), 49.

new identity in him. Our true life is now "hidden with Christ in God" (Col. 3:3).

In speaking of his new life "in Christ," and in his related declarations that for him "living is Christ" (1:21) and "I have been crucified with Christ; and it is no longer I who live, but it is Christ who lives in me" (Gal. 2:19–20; see also 2 Cor. 5:17–18; Rom. 8:1; Col. 3:3), Paul is not adopting a deterministic view of life, as though we are simply puppets of forces that operate over our heads. Our new life in Christ is God's gracious gift that we are called to appropriate freely in faith. We are summoned to gladly *become* who we truly *are* in Christ. We are to live out our new identity and our new freedom to serve God and others that we have been given "in Christ" by being conformed in our dispositions, decisions, and actions to his way of humility and self-expending love.

A second important dimension of the Pauline phrase "in Christ" is communal. Being "in Christ" means we are *members of Christ's new community.* The phrase expresses a new life of solidarity with others. Throughout the biblical writings, being human means belonging to a world of relationships with others, being part of a people gathered and sustained by God for the worship and service of God. Created as persons in the image of God, we are created and redeemed for life in community.

> **Persons become persons only in community, and a human community exists only in personal relationships.**
>
> Jürgen Moltmann, *Ethics of Hope* (Minneapolis: Fortress, 2012), 160.

In Bonhoeffer's phrase, reconciled and redeemed existence is "life together."[20] Thus to be "in Christ" is to participate in a new corporate life in which Christ reigns and we are inseparably bound together in him. Life in Christ redefines the meaning of personhood. In him we know that true human existence is coexistence, living gladly and freely with and for others.

Paul's description of the communal dimension of Christian life goes against the grain of much modern thinking and living. The relentless modern quest for personal identity takes many forms. The

---

20. Dietrich Bonhoeffer, *Life Together,* trans. John W. Doberstein (New York: Harper, 1954).

philosopher Charles Taylor characterizes modern society as "a society of self-fulfillers, whose affiliations are more and more seen as
revocable."[21] Personal identity is something individuals undertake
to "construct" from scratch, perhaps under the influence of a favorite
celebrity or the most recent cultural fad. Even the church is increasingly viewed as one of many voluntary associations, as simply one
organization among many others that individuals choose to join on
the major condition that it serves their own or their family's needs
and purposes. In partial reaction to this individualism of modernity,
there are numerous examples of persons and groups who seek to
define themselves primarily in terms of their particular nationality,
race, tribe, or social class. For Paul, life "in Christ" is altogether different from both modern individualism and its counterpart, exclusive
in-group loyalty.

There is still a third meaning of the phrase "in Christ" for Paul.
It refers to the *new vocation* of the believer. To be "in Christ" is not
only to receive a new personal identity and to find oneself in solidarity with other members of a new people among whom the gifts
of each are shared for the good of all. It is also to understand oneself and the community of faith to which one belongs as called to a
special vocation, a new life in the service of Christ and the gospel.
As apostle to the Gentiles, Paul understands his vocation to be the
proclamation of the good news of God's shattering of the age-old
boundary between Jews and Gentiles accomplished by the crucified and risen Christ. Other boundaries are also transgressed by the
world-renewing work of Christ. As Paul declares in another letter:
in Christ "there is no longer Jew or Greek, there is no longer slave
or free, there is no longer male and female; for all of you are one
in Christ Jesus" (Gal. 3:28). The gospel Paul proclaims and the new
vocation it inspires drives inexorably in the direction of breaking
down boundary lines of race, gender, ethnicity, religion, and culture, insofar as they become walls that separate people from the
grace of God in Jesus Christ and from one another.

There are, of course, obvious objections to this whole line of
thinking. First, is not the talk of life "in Christ" and "living is Christ"

---

21. Charles Taylor, *Sources of the Self: The Making of Modern Identity* (Cambridge, MA: Harvard,
1989), 508.

indicative of a kind of christocentric totalitarianism that threatens to empty all the ordinary joys of life? Is there nothing to be said for "living is fly fishing in a secluded stream" or "living is wrestling on the family room floor with your two-year-old"? The mistake here is to think that being in Christ is a constriction of life rather than its liberation, that the lordship of Christ brings domination rather than the release of human life for its full flourishing. Christ does not replace the goodness of everyday life but transforms, redirects, and enlarges it. For Paul, nothing truly human is alien to Christ and the new life in him.

Then, second, can we seriously think that the powerful sense of vocation that drove Paul might have anything to do with us? After all, Paul was called to be an apostle, and we have not been called to serve in this way. It is of course true that Paul was called to a special office in the life of the church, and it is also true that we are not apostles in the precise sense that Paul, John, Peter, and the other evangelists of the NT community are. Nevertheless, in dependence on their apostolic witness we too are called to be witnesses to Christ. In baptism we are blessed with the Spirit, given a new identity, and welcomed into new life "in Christ." At the Lord's Table we are bound in solidarity with Christ and with one another, strengthened for service in his name, and called to proclaim the Lord's death until he comes (1 Cor. 11:26). For all Christians, and not for Paul and the other apostles only, "living is Christ." As Karl Barth insists, all who are in Christ are called to be his followers and witnesses; all belong to a community essentially "summoned and impelled to exist for God and therefore for the world and [humankind]."[22]

---

22. Barth, *CD* IV/3.2:763.

1:27–2:18

The Humility of Christ as Paradigm of Christian Life

Most commentators agree that this section is the "centerpiece" or "linchpin" of Paul's Letter to the Philippians.[1] All the exhortations of the letter find their basis in the great hymn to the crucified and exalted Christ (2:5–11). When Paul urges the Philippians to live "in a manner worthy of the gospel" (1:27–30), he means a life that is conformed to the way of Christ, who in humility "emptied himself" (2:7) for our sake and became obedient to God even to death on a cross.

1:27–28
Just One Thing!

Having concluded the previous section with a promise to the Philippians to "come to you again" (1:26), Paul now marks an important transition in the letter with the single Greek word *monon* (literally, "one" or "only"). Standing by itself, this "one thing" might appear to be a mere throwaway word, a stylistic device to smooth over an otherwise awkward transition. In fact, however, it signals the beginning of what Paul wants most to say to his Philippian friends. He has thanked them for sharing in the gospel and the grace of God; he has told them that his imprisonment has actually helped spread the gospel; he has assured them that he will continue to speak boldly of Christ, whatever happens to him; and he has said how eager he is to return to Philippi and join them in their boasting in Christ. Then

---

1. Markus Bockmuehl, *The Epistle to the Philippians* (London: Hendrickson, 1988); Stephen E. Fowl, *Philippians* (Grand Rapids: Eerdmans, 2005).

Paul exclaims, "Just one thing!":[2] "Live your life in a manner worthy of the gospel of Christ."

This is not only the first exhortation of the letter; it is a fitting summary of all the exhortations that will follow. For Paul, of course, the gospel precedes every exhortation. In this and in his other letters, whether explicitly or implicitly, the indicative of what God has graciously done for us in Jesus Christ lies behind Paul's every imperative of what we are summoned and urged to do. That said, "Live in a manner worthy of the gospel" is Paul's strong reminder that the God of the gospel aims at the transformation of our lives individually and corporately. The apostle summons his readers not only to believe in Christ, not only to proclaim the truth of the gospel, but also to live in a manner worthy of that gospel. Not that Paul thinks what we believe is unimportant as long as we live an upright life. Rather, he is saying that Christian faith and life cannot be separated. The divorce of Christian conviction from Christian practice makes for a catastrophic distortion of the Christian calling.

But just what is a manner of life worthy of the gospel of Christ? Paul will answer this question in several steps leading up to the climactic hymn describing the way of Jesus Christ (2:5–11). Right off, however, it is important to emphasize that for Paul living in a manner worthy of the gospel encompasses not simply the personal behavior of believers but also the character of their common life. It would be easy enough for us to think that Paul's exhortations in this section are directed to members of the Philippian congregation simply as individuals. In a society like ours that prizes the freedom and self-realization of the individual, we may be inclined to conclude quickly that Paul is simply saying, "Each of you should live a life worthy of the gospel." However, if we limited the scope of Paul's exhortation in this way, we would miss a crucial part of the message of his letter. Life in Christ is a new way of living together. A new people, a new community (*koinonia*), comes into being in Christ, a community that confesses Christ as Lord, lives by his grace alone, shares in his Spirit, and follows his direction. As Paul proclaims the gospel, the new creation in Christ is not limited to the salvation and renewal

2. Karl Barth, *The Epistle to the Philippians* (Louisville, KY: Westminster John Knox Press, 2002), 45.

of isolated individuals. It declares what God has done in Christ to create a new human community of mutual love and service in him. Paul's gospel and the ethics that attend it emphasize the solidarity of believers in Christ and with each other.[3]

Paul's concern for the new life together in Christ is expressed in the main verb of 1:27. Although the Greek word *politeuesthe* is often translated "live your life" (NRSV), it has the more specific connotation of living in community, the common life of citizens in a city (*polis*) or political order.[4] This is language that the Philippians, as residents of a Roman colony, would readily understand. The word *politeuesthe* thus has unmistakable "political overtones" and would carry special "punch" with the Philippians.[5] After all, they are well aware of the many privileges and common responsibilities of Roman citizens. Later Paul will speak again of the new and true citizenship of believers (3:20), but already in this initial exhortation of the letter he instructs the Philippians that being Christian means belonging to "a new type of society, a radically new polis,"[6] one that is centered on Christ and "worthy of the gospel." An expanded paraphrase of the

> The formative biblical images which point to and describe the divine activity in the world are *political* images.
>
> Paul Lehmann, *Ethics in a Christian Context* (New York: Harper & Row, 1963), 90.

exhortation might read: "You are citizens of God's new order. Let your life together reflect the way of your Lord, not the prevailing way of life in a colony of the Roman Empire. Live like the people you truly are in Christ. Show that you are a new community in him. Live together 'in a manner worthy of the gospel.'"

Paul surely realizes that in urging the Philippians not to become carbon copies of other residents of their city, he risks that they may be accused of sedition or anarchy, of being enemies of the state, or of

3. See David G. Horrell, *Solidarity and Difference: A Contemporary Reading of Paul's Ethics* (London: T. & T. Clark, 2005).
4. Fowl underscores the communal/political meaning of Paul's imperative *politeuesthe* by his translation, "order your common life" (*Philippians*, 59).
5. Bockmuehl, *Philippians*, 97.
6. Bruno Blumenfeld, *The Political Paul: Justice, Democracy and Kingship in a Hellenistic Framework* (London: Sheffield, 2001), 294. While offering many insights, Blumenfeld's reading of "the political Paul," is, by his own admission, "extreme" (450).

having no respect for the law. But the charge would have been mistaken then and is mistaken now. Christians are neither conformists nor anarchists. Their life together has a different leader, is informed by a different narrative, reflects a different ethos, and moves toward a different goal. To be "in Christ" is to belong to a new form of human community based on the grace of God proclaimed in the gospel. Their life together, under the Lord Jesus Christ and led by the Spirit, is to constitute a communal witness to the gospel. This means that it is not only by their words but also by the quality of their common life and service that Christians either bear faithful witness to the gospel or obscure and even contradict it.

Paul goes on to explain that in the new community of Christ, members are to stand firm "in one Spirit" (1:27). Is this a lowercase spirit or an uppercase Spirit? That is, is Paul urging the Philippian church to show a robust communal spirit, a strong esprit de corps, much as a coach might rally his soccer players to exhibit a team spirit? Or is Paul thinking of the unity of the community that arises from the presence and activity of the Spirit of God at work among them? While NRSV translates "in one spirit" (lowercase), I follow Barth, Fee, and other commentators in understanding the Spirit (uppercase) as God's Spirit.[7] Paul is speaking here not of a sense of belonging together generated by the community itself. Instead, he is thinking of the Spirit as the gift of God's own uniting power. Paul leaves no ambiguity about the source of Christian faith and life or of the unity of believers. Unity in the Spirit of God is first of all a gift and only then also our task that is not to be evaded.[8]

In addition to "standing firm in one Spirit," Paul further describes the new community in Christ as one in which believers are "striving side by side with one mind for the faith of the gospel" (1:27). As we have already heard and shall hear again, Christian life for Paul is no settled, comfortable, conflict-free existence. It involves strenuous movement toward a goal, a continuous struggle against hostile forces in believers and in the world around them. Once again, however, it is important to note that for Paul this struggle is no individualistic

---

7. Barth, *Philippians,* 46–47; Gordon D. Fee, *Paul's Letter to the Philippians* (Grand Rapids: Eerdmans, 1995), 166.
8. Barth, *Philippians,* 47.

affair. It is not a contest we are expected to manage on our own. We belong to a community whose members strive and struggle "side by side," "in one Spirit," and "with one mind." Christians have a common Lord, a common commitment, and a common goal. Together they strive "for the faith of the gospel" (1:27).

Note that Paul does not say they are to strive "for *your* faith" or "for *our* faith in the gospel," as if the focus of Christians should be on *their* acts of faith. Paul's reference to "the faith of the gospel" does not place us as believers at the center of attention. Faith always points to its object, to the gospel of Christ that awakens and sustains faith. The point can be put this way: the gospel has to do with God's faithfulness to the world in Jesus Christ, and that message of God's faithfulness, God's gracious yes to us, summons us to faith. The faithfulness of God that moves us to faith is "the faith of the gospel."

There is another characteristic of the new community in Christ besides standing firm in the one Spirit and "striving side by side" for "the faith of the gospel." It is the refusal to be "intimidated" (1:28) in any way by opponents of the gospel. Recall that earlier Paul said that he is speaking out boldly in his imprisonment. Now he exhorts the Philippians in their own situation to be bold and not be "intimidated" by whatever opposition they may be facing (1:28a). Hansen notes that the word translated "be intimidated" or "frightened" occurs only here in the New Testament. He explains that it is used in the literature of the time to refer to the terror often exhibited by horses in battle. "Paul's instruction to stand firm without being frightened calls for Christians not to be agitated and terrified on the battlefield as horses often are."[9] The possibility of intimidation reminds us again that the Philippian Christians found themselves in a context where the power of Rome was pervasive and conspicuous. The Roman emperor was honored at every public gathering in Philippi. Since Christians in the city were worshiping another Lord, they would likely have been seen by other residents of Philippi as disturbers of the public order or even as being guilty of sedition.[10] In short, there was ample reason why the Philippians might be intimidated and in need of Paul's encouragement to stand

9. G. Walter Hansen, *The Letter to the Philippians* (Grand Rapids: Eerdmans, 2009), 98.
10. Fee, *Philippians*, 167.

together, have one mind, and remain firm in their convictions and practices.

With the Philippians' firmness in the faith and refusal to be intimidated in mind, Paul's next sentence reads: "For them this is evidence of their destruction, but of your salvation" (1:28b). The sentence is ambiguous, and commentators disagree about its precise meaning. Most commentators understand Paul to be saying that in standing firm and in struggling side by side for the gospel, the Philippians constitute a "sign" (O'Brien), "omen" (RSV), or "evidence" (NRSV) of the eventual "destruction" of their opponents and of the Philippians' coming "salvation."[11] This does not mean, of course, that the Philippian Christians and their opponents perceive what is happening in the same way. Indeed, they see matters in entirely different ways. As far as the opponents are concerned, the Philippians' refusal to conform would seem foolish and deserving of the destruction they were bringing on themselves. Paul, however, encourages the Philippian Christians to see God's hand at work in what they are going through. "This is God's doing," he assures them (1:28b). Their steadfastness in the faith in the face of persecution is a sign not of their coming destruction, as their opponents think, but of their coming salvation.

1:29–30
The Privilege of Suffering

Earlier Paul has assured the Philippians that his suffering and imprisonment should not unsettle or frighten them (as though it were evidence that the gospel is false or that the ministry of Paul is faltering).

> **We do not believe if we do not live in the neighborhood of Golgotha.**
>
> Karl Barth, CD II/1:406.

On the contrary, his imprisonment and suffering have served to spread the gospel (1:12). Now he calls the Philippians to view their present situation in a similar manner. Far from being a burden, or a mark of

---

11. Peter T. O'Brien, *The Epistle to the Philippians* (Grand Rapids: Eerdmans, 1991), 154.

God's displeasure, God has graciously granted them "the privilege [*echaristhe*] not only of believing in Christ, but of suffering for him as well" (1:29). God can use the suffering and even martyrdom of faithful disciples to bear witness to God's work of salvation in Christ. Notice that in speaking to the Philippians of the privilege of suffering for Christ, Paul is not addressing a few individuals in the Philippian church but the community as a whole. The "you" who having been granted this privilege is plural. The privilege is shared. Here again, Paul's summons to "solidarity" (Horrell) is evident, now in the form of a solidarity in suffering.

Contemporary readers of Paul's letter might well wonder whether speaking of suffering as something God has granted as a favor or "privilege" is not a rather hard pill to swallow. No doubt many readers of this passage today would be inclined to agree with Tevye in *Fiddler on the Roof*, who readily thanks God for giving Jews the honor of being God's elect people, together with all the suffering this has entailed, but then pleads with God to be so kind as to share the honor with other people from time to time. A response of this sort to Paul's talk about suffering for Christ as a gift or privilege is understandable. We must keep in mind, however, that Paul sees every aspect of Christian life in relationship to the life, passion, death, and resurrection of Jesus Christ. According to both Old and New Testaments, suffering can have a redemptive significance within the purposes of God. This is true preeminently of Christ's saving mission, but it may also be true in a "derivative and participatory" sense in the case of those who live in him and follow his way.[12] The qualification "derivative and participatory" emphasizes that Christ is "for us" in a way that we can never be "for him." Nevertheless, what Christians do and suffer for Christ can be a representation and proclamation of his redemptive work even though what they do and suffer can never be a repetition or completion of his saving life and death for them and for all. Paul's language of the "privilege" of suffering for Christ is the language of our free participation in and proclamation of God's free gift in him.

---

12. Bockmuehl, *Philippians*, 102.

In reading Paul's Letter to the Philippians, we should never let ourselves forget that, while the letter is laced with calls to rejoice, it is not naive about what Christians may be summoned to do and to suffer as witnesses to their Lord. To be in Christ, to be a witness and servant of Christ, is sheer grace, but the grace of God in Christ is not "cheap grace" (Bonhoeffer); it calls for us to follow him wherever this may lead. Of course, if one is committed to maximizing one's own comfort and well-being regardless of the plight and needs of others, it is simply impossible to imagine suffering for Christ and the gospel as, paradoxically, a gift or privilege.

> Cheap grace is grace without discipleship, grace without the cross, grace without Jesus Christ, living and incarnate.
>
> Dietrich Bonhoeffer, *The Cost of Discipleship* (New York: Macmillan, 1963), 47.

Note well how Paul emphasizes here his solidarity with the Philippians in suffering. We can paraphrase his point: "You are having the same struggle [*agona*, contest] that I have had and continue to have" (1:30). Paul does not sit in the grandstands of life viewing from a safe distance the runners below making their way on the arduous track of discipleship. He is on the field with them. Nor does Paul demean what they are going through in comparison with his own situation. He does not say, "You think you have it tough? Why complain? Look at how much more I am suffering than you are." For Paul, Christians are in the struggle of faith and the journey of Christian life together.

FURTHER REFLECTIONS
Suffering for Christ

While virtually all commentators would agree that the theme of suffering for Christ is deeply etched in this letter, the view that it is basically a summons to martyrdom is misleading. There are no grounds for thinking that Paul intended to make martyrdom an end to be desired or that he considered it a way to gain favor with God. The basic meaning of the Greek word *martyr* is simply "witness," and Paul exhorts all his fellow Christians to be firm and steadfast witnesses to their Lord in whatever circumstances they find themselves.

In the history of the church, there are, of course, many instances of Christians glorifying the act of martyrdom and yearning to die a martyr's death. The best known is Ignatius of Antioch (second century) who famously longed to be devoured by the wild beasts in the coliseum in order to become "a real disciple" and "get to God."[13] Paul, however, never urges believers to long to be killed for their witness, for two very basic theological reasons: Christ has already died for us and our salvation, and believers have already been baptized into his death (Rom. 6:3). Salvation is God's gift and not a reward for our being martyred. Paul does not shrink from bearing witness to the gospel even at risk of death because he is convinced that not even death can separate him from the love of God in Christ. Still, having affirmed that for him "living is Christ and dying is gain" (1:21), he chooses the life of service to his brothers and sisters rather than death.

The question for contemporary readers of Philippians, however, is whether the recurrent motif of suffering and the awareness of the possibility of martyrdom in the letter have anything to say to Christians today. There are several aspects of the question. One is that for some heirs of the modern Enlightenment project, like the philosopher Friedrich Nietzsche, Christianity is a sick and unworthy religion because it revels in weakness and suffering and banishes all joy from human life. Unfortunately, Christian teaching about suffering has sometimes been distorted in ways that have poisoned all longings for fullness of life, blunted opposition to unjust suffering, and given sanction to the plight of the poor and the abused. Paul's Letter to the Philippians, however, has nothing to do with the call to suffer for suffering's sake or to secure one's salvation. Far from diminishing concern for and love of others, and far from robbing life of joy, Paul's exhortation to suffer with and for Christ is at the same time a call to joyful confidence in the steadfast love of God and a summons to a life of generosity and loving regard for others.

Another aspect of the question of the relevance of Paul's talk of suffering for Christians today is whether he is attempting to justify

13. Ignatius, *Ephesians* 1.2; *Romans* 4.1, in *Early Christian Fathers*, LCC 1, ed. Cyril C. Richardson (Philadelphia: Westminster, 1963), 88, 104.

suffering as a general feature of the world in which we live. The brief answer is no. Paul is neither an ancient tragedian nor a modern theodicist. Unlike the Greek tragedians, he does not teach that suffering is the sorry lot of humankind governed by blind fate or the caprice of the gods, simply a brutal fact of life that must be heroically endured. Unlike modern theodicists, Paul does not try to construct theological arguments to explain why belief in a good and omnipotent God is compatible with the reality of suffering in the world, and especially with the horrendous evils that leave human beings overwhelmed and speechless. In other words, Paul does not speak of suffering in general. Instead, he speaks very specifically of suffering "for Christ" (1:13, 29) or "for his sake" (3:8). These phrases do not directly address the multitude of questions prompted by disease, accident, war, or natural disaster. The suffering Paul is experiencing and knows that the Philippians are experiencing too is not the result of creaturely frailty or of catastrophic events like earthquakes and floods. It is suffering that comes as a result of faithful proclamation of the gospel and service in the name of Christ. To make suffering-in-general the theme of Paul's letter and the dominant mark of Christian life is to obscure and distort the meaning of "suffering on account of Christ."

In the wake of recent world events, positing a necessary link between faith and suffering, or more specifically between faith and martyrdom, would strike many people today as deeply problematic and frankly dangerous. Terrorism haunts our world, and the very word *martyrdom* sends a chill down our spines. But the association of what Paul says in Philippians with modern terrorist activities would be bizarre. One can hardly imagine a more egregious distortion of Paul's Letter to the Philippians than to classify it with understandings of martyrdom circulating among religious extremists today. The notion that one can become a "martyr" and earn a reward for oneself in heaven by suicide bombings in crowded marketplaces, mosques, and churches is a moral monstrosity, not a martyrdom in the sense of having one's life taken on account of one's confession of the lordship of Christ, who comes to the world in humility and self-giving love.

Suffering for Christ, and its ultimate expression in martyrdom, is not a curious piece of ancient history. It takes place no less in the world today than it did in the first centuries of the church. When the facade of Westminster Abbey in London was renovated in 1998, niches that had been empty since the Middle Ages were filled with sculptures of ten Christian martyrs of the twentieth century, including Dietrich Bonhoeffer, Martin Luther King Jr., and Oscar Romero. These ten sculptures represent, of course, only a small fraction of the many thousands of Christians in our own era who have been persecuted or suffered a violent end because of their witness to the way of Christ. But what about all the other Christians who sleep safely at night? Can suffering for Christ have any personal meaning for comfortable and secure middle-class Christians in many Western societies proud of their tradition of religious toleration?

When the word *suffering* is used, the first thing that may come to mind is physical pain or bodily deprivation. Paul certainly experienced a lot of this sort of suffering (see 2 Cor. 11:25–27). However, in Philippians Paul does not provide a litany of physical sufferings. Rather, as we shall see, when he tells his readers he has "suffered the loss of all things" for the sake of Christ (3:8), he has in mind the loss of all the things he considered valuable prior to his meeting Christ, in particular his pride in being blameless before the law and his zeal in guarding the exclusivity of God's covenant with Israel. For the Philippians, too, their sufferings and losses would have included more than the possibility of incarceration or death. It would no doubt also have included loss of social standing in a colony of Rome whose residents were proud to be citizens of the world's greatest empire, with its vaunted history, fearsome military, and impressive cultural and political achievements.

The possibility of suffering *this* sort of loss is surely one of the costs that may attend a life worthy of the gospel even in modern democratic societies proud of their tradition of religious freedom. Christians in the United States, for example, are challenged like the Philippians to have the mind of Christ and to live out their faith as residents of a great empire with powerful military forces and a pervasive sense of exceptionality among the nations. This may well mean experiencing "losses" analogous to the significant losses that Paul experienced and that he called the Philippian Christians to endure as well. Can one be a Christian in Philippi or in New York or

Chicago or Los Angeles without a readiness to risk, with Paul, "the loss of all things" (3:8) that seem so precious but that threaten to get in the way of our witness to Christ and our reconciliation with others? Christ's way of humility and self-expending love for others is the unsubstitutable paradigm of the Christian life. It cannot be despised or ignored unless one wants to find oneself among those Paul describes in Philippians as "enemies of the cross" (3:18).

2:1–4
Be in Full Accord

Paul continues his appeal to the Philippians to live together in harmony by a series of "if" clauses: "if there is any encouragement in Christ," if there is "any consolation from love," if there is "any sharing in the Spirit," if there is "any compassion and sympathy, make my joy complete" (2:1). These "if" clauses should not be read as having only hypothetical force, as though Paul were not sure whether the Philippians have in fact experienced these realities "in Christ." Paul's meaning is better grasped if each "if" clause is replaced by a "since" clause: "since all of us find encouragement in Christ . . ." Paul is referring to realities that the Philippians are presently experiencing, not to possibilities they might experience in the future.

Paul's exhortations here and elsewhere in the letter show that he wants to nurture a particular kind of life together in Christ. He wants Christ to be formed in them, and his joy will not be complete until this happens (2:2; cf. Gal. 4:19, "My little children, . . . I am again in the pain of childbirth until Christ is formed in you"). Mutual encouragement, mutual consolation, mutual sharing, mutual compassion, and joy in the midst of suffering are markers of this new life together under the lordship of Christ. We might call these markers a sampling of the virtues of new community in Christ as long as we understand that such virtues do not have their source either in the individual members of the community themselves or in the inherent capabilities of the community as a whole. Rather, these virtues of the Christian life have their ultimate source and continuing power from the living Christ who by the Holy Spirit creates and sustains the community and its members.

Paul contrasts this new way of life together in Christ with its opposite. If there are virtues of the new community, there are also vices to be avoided: selfish ambition, conceit, looking out only for one's own interests. Over against such attitudes and motives, Paul urges: "In humility regard others as better than yourselves" (2:3). What is common to the vices Paul lists is the effort to make oneself the center of the world rather than looking to God and the needs of the neighbor. Luther aptly describes sin as basically *incurvatus in se,* "being curved in on itself."[14] In other words, sin is living in the closed circle of the self, a prison whose doors are locked from within. Proclamation of the gospel aims to unlock these closed prison doors and open the way to a new life together in Christ.

Outstanding among the markers of this new life in Christ is "humility" (*tapeinophrosyne*) (2:3). Far from being a virtue in the Greco-Roman ethical tradition of Paul's time, to be among the humble was deemed not only undesirable but base, even shameful.[15] Humility described the condition of those who were servile, lowly, obsequious, and ignorant, those who lacked the dignity, independence, and self-esteem of the Greek philosopher or the Roman citizen. For Paul, however, humility is understood altogether differently. This is because, as we shall see directly, humility is totally revalued by who Christ is and what he does. As Paul understands humility in the light of Christ, it describes those who know themselves to be radically dependent on the grace of God and who are therefore freed to place the needs of others above their own self-interests. For Paul, the gospel brings about a decentering and recentering of human life. To be in Christ is to be human in dependence on and with thanksgiving for the grace of God that is manifested in care and regard for others. When Paul exhorts the Philippians to be of one accord and of one mind, and in humility to look to the interest of others rather than their own interests, he is saying in effect, "Live as the new community you are by the grace of God in Christ! In your relationships

14. Luther, *Lectures on Romans,* LW 25, ed. Hilton C. Oswald (St. Louis: Concordia, 1972), 345.
15. Bockmuehl, *Philippians,* 110–11; Fee, *Philippians,* 187–88.

with one another, put into practice your new and true identity in your one Lord!"

Now take special note how Paul goes about encouraging this new manner of life "worthy of the gospel." He does not simply issue a set of commands: "Do this. Do not do that." A manner of life worthy of the gospel is not primarily a matter of obeying commands or adhering to a set of rules. Rather, Paul urges them to live as a community empowered and guided by the "mind of Christ." He reminds the Philippians of the story of Jesus Christ the Lord that is at the heart

> It is not abstract argument, but example, that gives the [church's] word emphasis and power.
>
> Dietrich Bonhoeffer, *Letters and Papers from Prison* (New York: Macmillan, 1971), 383.

of the gospel and of Christian faith. Retelling this story in the form of a hymn or poem, Paul exhorts the Philippians to let their minds and hearts, their dispositions and affections, their decisions and actions, be formed and patterned after the way of Christ. The living Christ of the Christ hymn is for Paul the supreme paradigm of the new life in Christ.

As we attend to this hymn, it quickly becomes apparent where Paul anchors Christian freedom and responsibility. If the new life in Christ is not simply following a set of rules, even less is it a frolic of unrestrained freedom, doing what one pleases, living an anything-goes life that ignores all discipline and direction. Christian life for Paul follows an altogether different logic from legalism on the one hand or libertinism on the other. In Philippians as in his other letters, Paul is indeed an apostle of Christian freedom: "For freedom Christ has set us free" (Gal. 5:1). Paul understands this freedom, however, as having a particular basis and content. Freedom for Paul is both a freedom *from* bondage to sin and a positive freedom *for* the service of God and neighbor. This freedom for God and others has its basis and paradigm in the free and gracious act of God for us in Jesus Christ. Christian freedom is patterned after the way of Christ. It is Christ-formed life. In other letters, Paul can speak of Christian life as bound to the "law of Christ." By the law of Christ Paul has in mind Christ's way of humility and self-expending love that is active in the life of Christians when they "bear one another's burdens" (Gal. 6:2), "associate with the lowly" (Rom. 12:16), and love their neighbors as themselves (Rom. 13:9). According to Paul, only a new life together grounded in and shaped by the way of Jesus Christ is "worthy of the gospel."

2:5–8

The Self-Emptying of Christ

We have now arrived at Paul's great Christ hymn that constitutes the center point of his letter. If the driving motive and the supreme paradigm of responsible life in Christ were only implicit in what Paul has previously written, they are now made crystal clear. In this hymn Paul describes the person, work, and way of Christ as the radiant power and supreme model of all who are in Christ.

In the NRSV this passage is formatted like a poem with two stanzas. In the first stanza (2:5–8), the hymn describes Christ Jesus as one who, though being in the form (*morphe*) of God and equal (*eso*) with God, emptied himself, taking the form of a servant, humbling himself, and becoming obedient even to death on a cross. In the second stanza (2: 9–11), the hymn speaks of God's exaltation of Jesus, giving him the name above every name, to the end that all creation, from the heights of heaven to the depths of the earth, should confess that he is Lord to the glory of God the Father. Since the early centuries of the church, this extraordinarily rich passage has been one of the most discussed texts in the New Testament. Its meaning cannot possibly be exhausted in a few pages. I limit my comments to a few of the more important questions prompted by the Christ hymn.

We may first want to know where this hymn originated. Some scholars have seen it as evidence of major Hellenistic influence in the thought of Paul. According to this view, the worship of Jesus, speaking of him as "in the form of God," or "being equal with God," was not part of the theology of the early Christian movement but was developed only as the gospel was extended into the Hellenistic world where the idea of descending and ascending angels and gods was prevalent. Once a widespread view, this view of the Hellenistic origin of this

passage is no longer held by many NT scholars. There is every reason to think that the "high Christology" present in this hymn is not
something Paul has imported from outside the Christian community but is an expression of the exuberant praise of Christ in early
Christian worship.[16]

We do not know whether Paul composed the text himself or is
quoting from a widely known hymnlike confession. If the latter, it
would simply confirm that Paul did not make up the gospel but proclaimed what he had "received" (1 Cor. 15:3). In any case, his own
touch is clearly evident in a phrase like "even death on a cross," which
coincides with the central importance of the cross in Paul's theology
(note how in 3:18 Paul speaks of his opponents as "enemies of the
cross"). Scholars increasingly agree that the content of this hymn
stands in continuity with the earliest confessions embedded in the
New Testament: Jesus is the Christ (Mark 8:29) and "Jesus is Lord"
(1 Cor. 12:3). In other words, the hymn is a powerful early summary of the central gospel narrative of God's presence and work in
the lowly servant Jesus. All this means that there can no longer be
any doubt that from earliest times, Jesus was the object of worship
and praise in the Christian community. Passages like Philippians
2:5–11 simply make explicit what is implicit from the beginning
of the Christian movement. The idea that Jesus was first viewed by
Christians as merely another prophet or great teacher and was only
much later elevated to the state of divinity does not fit the evidence.
As Richard Bauckham succinctly puts the matter, from the earliest
years of the church, the crucified Jesus was confessed as belonging
to the very identity of God.[17]

Another much-discussed question arises from the Pauline preface to the hymn (2:5). The NRSV translates the verse, "Let the same
mind be in you that was in Christ Jesus," whereas the RSV translates, "Have this mind among yourselves, which you have in Christ
Jesus." The former reading tends to emphasize the primarily ethical

---

16. "We cannot attribute the origins of the cultic worship of Jesus to Pauline Christianity.
    Instead, Pauline Christians took over and perpetuated from previous circles of Christians
    a devotional pattern in which Jesus functioned with God as subject matter and recipient of
    worship." Larry W. Hurtado, *Lord Jesus Christ: Devotion to Jesus in Earliest Christianity* (Grand
    Rapids: Eerdmans, 2003), 136–37.
17. Richard Bauckham, *God Crucified* (Carlisle: Paternoster, 1998).

purpose of the hymn: "In your thinking and acting, follow Christ Jesus." The latter translation tends to emphasize the soteriological presupposition of the hymn: "You Philippians already have new life in Christ Jesus and should allow this reality to shape and govern all your thinking and your relationships with your brothers and sisters." Some scholars see a major difference between these readings of the verse, but I regard the ethical and the soteriological aspects of the hymn as inseparable and see no compelling reason to have to choose between them. The soteriological reading implies the ethical, and the ethical reading presupposes the soteriological.

More important than the questions about the origin of the hymn or the nuances of Paul's preface is the fact that the hymn narrates the event of the coming of Christ Jesus from God in two acts reaching from eternity to eternity. In the first part of the drama we are told of God's astonishing love in Jesus Christ in which he humbled himself for our sake, even to the point of dying a criminal's death on a cross. In the second part we are told of the equally amazing divine vindication of the crucified Christ, his exaltation, and his being given a name that is above every name.

We begin with the central claims of the first stanza of the hymn (2:6–8). Two possible lines of interpretation are widely discussed. Does the hymn say, as some commentators argue, that Christ Jesus was "equal with God" from all eternity but that he gave up this equality, and in this sense "emptied" (*ekenosen*) or divested himself of divinity and took on a human form for our sake? Or does it say, as other commentators contend, that Christ did not regard his equality with God as something to be "grasped" or selfishly "exploited" (*harpagmon*) but instead poured out his love for us, taking on the life of a humble servant and living and dying as an obedient servant of God for our salvation? Answers to these much-discussed questions hang largely on how the Greek words *harpagmos* and *ekenosen* are translated and understood. *Harpagmos* can mean seizing something that one does not own or exploiting or making selfish use of one's own possessions.[18] I agree with those commentators who contend that the latter rendering not only best fits the overall meaning

18. See N. T. Wright, "Harpagmos and the Meaning of Philippians 2:5–11," *Journal of Theological Studies* (1986): 321–52.

and purpose of the hymn in the Letter to the Philippians but is also most congruent with Paul's understanding of Christ in his letters as a whole. Christ did not take advantage of his status or rights as equal with God but instead looked not to his own interests but to the interests of others (2:4).

Consistent with this understanding of *harpagmos*, the affirmation that Christ "emptied" (*ekenosen*) himself on our behalf should not be taken to mean that he vacated or abandoned his divinity and underwent a kind of ontological change. In other words, "emptied" does not mean that, although originally equal with God, Christ voluntarily ceased to be divine when he became human. Rather, his self-emptying refers to his pouring out his life for human redemption, not to some kind of ontological metamorphosis into something less than divine. It is an act of astonishing humility and self-expenditure for the sake of others, but by no means an act of self-contradiction or even self-annihilation. Barth puts the matter this way: God's giving is a self-giving, but not a giving up of being God.[19] We will have occasion later to note that Paul—surely with the self-emptying of Christ in mind—uses the metaphor of his own life being poured out like a libation over the sacrifice and faith of the Philippians (2:17).

The first stanza of the Christ hymn is, along with John 1:14— "The Word became flesh"—one of the key texts for later doctrines of the incarnation of Christ. It must be emphasized, however, that the event of incarnation should not be thought of as completed with the birth of Christ. No doubt "born in human likeness" (2:7; cf. Gal. 4:4) emphatically affirms Christ's full humanity. Yet when the hymn further declares that his self-emptying, self-humbling, and voluntary obedience were "to the point of death—even death on a cross" (2:8), we are clearly to understand that throughout the course of his life, passion, and death Christ gave himself in free and faithful obedience to the will of his Father. Rightly understood, then, the incarnation of Christ refers not simply to the moment of his birth or his death but to the whole course of his life that culminated in his crucifixion and resurrection in fulfillment of the eternal purpose of

19. Barth, *CD* IV/1:184-85.

God. We read the Christ hymn properly when we say that in all that Christ said and did—his preaching and teaching of the kingdom of God, his healing of the sick, his blessing of children and the poor, his table fellowship with sinners, and most decisively, his passion and death—he was pouring out his love, giving of himself, and freely obeying the will of God for our salvation.

But, it may be asked, where does the text say anything about the saving purpose of this self-emptying, self-humbling, and obedient act of Christ? In other words, does Paul's Christ hymn contain any explicit soteriological point? Are we not simply given an impressive example of humility to follow? Is not the intent of the hymn strictly ethical? In response to these questions, it does seem clear that Paul's reminder to the Philippians of Christ's act of self-expending love serves the purpose of clarifying for them what constitutes the definitive Christian paradigm or model of the new life in Christ. That said, however, it would be a serious distortion of Paul's theology if we were to understand Christ's act of self-emptying and self-giving as only exemplary, as if the work of Christ were on the same level, so to speak, as what his followers are now urged to do (2:4). On the contrary, Paul's gospel is surely far more than a list of things for us to do. It is first of all a message of what God in Christ has done for us: "in Christ God was reconciling the world to himself" (2 Cor. 5:19). Christ's act of self-donation, of pouring himself out for others, is singular. He is the basis and power of the new life in communion with God and others. The reference to the cross of Christ in the hymn ("even death on a cross") is more than a hint of Paul's theology of the cross that stands in the background.

Just how Christ's self-emptying and obedience even to a cross accomplishes our salvation is not explained by Paul either here or elsewhere in the letter. We find here no *explicit* theory of atonement. There is no obvious *Christus Victor* theory, according to which Christ defeats the forces of sin, evil, and death by his crucifixion and resurrection;[20] no clear satisfaction theory, according to which he dies on our behalf and in our place to satisfy the justice of God;[21] no definite moral influence theory, according to

---

20. See Gustaf Aulén, *Christus Victor* (New York: Macmillan, 1956).
21. See Anselm, *Cur Deus Homo,* trans. Sidney Norton Deane (La Salle, IL: Open Court, 1951).

which our salvation is achieved by our being moved and transformed by the example of Christ.[22] Nevertheless, neither the letter as a whole nor the Christ hymn in particular should be read in a vacuum. In other letters Paul says much about the saving work of Christ, as an event "for us." Christ "gave himself for me" (Gal. 2:20); he died "for the ungodly" (Rom. 5:6), "for our sins" (1 Cor. 15:3), "for us" (Rom. 5:8; 1 Thess. 5:10), "for all" (2 Cor. 5:14). This emphatic "for me," "for you," "for us," and "for all" is a signature component of Paul's theology of the cross, and it should not be marginalized or neglected even as we acknowledge the primarily ethical purpose for which Paul employs the Christ hymn in Philippians 2:5–11.

A passage in Paul's Corinthian correspondence is especially close to the implicit soteriological meaning of the Christ hymn in Philippians. "You know the generous act of our Lord Jesus Christ, that though he was rich, yet for your sakes he became poor, so that by his poverty you might become rich" (2 Cor. 8:9). It is largely on the basis of this expression of Paul's theology of the cross that from ancient times, Christian theologians have understood the saving work of Christ as a "wondrous exchange." That Christ humbled himself and became poor for us that we might be rich in him has been understood as the very heart of the gospel. Irenaeus: Through his immeasurable love, our Lord Jesus Christ "became what we are in order that he might bring us to be even what he is himself."[23] Athanasius: "He was humanized that we might be deified."[24] Cyril of Alexandria: "He took what was ours to be his so that we might have all that was his."[25] The twentieth-century theologian Karl Barth also often speaks of the saving work of Christ as a "wondrous exchange." In a prayer before one of his sermons on a text from Philippians, Barth says: "Lord our God. You have humbled yourself in order to lift us up. You became poor so that we might be rich. You came to us so that we might come to you. You

---

22. See R. E. Weingart, *The Logic of Divine Love: A Critical Analysis of the Soteriology of Peter Abailard* (Oxford: Clarendon, 1970).
23. Irenaeus, *Against Heresies* 5 (*ANF* 1:526).
24. Athanasius, *On the Incarnation*, in *Christology of the Later Fathers*, LCC 3, ed. E. R. Hardy (Philadelphia: Westminster, 1954), 107 n. 79.
25. Cyril of Alexandria, *On the Unity of Christ* (Crestwood, NY: St. Vladimir's, 1995), 59.

became a human being like us in order that we might participate in your eternal life."[26]

To summarize: in the first stanza of the Christ hymn we are told that Jesus Christ, who is equal with God, freely *emptied* himself; freely *humbled* himself, taking the form of a servant; and freely *obeyed* God even to death on a cross. These three verbs comprise the very heart of the first stanza:

— *Emptied:* not in the sense of a loss of self but in the sense of pouring out his grace and goodness to creatures in need
— *Humbled:* not in a condescending way but by willingly entering into solidarity with those of low estate, bridging the great gulf between God and creatures, God and sinners
— *Obeyed:* not in the sense of his involuntarily bending to a higher coercive force but freely consenting to the will of God for the benefit of others

What could be more astonishing? The Lord of heaven and earth empties himself, humbles himself, becomes obedient even to death on a cross. As Kierkegaard noted, the lordly humility and humble lordship of Christ constitutes the real "infinite qualitative difference" between God and us. The greatest difference between God and us is not that God is Creator and we are creatures. Not even that God is holy and we are sinners. Those are indeed immense chasms. But the greatest chasm of all is that God in Christ does what we in our overweening pride and self-centeredness refuse to do and what we presume God is incapable or unwilling to do. God in Christ loves

> God is not greater than he is in this humiliation. God is not more glorious than he is in this self-surrender. God is not more powerful than he is in this helplessness. God is not more divine than he is in this humanity.
>
> Jürgen Moltmann, *The Crucified God* (New York: Harper & Row, 1973), 205.

---

26. Karl Barth, *Predigten 1954–1967*, hg. Hinrich Stoevesandt, Gesamtausgabe 1.2 (Zurich: TVZ, 1979), 97 (my translation).

extravagantly, living and dying among us in great humility, doing for us what we could not do for ourselves. According to the first stanza of the Christ hymn, *this* is who God is; *this* is what God is like; *this* is the heart and mind of God as embodied and revealed in Jesus Christ. The first stanza of the Christ hymn is a veritable revolution in our understanding of who God is and what constitutes God's power and glory. The world-disrupting message of "Christ crucified" is, as Paul writes in another letter, "a stumbling block to Jews and foolishness to Gentiles" (1 Cor. 1:23).[27]

Here then is the primary theological basis of all of Paul's exhortations to the Philippians: "Let the same mind be in you that was in Christ Jesus." In humility, regard each other in a way that bears a likeness to Christ's way. In humility, relate to each other and all others as God has related to you and acted on your behalf. By the grace of God and the power of the Holy Spirit, let your life together be a reflection of, a correspondence to, God's astonishing humility, freely accepted servanthood, and self-giving love in Jesus Christ.

FURTHER REFLECTIONS
Kenosis

From earliest times, Christian theologians have debated the meaning of the "self-emptying" (*kenosis*) of Christ described in the hymn of Philippians 2:5–11. The issue has not been whether the hymn, together with other NT passages, affirms both the full deity of Christ (he was "in the form of God" and was equal with God, 2:6) and his full humanity (he was "born in human likeness" and was "found in human form," 2:7). That issue found a doctrinal resolution in the historic Declaration of Chalcedon in 451 CE, according to which Jesus Christ is "truly God, truly human, two natures united in one person, without confusion, change, division or separation."

However, in spite of this doctrinal consensus of classical two-natures Christology, the affirmation of the Pauline hymn that Christ

---

27. Origen, the great biblical scholar and theologian of the third century CE, responded to the taunts of the philosopher Celsus that Christians incredibly worship a God who changed from the best to the worst by becoming human. *Against Celsus* (*ANF* 4:502).

"emptied himself" has long posed difficulties for theologians.[28] The problem is well summarized by David Brown: "Whatever popular piety may have thought to the contrary, in expounding this two-natures Christology the Church's theologians adamantly maintained that in that union the divine nature was never, and could never have been, subject to the perils of being human: to temptation, ignorance, suffering and death. Instead, strictly speaking, such notions were applicable only to Christ's human nature. So although in virtue of the union, human experience was attributable to God in Christ, these huge qualifications were always seen to follow on more careful analysis."[29]

During the Reformation period, Lutheran and Reformed theologians argued about whether the majestic attributes of God could appropriately be ascribed to the human nature of Christ. The Lutherans, fearful of dividing the person of Christ, answered yes; the Reformed, fearful of denying the full humanity of Christ, responded no. A point of agreement was that the self-emptying or self-limitation of Christ refers to the temporary hiddenness of his glory in the time between his birth and resurrection. Both sides, however, rejected any idea that Christ had actually given up his divinity, or any of the divine attributes such as immutability or impassibility, in assuming human nature.

In the nineteenth century, especially in Germany, England, and Scotland, the Christ hymn became the focus of numerous "kenotic" Christologies. The idea of a real *kenosis* or emptying of Christ in the incarnation seemed to offer to the modern mind a way of making more intelligible the mystery of how the incarnate Lord could be both fully God and fully human. Convinced that the presentation of Christ in classical Christology had a taint of docetism (Christ only seemed to be human and was in fact divinity in human garb), the kenotic christologians aimed to affirm the divinity of Christ without hedging on his full humanity, with all the limitations that being human necessarily entails.

---

28. See David Brown, *Divine Humanity: Kenosis and the Construction of a Christian Theology* (Waco, TX: Baylor University Press, 2011); also, *Exploring Kenotic Christology: The Self-Emptying of God,* ed. C. Stephen Evans (New York: Oxford University Press, 2006).
29. Brown, *Divine Humanity,* 1.

According to the ingenious proposal of Gottfried Thomasius (1802–1875), for example, although Christ was fully divine, when he assumed a real human nature, he relinquished or "emptied himself of" divine properties such as omnipotence, omniscience, and immutability that are simply incompatible with existence as a finite human being. Other properties of divinity, however, such as love and wisdom, were retained by the Lord in his incarnate state.[30]

A far more radical form of kenotic Christology emerged in the United States in the 1960s. Drawing on the philosophies of Georg Hegel and William Blake, these later kenoticists interpreted the *kenosis* of Philippians 2:7 to mean that God had simply abolished God's transcendent being, emptying God's self entirely into humanity, thereby liberating humanity from every thought of an alien transcendent realm. After the self-abolition or "death of God," Christ is present in every moment of human life as incarnate love.[31]

Karl Barth offered one of the most trenchant theological criticisms of nineteenth-century kenotic Christology and, by extension, of the still more drastic later readings of the *kenosis* text. His basic objection to these Christologies can be summarized in his comment that "God gives himself but he does not give himself away."[32] This does not mean that Barth simply reverts to the old orthodox treatment of the kenotic passage in Paul. On the contrary, in Barth's reading, the Christ hymn declares that humility, obedience, suffering, and sacrificial love, far from being alien to God, belong to God's eternal being.

> One cannot simply say, as in Nazi times, that one believes in God. It is necessary to be precise about who our God is.
>
> Ernst Käsemann, *On Being a Disciple of the Crucified Nazarene* (Grand Rapids: Eerdmans, 2010), 175.

Jesus Christ in his incarnation and crucifixion reveals the deepest nature and character of God.[33] If we think that God cannot be God,

---

30. See Claude Welch, *God and Incarnation in Mid-Nineteenth-Century German Theology: G. Thomasius, I. A. Dorner, A. E. Biedermann* (New York: Oxford University Press, 1965); Brown, *Divine Humanity,* 42–55.
31. See Thomas J. J. Altizer, *The Gospel of Christian Atheism* (Philadelphia: Westminster, 1966).
32. Barth, *CD* IV/1:185.
33. For an excellent discussion of Barth on this topic, see Bruce McCormack, "The Humility of the Eternal Son: A Reformed Version of Kenotic Christology," *International Journal of Systematic Theology* 8 (2006): 243–51.

cannot remain faithful to God's self in assuming and experiencing human life to its utmost depths, our concept of God is, as Barth puts it, "too narrow, too arbitrary, too human—far too human."[34]

Two more recent interpretations of the *kenosis* passage deserve mention. Both ask: with what or whom is Paul contrasting the way of Christ in the Christ hymn? One answer is that Paul is contrasting the way of Christ with that of Adam and Eve in the garden of Eden. According to the Genesis story, the first human couple refused to walk the way of humility before God. Instead, they proudly grasped after divinity, wanting to be "like God" (Gen. 3:5). Christ, on the contrary, did not consider divinity something to be seized or exploited for his own benefit but humbled himself for our sake.[35]

Another recent interpretation of Paul's Christ hymn emphasizes its political context. Paul is contrasting the way of Christ with the way of the Roman emperor and the ethos of empire. The emperor is acclaimed as lord and savior, but his kind of lordship is built on pride, power, and violence. The way of Christ is the exact opposite; the Lord Jesus Christ exhibits humility, rejects violence, and achieves victory paradoxically by the exercise of self-giving love.[36] While both of these interpretations have their merits, neither should be adopted as a replacement for the affirmation that in the self-emptying, humility, and obedience of Christ, it is no less than *God* who is at work to save humankind, and that this act of self-humbling love, far from being impossible or demeaning to God, reveals the deepest truth and inmost reality of God.

The *kenosis* passage and the history of its interpretation speaks to us today in at least two ways. First, it underscores that theology matters. It matters whether Christ is confessed as truly human and truly divine. On the one hand, "if human beings are to be helped in their imitation of Christ, it must be a fully human life that engages with us."[37] On the other hand, it matters whether the self-giving and other-affirming human life that Christ lives

---

34. Barth, *CD* IV/1:186.
35. See James D. G. Dunn, *The Theology of Paul the Apostle* (Grand Rapids: Eerdmans, 1998), 284–86.
36. See Marcus Borg and John Dominic Crossan, *First Paul: Reclaiming the Radical Visionary behind the Church's Conservative Icon* (New York: Harper, 2009), 211–13.
37. Brown, *Divine Humanity*, 200.

> God's transcendent power is not so much displayed in the vastness of the heavens, or the luster of the stars, or the orderly arrangement of the universe . . . as in his condescension to our weak nature.
>
> Gregory of Nyssa, *Address on Religious Instruction, in Christology of the Later Fathers*, ed. E. R. Hardy, LCC 3 (Philadelphia: Westminster, 1954), 301.

incarnates the very life of God. Christ is more than an example; he is our Lord. It matters therefore how we think and speak of him, whether we are prepared to confess him not simply as a good teacher and a moral exemplar but as our Lord and Savior. It matters whether we are prepared to think and speak of *God* in the light of the humility, self-emptying, and obedience of Christ. Briefly stated, your God is too small if you think of the majesty of God as invulnerability to suffering or of the power of God as sheer domination.

The Christ hymn shatters all conventional misunderstandings of God. The God of the gospel is revealed in the humility and "weakness" of the cross. Paul does not say: "Listen, there once was a man named Jesus who led a very noble life and died a very heroic death." He says: "Consider well, the one we confess as our Lord and Savior is the very God who for our sake humbled himself, assumed our human nature, and was obedient even to death on a cross."

Second and equally important, Paul's use of the Christ hymn underscores that right Christian practice matters no less than sound Christian theology. In other words, orthopraxis is as important as orthodoxy. Paul recounts the self-emptying of Christ to summon the Philippian community to unity and harmony in Christ and to a Christlike humility that places the interests and welfare of others above one's own. The Pauline appeal to the kenotic way of Christ speaks as directly to the church today as it did to the church in Philippi. The church today needs to hear both of these words: our theology, our way of thinking and speaking about Christ and God, matters deeply; and our conformity to Christ in our personal and corporate life—in our everyday attitudes, relationships, decisions, and actions—matters deeply too.

2:9–11
The Exaltation of Christ

When we move to the second stanza of the hymn, a 180-degree turn
in the story poses many new questions. How should we understand
the relationship between the first and second stanzas? In view of
the strong "therefore" (*dio*) that links the humble descent of Christ
described in the first stanza to the second stanza's declaration of
Christ's exaltation to the highest possible honor by God (2:9–11),
are we to understand that Christ's exaltation by God comes as a
reward for what Christ has done? Is it a kind of prize given to him
because he has perfectly obeyed and greatly suffered? Is the "cross of
Christ" (3:18), so central to Paul's message, simply a means endured
to assure a glorious end?

The short answer to these questions is no. Paul does not for a
moment think about the hymn in this way. He does not exhort his
readers to have the mind of Christ because following his example
guarantees that every suffering will be followed by success. To put
it bluntly, Paul does not offer a prototype of Disney theology in
which the pauper predictably becomes a prince. There is no implication in the Christ hymn that the motive of his self-humbling was
the reward that awaited him on the other side of death. What sort of
humility and concern for others would that be? Christ's "death on a
cross" and his being "highly exalted" are not connected as payment
for a job well done or as sunrise follows the night with complete
predictability.

In contrast to the idea of reward, the second stanza is basically a
declaration of the lordship of the crucified Christ, a lordship already
a reality (God has "highly exalted" him), but whose acknowledgment is not yet universal (every knee "should bend," every tongue
"should confess"). The tenor of these verses is comparable to the
soaring acclamations in Romans 8:38–39 and Colossians 2:15 of
God's victory in Christ over death and all other powers and principalities of the world that oppose God's purposes. In all instances
the note of triumph is present, the horizon of victory is undeniably
cosmic, and the voice is doxological: "Praise to Christ! Glory to
God! All creatures will give homage to Christ! The crucified Lord

reigns at the right hand of God!" Make no mistake: for Paul the "weakness" of God in the cross of Christ is not ineffectual; it is paradoxically "stronger than human strength" (1 Cor. 1:25).

Another strong theme of the second stanza is God's freely gracious vindication of Christ and his way of humility, obedience, and self-giving love, even to death on a cross. In the background are OT passages like Isaiah 53:12 and 61:7, where the prophet speaks of God's faithfulness and God's vindication and deliverance of the suffering, faithful believer.[38] In other words, if the cross is the verdict of sinful humanity on Christ, his resurrection and exaltation are the "verdict of God" that reverses the human verdict.[39] The victory and vindication themes of the second stanza are complementary. Whereas the first stanza of the hymn depicts the astonishing humility and generosity of the love of God, the second stanza affirms that this love is both just and victorious.

> God, in raising Jesus, has said, "This is *my* work, *my* life: what is done in Jesus is what I do, now and always."
>
> Rowan Williams, *Resurrection: Interpreting the Easter Gospel* (Cleveland: Pilgrim, 2002), 55.

A remarkable feature of the second stanza is its unmistakable allusion to Isaiah 45:21–23, in which God declares: "There is no other god besides me. . . . 'To me every knee shall bow, and every tongue shall swear.'" Since this is "one of the most unyielding monotheistic passages in the whole Bible," applying these words to Christ, as the hymn does, is nothing short of "astounding."[40] The identity of God can no longer be separated from Jesus. The power and glory of the Lord of heaven and earth are identified with this crucified and resurrected Nazarene.

What is "the name that is above every name" and is given to Christ by the Father (2:9)? It is none other than the name of "Lord" (*kyrios*, 2:11). This is the Greek form of the very name by which YHWH, the Holy One of Israel, is known and praised.[41] That Christ bears this name is a truly momentous affirmation. Anyone who thinks that the

38. Bockmuehl, *Philippians*, 141.
39. Barth, *CD* IV/1:305–9.
40. Dunn, *Theology of Paul*, 251.
41. See Kendall Soulen, *Divine Name(s) and the Holy Trinity* (Louisville, KY: Westminster John Knox Press, 2011).

view of Christ in the early church was a "low Christology" in contrast to the "high Christology" of later centuries culminating in the Nicene Creed (325) should ponder this passage in Philippians with great care. In the first stanza Christ, who humbled himself for our sake, is declared to be equal with God; in the second stanza Christ is given the name of "Lord," the name that, according to the OT witness, belongs to none other than YHWH, the Creator of heaven and earth and the Savior of his people.

But one might ask: If, according to the first stanza, Christ from the beginning was equal with God, how can the second stanza say Christ was exalted by God and given the name of Lord? Does not the idea of Christ's being given this name in his exaltation imply that he was not Lord and equal with God before his exaltation? Paul does not ask this question, but the classical theological tradition, building on the Christ hymn, does ask it and offers this answer: from all eternity the Father loves and gives all to the Son, and the Son loves and gives all to the Father. The gift of the name that is above every name has to do with the Son in his incarnate form, in his union with our human nature.[42]

In other words, we are not to think of the two stanzas as describing a relationship between Christ and God the Father that has the form of a transaction such as, "I will give you something if you give me something in return." This is certainly not the point of the Christ hymn. There is indeed an act of giving, both on the part of Christ and on the part of God the Father. But it is not obligation or duty or reward that moves the giving on either side. On both sides, the giving is free and uncoerced. Just as the obedience of Christ to the Father, even to death on a cross, is completely free and in no way motivated by obligation, duty, or fear, so the gift from the Father to Christ of the name that is above every name is completely free and in no way mandated, extorted, or coerced. This mutual giving of Christ and God the Father depicted in the Christ hymn will be fully elaborated in later Trinitarian theology as rooted in the mutually free and mutually self-giving love that binds Father and Son in their common Spirit. The love of the triune persons for one another is given freely,

42. Cyril of Alexandria, *On the Unity of Christ*, 122–24.

spontaneously, and boundlessly. It arises not from any lack or need or obligation but simply from the sheer plenitude and joy of their shared life and love together.[43]

Finally, to the Lord Jesus Christ, the hymn proclaims that every knee shall bow "in heaven and on earth and under the earth" (2:10; cf. Isa. 45:23; Rom. 14:11). This is a way of saying that all beings in all regions of God's creation, from the highest to the lowest, shall one day give their allegiance to the Christ and worship him. If there is a hint of the *Christus Victor* motif in the hymn, it is here. Does this acclamation guarantee universal salvation? Or does it mean that all creatures will one day confess Christ as Lord, if not voluntarily, then by compulsion? The hymn does not take us in either of these directions. What it joyously affirms is that what God has done in Christ is and will be victorious over all the forces that threaten to ruin God's creation. God's work in Christ, being intrinsically good and profoundly beautiful, is on the way to its universal completion. But it reaches its goal in the free and glad response of the human heart. The triumph of God's gracious work in Christ does not come by way of coercion.

In sum, the connection between the two stanzas of the hymn is to be found not in the idea of reward but solely in the character and purposes of the sovereign and gracious God of Scripture.[44] Taken together, the two stanzas of the Christ hymn identify God as the faithful God of Israel, the God of compassion and righteousness, the God whose "love in freedom" is greater than any power of this world.[45] Both movements described in the Christ hymn—the movement downward and the movement upward—are acts of God's free grace. Just as the self-humbling, self-emptying, and obedience of the one who is equal with God is breathtaking grace, so too God's exaltation of Christ who humbled himself for us is superabundant grace. Christ died for us, and Christ was raised for us, and both are events of sheer grace.

Understanding the freedom and generosity of the grace of God as it is depicted in the Christ hymn should inform the church's

43. Fowl, *Philippians*, 101.
44. Ibid.
45. Karl Barth, CD II/1:257; Fowl, *Philippians*, 101.

celebration of its Holy Week. When our observance of Good Friday and Easter Sunday becomes a routine ritual stripped of surprise, when we consider the empty tomb as the inevitable or predictable follow-up to Golgotha, just as the sun predictably rises each morning after a period of darkness or spring flowers predictably follow the snows of winter, the deep mystery of both Good Friday and Easter are lost. In between the darkness of Good Friday and the light of Easter morning is the terrible silence of Holy Saturday.[46] Easter begins not with a yawn but with a surprising and joyful shout: he is risen!

The political implications of the hymn's naming Christ "Lord" are not to be overlooked. Bockmuehl rightly sees in the Christ hymn "a profoundly double-edged political point."[47] On the one hand, to confess the lordship of Christ is to refuse to give unconditional allegiance to Caesar or to any other claimant to ultimate authority. Put bluntly, if Christ is Lord of all, Caesar is not.[48] The exaltation of the crucified Christ forever shatters the equation of divine power with tyrannical and oppressive rule. On the other hand, if the Lord has become a servant, service to others is no menial and inferior task but a divine calling. Still more, if God in Christ has taken to himself human life in its most vulnerable and despised form of a slave nailed to a cross, the dignity and value of every human being—not just the healthy, educated, wealthy, and powerful—receives its supreme and irrevocable affirmation.

> How can "dignity" be denied to even the most miserable of men when the glory of God himself was the honor of this man nailed in supreme wretchedness to the cross?
>
> Karl Barth, *CD* III/4:654.

At the conclusion of our reflections on Paul's magnificent Christ hymn, we return to the question whether the purpose of the hymn is primarily christological and soteriological or primarily ethical in

---

46. See Alan E. Lewis, *Between Cross and Resurrection: A Theology of Holy Saturday* (Grand Rapids: Eerdmans, 2001); also, Hans Urs von Balthasar, *Mysterium Paschale* (Grand Rapids: Eerdmans, 1990).
47. Bockmuehl, *Philippians*, 147.
48. This theme occurs frequently in the writings of N. T. Wright. See "Paul's Gospel and Caesar's Empire," available at http://www.ntwrightpage.com/Wright_Paul_Caesar_Empire.pdf.

nature. Does it purport to tell us something about the mystery of the relationship between Christ and God the Father or does it function mainly as an ethical model? In the light of the preceding comments, it is clear that these questions pose a false alternative. Paul's principal purpose in reciting this hymn is indeed ethical, as the context of the passage demonstrates. However, the ethical force of the passage lies in the truth that it affirms. The hymn declares the truth of who Christ is and how God in Christ has dealt and continues to deal with us. In other words, the gospel, encapsulated in the hymn, tells us how things truly are. A moral imperative is contained within a christological indicative. We who are in Christ are called to think and act in accordance with Christ if our thinking and acting are to be in alignment with truth and reality. Richard Hays aptly summarizes the foundation and motive of Christian life in Paul's thinking: "Insofar as we perceive the truth about God's redemptive work in the world, we will participate gladly in the outworking of God's purpose."[49]

As is evident in the Christ hymn and the use to which Paul puts it, theology and ethics are closely bound together. God in Christ acts on our behalf, and we are called to respond in a manner corresponding to that action. The obedience, humility, and self-giving love of Christ provide the foundation, motivation, and direction of Christian ethics. Basically, Christian ethics is the practical outworking of faith in the living Christ whose way is proclaimed in the Gospels and summarized in the Pauline Christ hymn. When empowered by his Spirit and strengthened in Christian community, followers of the crucified and exalted Lord will hasten to serve him in deeds of love and the works of justice and reconciliation. As Paul writes to the Corinthian church, "If I have all faith, so as to remove mountains, but do not have love, I am nothing" (1 Cor. 13:2). James says the same: faith that does not manifest itself in the works of love is dead (Jas. 2:17).

Gathering together the strands of our reflections, it is clear that the Christ hymn represents a revolution in our understanding of both God and humanity. It depicts God as coming to us in humility and self-giving love and in so doing dignifying all human beings

---

49. Richard Hays, *The Moral Vision of the New Testament: Community, Cross, New Creation* (San Francisco: Harper, 1996), 39.

as persons included in this love. We have also contended that two things are to be avoided in any interpretation of Paul's beautiful and enormously influential Christ hymn. We should not underplay the ethical and political thrust of Paul's weighty hymn by quickly driving it onto the highway of christological speculation, where it often remains indefinitely. That would be a serious misreading of Paul, who never separated belief and practice. We must, however, quickly add: it is equally possible to subvert Paul's christological and soteriological affirmations by making the hymn no more than an ethical ideal to be emulated. Jesus is indeed the paradigm without peer for Christian life, but he is so as the one who is equal with God and who has acted for our salvation. He is far more than, even if he is also, a unique example. He is our Savior (3:20).

2:12–18
Work Out Your Salvation

After telling the story of Christ humbled and exalted for us, Paul now renews and recapitulates the ethical exhortations that originally prompted the introduction of the hymn ("live your life in a manner worthy of the gospel of Christ," put aside "selfish ambition," "in humility regard others better than yourselves"). Paul begins by commending the Philippians for their past obedience when he was present with them and urges them to continue to obey now in his absence. In Greek, the verb "you obeyed" has no object, and the question arises whether Paul is commending the Philippians for obeying him or for obeying God or Christ or the gospel. O'Brien aptly comments, "A wedge should not be driven between Paul and Christ at this point."[50] Paul is commending the Philippians' obedience to Christ and the gospel as proclaimed by Paul. In other words, Paul never claims a right to obedience that resides in his own person. His authority is not his own. Obedience is properly rendered only to the living Lord and secondarily to Paul only as the commissioned apostle, servant, and ambassador of Christ and the gospel.

---

50. O'Brien, *Philippians*, 275.

Paul wants to assure the Philippians that even though he is not personally present with them, they are far from helpless in responding to his exhortation to have the same mind as was in Christ Jesus. Despite my absence, Paul says, God continues to work in you as you persevere in faith and service. "Work out your own salvation" (2:12) clearly does not mean "work for your salvation" or "work to earn your salvation," as though our salvation is dependent on what we are able to achieve. That would run utterly counter to Paul's core convictions throughout this and his other letters. So Paul immediately continues, "for it is God who is at work in you" (2:13). As we will hear especially in chapter 3, our righteousness and our salvation come not from our own achievements, however impressive they may be, but from the grace of God in Jesus Christ. Paul undeviatingly sees God as the primary actor in the drama of salvation. By God's grace we are indeed participants in this drama, but always as subjects entirely dependent on his prior and superior working. As Paul says in another letter, "I worked harder than any of them—though it was not I, but the grace of God that is with me" (1 Cor. 15:10).

> The action is from both [God and believers] . . . [but] the whole process is credited to God.
>
> Augustine, *Enchiridion* 9.32, in *Confessions and Enchiridion*, LCC 7, ed. Albert C. Outler (Philadelphia: Westminster, 1955).

Note, too, that the summons to *work out* your own salvation" looks to the future, to the end of what God has begun. Just as Paul has assured his readers earlier that God will complete the good work begun in them by God (1:6), he now urges them to take an active part in living out the grace of God still at work in them. To paraphrase Paul: keep on living out the salvation begun in you in Christ to its final goal and do it with wholehearted dedication.

But why are we to work "with fear and trembling"? This phrase appears several times in the biblical witness. In OT passages (e.g., Deut. 2:25; Isa. 19:16) it describes an attitude of "awe and reverence in the presence of God."[51] Paul himself uses the phrase "fear and trembling" on several occasions, including his description of his

51. Ibid., 284.

attitude when he first preached to the Corinthians: "I came to you in weakness and in fear and in much trembling" (1 Cor. 2:3). The apostle was fully aware that apart from the strength he received from God he was totally inadequate to fulfill his God-given commission to preach the gospel of Jesus Christ, especially in a metropolis like Corinth, known for its freewheeling lifestyle as well as its commercial prominence.

The phrase "fear and trembling" has been made famous in modern theology by Søren Kierkegaard's book with that title.[52] Kierkegaard pondered deeply the story in Genesis 22 where Abraham is commanded by God to sacrifice his beloved son Isaac. In a series of retellings of the story, Kierkegaard imagines what must have been the anguish and turmoil of Abraham as he seeks to remain faithful to the will of God. Of course, Paul knew nothing of Kierkegaard. Nevertheless, Kierkegaard's reflections on the mystery of God's will in the changing circumstances of our lives may illumine Paul's call to the Philippians to live out "with fear and trembling" the grace and salvation with which they have been entrusted. We never know all the reasons why or how particular events of our lives fit into the purposes of God. They are frequently shrouded in darkness. Even Christ on the cross cried out with the words of the psalmist, "My God, my God, why have you forsaken me?" (Mark 15:34).

It must be emphasized, however, that the obedience of Christ and the obedience of his disciples is not blind obedience. It rests not on fear but on the faithfulness of God. There is no indication that Paul speaks of "fear and trembling" in this passage to frighten the Philippians. As Bockmuehl notes, "Paul does not imply cowering in terror."[53] The point is not that since God is out to get us, we had better watch out. Instead, the phrase speaks of appropriate reverence in God's presence and the awareness of our radical dependence on God's grace. In context it is clear that Paul's aim is to strengthen the Philippians' confidence in living the Christian life and bearing a faithful witness. At the same time, he wants them to take their responsibility as Christian disciples seriously and not assume that

---

52. Søren Kierkegaard, *Fear and Trembling*, trans. Howard Lowrie (New York: Doubleday, 1955).
53. Bockmuehl, *Philippians*, 153.

since God is at work in them, they can be complacent or indifferent. As so often, Calvin gets to the heart of the matter. "By the term *work*," Calvin says, "[Paul] reproves our indolence . . . but he immediately represses arrogance by commending fear and trembling."[54]

Calvin's point is on-target, but I venture to suggest we can go a step further than he does. There is another dimension of "fear and trembling" alongside the disturbing awareness of the holiness and majesty of God, the mystery of God's will, and the recognition of our own frailty. As recipients of the grace of God in Jesus Christ, we are struck by awe and amazement not out of terror of a God who is against us and seeks to destroy us, but by the astonishing goodness and generosity of God who wills to be for us and comes to us as a humble servant. We are to live out our salvation in awe and reverence before this gracious God from whose love in Jesus Christ nothing can separate us.

This way of thinking of "fear and trembling" is not as far-fetched as it might at first appear. How else could we explain the fact that within a few lines of the "fear and trembling" phrase, Paul exhorts the Philippians to "be glad and rejoice with me" (2:18), even as he is "glad and rejoice[s]" with all of them (2:17)? There is, in other words, a healthy fear of the Lord that is the beginning of wisdom (Prov. 1:7) and a joyful trembling that arises with the awareness of God's unspeakable gift that we have been given in Christ. Such fear and trembling is altogether different from the dread we experience and the punishment we are inclined to expect when we fail to live up to all that is commanded of us by the tyrannical and unforgiving deity of our own imagining.

As we have seen, Paul calls the Philippians to responsible Christian life both before and after introducing the Christ hymn. Before, he writes: Be in full accord and of one mind. Avoid selfish ambition. Consider the interests of others above your own (2:2–4). After, he writes: Do not murmur or complain if you are now undergoing hardships. Do not argue with one another (2:14). In other words, living in accordance with the crucified and exalted Lord is not simply a matter of verbal confession but, equally important, a matter of the

---

54. John Calvin, *Ephesians, Philippians, and Colossians*, CNTC, ed. David W. Torrance and Thomas F. Torrance (Grand Rapids: Eerdmans, 1965), 255.

particular ways we relate to others. Paul assures his Philippian friends that when they are of one mind and live in harmony with one another, they will "shine like stars" (2:15) in a dark ("crooked and perverse") world. Some commentators see an allusion here to the well-known servant passages of Isaiah, where the servant is called to be "a light to

> **The believing community manifests the risen Christ: it does not simply talk about him, or even "celebrate" him. It is the place where he is shown.**
>
> Rowan Williams, *Resurrection: Interpreting the Easter Gospel* (Cleveland: Pilgrim, 2002), 56.

the nations" (Isa. 42:6; 49:6).[55] Offering light to the nations—shining like stars—certainly cannot be exhausted in words alone. It is in living together under the grace of God and in peace with and love for one another that the Philippian community will become like stars in an otherwise dark night, a luminous and abiding witness to the nations.

Paul concludes this section of the letter by returning to the theme of joy. If the Philippians now experience suffering because of their faith, they should know that Paul rejoices in his own suffering and invites them to rejoice as well. He likens his life as witness of Christ to a libation "poured out" and mingled with their own offering of sacrifice and suffering (2:17). This is a remarkable image. Having reminded the Philippians of the self-humbling and obedience of Jesus Christ—his "emptying," his "pouring out" of his life for our sake—Paul now describes his own life and that of the Philippians as a common offering, a common pouring out of life in the service of Christ and the gospel. Of course, the outpouring of the life of the Christian in love and service is not to be understood as actions that somehow make up for a supposed deficiency in the saving work of Christ. Rather, it is a thankful and joyful witness to and participation in the saving work of Christ for us and for the world. "I am glad and rejoice with all of you," Paul says, and "you also must be glad and rejoice with me" (2:17–18) In the next section of the letter, he proceeds to commend two of his helpers as examples of costly participation in the way of Christ and the work of the gospel.

---

55. Bockmuehl, *Philippians*, 158.

FURTHER REFLECTIONS
God's Working and Our Working

In several places in Philippians, Paul places the working of God and human working in paradoxical proximity (1:19; 3:12; 4:13). In each of these instances, human action and divine action are somehow conjoined. The most explicit example, however, is found in 2:12–13, where Paul exhorts: "Work out your own salvation with fear and trembling; for it is God who is at work in you, enabling you both to will and to work for his good pleasure."

Broadly speaking, there are at least two ways in which the mystery of God's working and human working can be misconceived: synergism and monergism. According to synergism, we cooperate with God in such a way that our working complements or completes the working of God. The basic assumption here is that the relationship between God and humanity is a zero-sum game. The more God works, the less there is for human beings to do. Conversely, if human beings act, to that extent God cannot be acting. In this schema, the activity of God and human beings is parceled out between them: God does this much, and humanity does that much. In the history of Christian doctrine, this synergistic view is called Pelagianism, named after Pelagius, a fifth-century British monk who taught that human sin was not as drastic as Augustine held it to be. Human beings, Pelagius argued, are able to make a significant contribution to their salvation. Synergism is certainly not Paul's way of understanding the co-presence of divine and human activity.

The other errant possibility of resolving the mystery is monergism. According to this view, God does everything and humanity nothing. Since God is omnipotent, when God works there is nothing left for human beings to do other than *appear* to be actors freely deciding and acting. Humans are really like puppets moved in this or that direction by an unseen puppeteer. Here again, as in the case of synergism, monergism presupposes the model of a zero-sum game. If synergism offers a God who is in need of our help, monergism offers an alien and inhuman God.

Paul's proclamation of the gospel does not fit the mold of either synergism or monergism. In contrast to both, the God of the gospel establishes a covenantal relationship marked by the free grace and guidance of God on the one hand and the free thanks and obedience of God's people on the other.

Paul's resolution of the classic conundrum of divine grace and human freedom is to be found in his Christology. As the Christ hymn implies, divine grace and human freedom are not in competition. The action of God in Christ does not crush human freedom; it brings human freedom to its full and proper realization. We are never more fully human, and never more fully free, than when we live by the grace of God and in loving community with others.

> **The glorification of God does not come at the expense of creatures.**
>
> Kathryn Tanner, *Jesus, Humanity and the Trinity* (Minneapolis: Fortress, 2001), 2.

This is, to be sure, a distinctive understanding of human freedom. It is quite different from a view of freedom as absolute autonomy or doing anything you want to do. It is a world away from the understanding of freedom that drives the characters of Jonathan Franzen's novel *Freedom,* who for all their many choices and all their celebrated "freedom" remain stuck in the inability to make wholehearted commitments and often find themselves lonely and confused.[56] For Paul, human beings are called to freely correspond in their decisions and actions to what God freely does for them in Christ. What God freely and graciously accomplishes for humanity in Christ is, of course, sufficient and complete. We are not called to supplement it or to make up for the insufficiency of the work of Christ. Rather, we are called to freely and gladly live out the grace of God freely and graciously given to us in Christ. This is the "privilege" (1:29) we have been given: to bear witness to the grace of God in Jesus Christ not only in words but in lives that correspond to his.

Whether Paul's reference to the co-working of God and humanity in Philippians 2:12b–13 makes any sense to us will largely depend on the understandings of freedom that we bring to our inquiry. Recall Paul's opening benediction of grace and peace "from God our Father and the Lord Jesus Christ." The freedom of "God our Father and the

---

56. Jonathan Franzen, *Freedom* (New York: Farrar, Strauss & Giroux, 2010).

Lord Jesus Christ" is not the arbitrary freedom of the paterfamilias of a Roman household or the authoritarian freedom of an imperial lord. Rather, it is the freedom of one who, though equal with God, emptied and humbled himself for our salvation. Human freedom flourishes when it is grounded and directed by the freedom of this Lord. The well-known collect for peace in the Book of Common Prayer says it well when it praises the God "whose service is perfect freedom."

In recent years, the relationship between divine and human action has been much discussed under the topic of *double agency*. For Christian faith, the central paradigm of double agency is the incarnation. Since Jesus Christ is both truly God and truly human, what Jesus does and suffers as a human being, God does and suffers. Jesus says, "My Father is still working, and I also am working. . . . Whatever the Father does, the Son does likewise" (John 5:17, 19). While there is, of course, a vast difference between the singular union of God and humanity in Christ, on the one hand, and God's working in our working, on the other, it is nevertheless the testimony of Christians, beginning with Paul, that being in Christ includes a coactivity of Christ and the believer. "It is no longer I who live, but Christ who lives in me. And the life I now live in the flesh I live by faith in the Son of God" (Gal. 2:20; cf. 1 Cor. 15:10). Donald Baillie called the mysterious co-working of God and the believer "the paradox of grace."[57]

The most striking example that Paul gives us of the co-working of God and the creature in Christian life is the practice of prayer. Recall that Paul is convinced that all will work out for his deliverance "through your prayers and the help of the Spirit of Jesus Christ" (1:19). As he states more fully elsewhere, the Spirit of Christ is at work both in our praying (Rom. 8:26) and in our working (1 Cor. 15:10). So Paul constantly prays as he works and works as he prays, knowing that, in the final analysis, his praying and working for the spread of the gospel will bear fruit only insofar as God works in and through him. The practice of prayer, invoking God's presence and activity at the beginning, middle, and end of our activity, reminds us that "unless the Lord builds the house, those who build it labor in vain" (Ps. 127:1).

57. Donald Baillie, *God Was in Christ* (New York: Charles Scribner's Sons, 1948), 106–32.

2:19–3:1a

Two Exemplary Helpers

2:19–30
Regarding Timothy and Epaphroditus

In this section Paul tells of his plans to send Timothy and Epaphroditus, two of his coworkers, to Philippi in the near future. He does so with warm and strong commendations. Timothy has served Paul in the work of the gospel "like a son with a father" (2:19–24). Epaphroditus, called by Paul "my brother and co-worker and fellow soldier," is sent with praise for his brave service in the work of Christ (2:25–30).

The transition from the mountaintop heights of the Christ hymn and its accompanying exhortations to the valley of practical church concerns is noticeably abrupt, and it is not surprising that some commentators see little connection between this and the preceding section. They conjecture that we have here a fragment of a different letter that Paul wrote to the Philippians on another occasion. However, a careful reading of the passage in the context of the letter as a whole leads to a different conclusion. While it may seem that Paul shifts almost randomly from theological confession and ethical exhortation to practical matters regarding two coworkers, we can nevertheless discern important continuities between this and the preceding section.

The return of Timothy and Epaphroditus to Philippi as joyful news is one clear connection. Recall that the previous section concludes with Paul's exhortation to his friends to rejoice with him despite the sufferings that both they and he are experiencing: "I . . . rejoice with all of you . . . rejoice with me," he writes (2:17–18). Now Paul gives the Philippians concrete reasons for rejoicing. He is sending Epaphroditus home at once, and he will soon be sending

Timothy to Philippi as well to assist the Philippians for a time in Paul's absence. He expects this news will bring joy to the Philippians and will in time add to Paul's own joy. He will be cheered by hearing news of his friends in Philippi when Timothy returns from his trip, and on top of this is the hope that Paul himself will be able to visit them soon. As for Epaphroditus, he should be welcomed home "with all joy" (2:29). These events provide ample reasons for the Philippians to rejoice with Paul.

Christian joy for Paul is rooted in the redemptive work that Christ has already accomplished and in the confidence that he will return to bring this work to its consummation. However, the good news that awakens joy is not simply a matter of remembering a past event and expecting an event in the future. For Paul, Christ is risen and is present here and now among his people in the power of the Spirit. Paul rejoices in the fellowship of believers in Christ. Their quality of life together in Christ—their deep friendship, common service, and mutual support and love—awaken joy. Paul thus sees the work of Timothy and Epaphroditus and their coming reunion with fellow Christians in Philippi as occasions to celebrate. Clearly for Paul, the company of fellow Christians and their sharing of love and service make Christian life and discipleship a joyful experience rather than a heavy burden.

But there is another and equally important connection between this section of the letter and the one preceding it. Earlier Paul rehearsed the story of Christ as the supreme paradigm of Christian life. The mind-set of Christians, their dispositions, decisions, and actions, are to be guided and formed by the way of Christ recounted in the great Christ hymn. The life of Christians, personally and in community, is to reflect, to correspond, to his. In all circumstances, they are to discern what is best and decide what to do in a manner that is directed and governed by the mind of Christ and with the help of his Spirit. No other model of living "in a

> **Paul strikes a positive note in these verses as he presents first Timothy and then Epaphroditus as godly examples for the Philippians to follow.**
>
> Peter T. O'Brien, *The Epistle to the Philippians* (Grand Rapids: Eerdmans, 1991), 323.

manner worthy of the gospel of Christ" (1:27) can ever replace or compete with his own. Nevertheless, for Paul there are also dependent and secondary examples of the Christian life, and he clearly finds two in his coworkers Timothy and Epaphroditus. Notable are the "striking verbal parallels" between the brief descriptions of Paul's two coworkers and the way of Christ presented in the Christ hymn. Their stories thus also serve Paul's larger purpose of helping the Philippians in their "progress and joy in faith" (1:25).[1] As secondary but nonetheless noteworthy examples, the portrayals of Timothy and Epaphroditus assist in the Christian formation of the Philippian community, the strengthening of its life together in Christ, and its readiness to serve him even at great risk.

2:19–24 *Timothy*

The two Letters to Timothy in the New Testament are widely viewed today by scholars as having been written by someone other than Paul. In these letters Timothy is portrayed as a rather inexperienced young man in need of a mentor. In Philippians, however, while Paul speaks of Timothy as a young man, he is presented as an experienced coworker. In any case, the relationship of Paul and Timothy was clearly a close one. Their names are linked in the salutations of at least four of Paul's letters (1 Thess. 1:1; 2 Cor. 1:1; Phil. 1:1; Phlm. 1). Writing of Timothy in one of these letters, Paul calls him his "beloved and faithful child in the Lord" (1 Cor. 4:17).

Here in Philippians, Paul goes still further in his commendation. He speaks of Timothy's relationship with him as "like a son with a father" (2:22). The metaphor expresses not only a strong personal tie between them but also the depth of their cooperation in the work of the gospel (2:22). So close is the relationship of Timothy and Paul that, while promising to send Timothy to Philippi "soon," Paul wants to keep him by his side until he sees "how things go with me" (2:23). In other words, if Paul's situation gets worse and should even come

---

1. Peter T. O'Brien, *The Epistle to the Philippians* (Grand Rapids: Eerdmans, 1991), 315. Markus Bockmuehl, *The Epistle to the Philippians* (London: Hendrickson, 1998), 167, agrees: The language used of Timothy by Paul is "deliberately evocative" of the attitude and way of Christ portrayed in the Christ hymn.

to his receiving a death sentence, it is Timothy whom Paul wants by his side. Timothy is for Paul a person of "worth," and he takes for granted that Timothy's Christian commitment and his leadership abilities are well known in Philippi as well (2:22).

Paul's remark "I have no one like him who will be genuinely concerned for your welfare" (2:20) not only indicates how highly Paul thinks of Timothy and how much he counts on him; it also expresses Paul's great confidence in the exemplary value that Timothy's faithful service will have for the Philippians. Timothy is not like all the others around Paul who "are seeking their own interests, not those of Jesus Christ" (2:21). We do not know to whom Paul is referring here as "seeking their own interests," although one good possibility is that he has in mind those mentioned earlier who "proclaim Christ out of selfish ambition" (1:17). Timothy is clearly not of this ilk. With Paul, he has faithfully "served in the work of the gospel" (literally, is "enslaved for the gospel"). In Paul's view, the Christlike attitude and caring behavior of Timothy, the subordination of his own interests to the interests of others, and his genuine concern for the welfare of the people whom he will serve as pastor are precisely the marks that commend him for service in the name of Christ.

In brief, the demeanor and practice of Timothy offer a likeness or analogy of the mind of Christ who poured out his life for our salvation. Timothy's concern for others rather than for himself is a reflection of the humility of Christ and of the love that Paul describes elsewhere as "patient," "kind," not "arrogant" or insisting "on its own way" (1 Cor. 13:4–5). In effect, then, we have in Paul's commendation of Timothy a compressed narrative of exemplary Christian discipleship. For Paul, the faithful service of Timothy embodies a way of life that is "worthy of the gospel." In looking not to his own interests but to the interests of others, he corresponds in some small degree to the self-emptying and other-regarding love of Christ (2:6–8).

2:25–30 *Epaphroditus*

Unlike Timothy, who is mentioned several times in the New Testament, we know of Epaphroditus only from this brief passage of Paul's Letter to the Philippians. A native of Philippi, he was sent by the church there to take a gift of money to Paul and to serve as his helper on their behalf. For a period, Epaphroditus faithfully persisted in this service despite a serious illness that almost proved fatal. Paul then explains that Epaphroditus had been "longing" to see his friends in Philippi and was worried because they had been told he was ill. When Paul decides to send him home, he commends him warmly and urges the Philippians to "welcome him then in the Lord with all joy" (2:29). Receiving him in this way would be another opportunity for the Philippians to rejoice with Paul in spite of the challenges both he and they face (2:18).

Just as Paul gives Timothy high praise by describing him as a servant of Christ who is genuinely concerned not for himself but for the welfare of others, so Paul is generous in his commendation of Epaphroditus. He describes him as "my brother;" "co-worker," and "fellow soldier" who "came close to death for the work of Christ, risking his life to make up for those services that you could not give me" (2:30). In the three descriptors, Paul portrays Epaphroditus not only as a fellow believer in Christ ("my brother"), not only as someone who has worked with him in the service of Christ and the gospel ("co-worker"), but also as someone who, like Paul, has been on the front lines of the proclamation of the gospel, even to the point of risking his life ("fellow soldier"). This last title reminds us again that Philippi was a Roman colony, and Paul's use of a military metaphor would surely find resonance in the church located there. "Fellow soldier" also underscores that, for Paul, Christian life and ministry involves believers in a struggle (*agon*), a battle with forces hostile to the gospel. Taking part in this struggle had almost cost Epaphroditus his life. Thus, like Timothy, Epaphroditus is described by Paul as someone whose service gives exemplary witness to the way of Christ. There is a kind of reverberation and reflection of the way of Christ in Paul's brief story of Epaphroditus.

Curiously, Barth casts a pall of suspicion over this coworker of Paul. Noting the serious illness Epaphroditus experienced, Barth wonders about Epaphroditus's motives for wanting to return to Philippi. Did he really long for all the members of the Philippian church, or only for his family? Did Epaphroditus really worry about the Philippians' worry for him? "What a very strange motive for the behavior of a mature man!" Barth remarks.[2] Barth seems to suggest that longing for family and friends at home is unworthy of a servant of the gospel, despite the possibility that Epaphroditus may actually have been younger than "a mature man," and despite the fact that Paul had earlier described himself as longing for his friends in Philippi (1:8). Barth goes so far as to suggest that Epaphroditus's desire to return home, leaving unfinished the work to which he had been commissioned, might even qualify as an act of "desertion" similar to one reported in Acts 15:38.[3] Barth does not press the point any further, and in the end acknowledges that Epaphroditus did risk his life to minister to the gospel and should be honored for his service. He rightly calls attention to Paul's gracious way of dealing with all the "questionable circumstances" in which Epaphroditus will be returning to Philippi.

I read this passage rather differently from Barth. While Paul may have felt he had to defend Epaphroditus from possible criticisms of his behavior by members of the Philippian community, Paul emphasizes the readiness of Epaphroditus to risk illness and even death in the ministry of the gospel. Even if his service was cut short, his risk of life is a witness to the great sacrifice Christ has made for us all and an example of our calling to bear a bold witness to the gospel despite the danger this may entail. As we have emphasized repeatedly, there cannot be the least doubt that, for Paul, what Christ did in emptying himself and becoming obedient even to death on a cross stands far above any acts of humility, love, service, and sacrifice on the part of his disciples. Christ is the supreme example because he is also and exclusively our Savior (3:20). Yet the free grace of God in Christ by the power of the Holy Spirit enables his followers to participate in and bear witness to—sometimes costly witness to—his work.

All this is to say that for Paul, an analogy can be discerned between the way of the Savior and the way of his faithful servants Timothy and Epaphroditus. No more than an analogy! No more than a faint resemblance! In no way do Timothy and Epaphroditus stand on the same level with Christ as models of Christian life, let alone replace him. Nevertheless, an imperfect but real correspondence can be seen

2. Karl Barth, *The Epistle to the Philippians* (Louisville, KY: Westminster John Knox Press, 2002), 88.
3. Ibid., 87.

> **Sometimes witnesses are all Christians have to offer, and sometimes witnesses are enough; for what could be more powerful than the discovery that human beings have been made part of God's care of creation through the cross and resurrection of Jesus of Nazareth.**
>
> Stanley Hauerwas, *With the Grain of the Universe* (Grand Rapids: Brazos, 2001), 241.

between the way of Christ and the way of these two witnesses. When Christians are truly concerned for the well-being of their neighbors, when they risk all for the sake of the gospel and the community that it gathers, they live, as we might put it, "eccentrically"—they live not for themselves but for others.[4] The Christlikeness of their service should not be ignored or devalued. In their small, imperfect way, their lives bear witness to the self-giving way of Christ. Paul's position is unmistakable: look first of all and always to Christ as the perfect archetype of the life "worthy of the gospel," but do not disregard the life witness of disciples like Timothy and Epaphroditus who in their small but important way bear a likeness to the "mind of Christ."

We conclude, then, that two themes stand out in this section of the letter. There is first of all the recurrence of the theme of joy. The coming visit of Timothy and the return of Epaphroditus will increase the Philippians' joy in Christ, giving them concrete occasions to rejoice with Paul, as he enjoins them to do. The section thus appropriately concludes with the exhortation: "Finally, my brothers and sisters, rejoice in the Lord" (3:1a).

Second, and equally important, these paragraphs about Timothy and Epaphroditus, seemingly marginal on first glance, reflect in small measure the Christ hymn of the preceding section. In his earlier retelling of Christ's singular act of self-humbling, and now in what amount to very compact stories of two servants of Christ, Paul is providing concrete narratives that serve as examples of the life worthy of the gospel. Just as earlier the Philippians were exhorted to have the mind of Christ, so in the present section Timothy and Epaphroditus are described in a way that suggests they are secondary and

---

4. On "eccentricity" as a marker of Christian life, see David H. Kelsey, *Eccentric Existence: A Theological Anthropology*, 2 vols. (Louisville, KY: Westminster John Knox Press, 2009).

dependent, yet noteworthy, examples of Christian life in service of God and others. I emphasize again the words "secondary and dependent." Paul has no desire to make Timothy and Epaphroditus into icons. Nevertheless, Paul does not shy from pointing to followers of Christ whose lives of service should inspire and motivate others. To clinch the point he wants to make about Timothy and Epaphroditus, Paul calls on the Philippians to "honor such people" (2:29). Later in the letter, Paul speaks about the importance of attending to all that is "honorable" (4:8), including what is honorable in the wider world beyond the bounds of the church. Here, however, his thoughts are particularly focused on the honorable work of Timothy and Epaphroditus, two servants of Christ, dedicated to the interests of others and willing to take risks for the ministry of the gospel.

Previously, Paul has described his own life as "being poured out as a libation" (2:17). In the next section of the letter and at even greater length than in his commendations of Timothy and Epaphroditus, Paul exhorts the Philippians to imitate him in his dedication to and service of their common Lord.

FURTHER REFLECTIONS
Honor

Giving and receiving honor has an important place in all human societies. In our schools we commend students for their achievements by putting their names on an honor roll. "On a scout's honor" is part of the code of the Boy and Girl Scouts. When someone retires after years of service to an institution, we may arrange a dinner or some other special occasion in their honor. We decorate military personnel or other citizens for their special contributions to public life with medals of honor.

The Bible also speaks of people of worth who have a claim to receive honor from us. Think of the commandment of the Torah that calls us to "honor your father and your mother" (Exod. 20:12). Many of us have received love, care, and guidance from our parents, and they in turn deserve honor for their love and service. Even those for whom this commandment has a bitter taste because they have experienced abuse at the hands of their parents or have grown up in families where one parent has been absent can nevertheless recognize other people in their lives who have acted as father or mother to them and to whom therefore honor is due. By extension, the command to honor our father and mother embraces all those who have schooled us, who have guided and advised us, supported and affirmed us, and passed on to us wisdom born of experience. Such people, all would agree, should be honored.

In the perspective of the biblical witness, it is above all God who is "clothed with honor and majesty" (Ps. 104:1). When God does a new thing, even "the wild animals" will honor God (Isa. 43:20). It is this God who has humbly come to us in Jesus Christ who is worthy of supreme honor: "You are worthy, our Lord and God, to receive glory and honor and power, for you created all things" (Rev. 4:11). "Worthy is the Lamb that was slaughtered to receive power and wealth and wisdom and might and honor and glory and blessing!" (Rev. 5:12). God alone deserves our highest honor.

Yet the God who alone is worthy of our greatest honor, honors us. Honor is ultimately something that we neither give to ourselves nor that others give to us. Every human being is honorable because God has honored us all by creating us in God's image, by endowing us with such talents and abilities as we have, and by reconciling us through the work of Jesus Christ. In biblical perspective, then, being honored cannot be an occasion of self-congratulation or boasting. "What do you have that you did not receive?" Paul asks (1 Cor. 4:7). Our inalienable worth as human beings has its basis in God our Creator and Redeemer.

But—and here we come directly to Paul's exhortation to "honor such people" as Timothy and Epaphroditus—there is an added honor that God bestows on us as God's beloved creatures and forgiven sinners. This is the honor of being called by God to a new way of life in the service of Christ. Hence, for Paul and for Christians who attend seriously to his message, what is especially deserving of honor is a form of life that, however imperfectly, participates in and corresponds to the way of Jesus Christ.

While honoring the saints has always been part of the Roman Catholic tradition, Protestants are often uneasy about this practice for fear of replacing Christ as the center of faith and worship. Yet even the most squeamish Protestant will probably recognize the need for a category of honorable ones in the case of such people as Dietrich Bonhoeffer, who was executed for the witness he bore in Nazi Germany; and Martin Luther King Jr., who was assassinated for his leadership in the civil rights movement; and Mother Teresa, who dedicated her life to service among the very poor of India. There are, of course, countless "such people" of honor, as Paul puts it. These people deserve our honor because they placed the interests and needs of others over their own. Indeed, risking everything for others, their lives reflect in some small part the mind of Christ. That is the direction in which Paul points his readers with reference to Timothy and Epaphroditus when he urges them to "honor such people."

Now does this mean that Paul thinks only "such people" are deserving of honor? Are most of us consigned to live our lives as Christians in ways that are bound to appear as rather quiet, undistinguished, and unheralded, or even as rather mediocre Christians in comparison with the faithful Timothy and the risk-taking Epaphroditus, or the likes of Bonhoeffer, King, and Mother Teresa? No, honor is given to us too, by virtue of the fact that we also have been created by God and reconciled by Christ and are thus persons of great worth. Moreover, we too have been called to serve the purposes of God—certainly not to apostleship and perhaps not to putting our lives at risk in some dramatic way—but nevertheless to such witness to the gospel of Jesus Christ as it may please God to call us.

Recall what Paul says in another letter about the body of Christ and its many diverse members (1 Cor. 12:4–26). Every member of the body has been honored with a gift. No member of the body can say to another, I have no need of you, or I am superior to you, or you are not deserving of honor. On the contrary, even the so-called lesser members and their gifts are honorable.

> **If one member suffers, all suffer together with it; if one member is honored, all rejoice together with it.**
>
> (1 Cor. 12:26)

Even if only a relatively few Christians may be publicly recognized by the church for their risk-taking stand for the freedom of the gospel or the cause of justice and human dignity that it promotes, there is honor in offering one's witness and service with integrity and joy in one's own place and time.

That said, nothing is to be taken away from Paul's exhortation to honor the special ministry of those like Timothy and Epaphroditus who provide exemplary witness to the way of Jesus Christ. The church needs such witnesses to avoid the complacency and dullness that can all too easily become the standards of Christian existence. Barth says it well: "The life of the community would not be healthy, nor its witness eloquent, if it did not have such proponents."[5]

5. Barth, CD IV/3.2:887–88.

3:1b-4:1

Losing All to Gain Christ

The transition from "rejoice in the Lord" (3:1a) to "beware of the dogs" (3:2) is abrupt, prompting some commentators to judge that much of the material in 3:2–4:3 is a fragment of a separate letter of Paul. They contend that the call to rejoice in 3:1 is followed more smoothly by the repetition of the call to rejoice in 4:4. As noted previously, although the theory that Philippians is a compilation of multiple letters has some plausibility, there are good reasons to read the letter as a literary unity, as I hope the following discussion will show.

After an initial threefold warning (3:1b–3), the centerpiece of the section is Paul's account of what having the mind of Christ has involved for him personally (3:4–14). To the master paradigm of the self-expending Christ (2:5–11), and the two lesser examples of self-giving service found in the brief descriptions of Timothy and Epaphroditus (2:19–30), Paul now adds the witness of his own life. His account describes the radical changes in perception, the losses and gains, and the forward movement that characterize his new life in Christ. He has found a new identity in Christ, has surrendered his cherished past, and now strains forward in response to the call of his crucified and risen Lord.

The point of Paul's narrative is not to present himself as an object of admiration and praise. Rather, it is to exhort and inspire the Philippians to join in imitating him in imitating Christ. The section thus drives toward Paul's exhortation to the Philippians to "stand firm in the Lord" and to live according to his and his fellow workers' examples rather than being influenced by the "enemies of the cross of Christ" (3:15–4:1).

3:1b–4a

A Warning

Paul begins this section of the letter with the admission that he will now be repeating what they have already heard from him. But he thinks the repetition is for their own good (literally, it is a "safeguard"; 3:1b). Then he launches into a stern, threefold warning: "Beware of the dogs, beware of the evil workers, beware of those who mutilate the flesh!" Who are the targets of these harsh words of Paul against those who place their "confidence in the flesh" (3:2, 4)? New Testament scholars offer no consensus on the question. Most likely, however, they are Jewish Christian converts who, not content with the gospel Paul preaches, insist on the necessity of some of the practices and rituals of Judaism, such as circumcision. After all, Jewish Christians like Paul himself might reasonably have argued: Are not the Scriptures of Christians identical with those of the Jewish community, and do not these Scriptures describe circumcision as the essential mark of membership in the covenant community?

Moreover, the teachers Paul is opposing here may have sugarcoated their message of the necessity of circumcision by noting its political advantage. Under the umbrella of its dominant imperial cult, Rome tolerated and protected a number of ethnic religions, including Judaism. Since the new Christian movement was not among these recognized religions and was thus, strictly speaking, illegal, its confession of Christ, and particularly the claim of his universal lordship, was bound to evoke suspicion. Being more closely associated with Judaism would no doubt have had appeal for Christians in Philippi in face of the danger of opposition from representatives of the imperial cult.[1] Whatever their identity and their rationale, however, Paul sharply attacks those who are urging the recovery of Jewish practices among members of the church at Philippi. He calls them dogs, evildoers, mutilators.

In the Old Testament, dogs are looked on as despicable animals. Roaming about in search of food, they are associated with

---

1. Markus Bockmuehl, *The Epistle to the Philippians* (London: Hendrickson, 1998), 190; Stephen E. Fowl, *Philippians* (Grand Rapids: Eerdmans, 2005), 146.

"indiscriminate and base behavior."[2] As a pejorative label, "dog "was sometimes used by observant Jews to describe Gentiles who were considered ritually unclean. Even Jesus is reported to have used the epithet in his reply to the Syrophoenician woman who pleads with him to heal her daughter: "Let the children be fed first, for it is not fair to take the children's food and throw it to the dogs" (Mark 7:27). If Paul's opponents are Jewish Christian converts, there is irony in his use of *dogs* to characterize them. In effect, Paul turns the sharp epithet around and says it is these opponents who think of them-selves as super-Jews who are the real "dogs."

As for the charge against evildoers (NRSV "evil workers"), Barth follows Bultmann in construing the phrase as meaning "work-heroes," that is, people who think that busying themselves with a lot of religious rituals and moral regulations constitutes the essence of faith.[3] The further warning against mutilators of the flesh (Greek *katatome*) is a scathing and sarcastic reference to the rite of circumci-sion (Greek *peritome*).

It is possible that Paul sees his opponents whom he labels so harshly as the very opposite of having the mind of Christ, the way of humility, dependence on God's grace alone, and love for and solidar-ity with others. They are, in his view, like wild dogs whose only con-cern is for their own survival; they are evildoers, not because they are necessarily morally corrupt but because they want to substitute their own works for God's gift of salvation; they are mutilators of the flesh because they arrogantly insist on physical circumcision for all members of God's covenant community. In brief, they lack the humility to recognize and honor a deeper, spiritual circumcision of the heart that binds together Jewish Christian and Gentile Christian in Christ. Their ways represent the very opposite of the Christlike attitudes and practices that Paul is exhorting the Philippians to fol-low throughout the letter. Paul finds the root of all his opponents' faults in their "confidence in the flesh" (3:3–4).

Still, even if the irony of Paul's reverse name-calling is taken into account, and even if his biting sarcasm is explained as a product of

---

2. Bockmuehl, *Philippians*, 185.
3. Karl Barth, *The Epistle to the Philippians* (Louisville, KY: Westminster John Knox Press, 2002), 93.

heated controversy, the harshness of his "outburst"[4] remains. Like a "rhetorical flame-thrower,"[5] Paul's language here will strike many readers as over the top and may seem strangely inconsistent with the joyful and confident tenor of the letter as a whole. Did not Paul claim that he will rejoice in whatever way Christ is proclaimed, even if it is out of envy and rivalry (1:15–18)? Yes, but in the present context Paul is not confronting the issue of different motives for preaching the gospel. Rather, he is talking about those who, he is convinced, are in effect proclaiming a different gospel. When Paul determines that the gospel itself is at risk, he can be fierce (cf. Gal. 1: 7–9). He is prepared to pull out all the rhetorical stops in describing his opponents. Calvin does much the same thing in rebuttals of his "papist" opponents during the Reformation. Barth, too, minces no words in his repudiation of the "German-Christian" sympathizers with Hitler and the Nazi regime. However, while understandable in context, Paul's heated language still seems out of line with his effort, especially in this letter, to persuade and exhort rather than to pummel and excoriate. Even Calvin is a bit concerned that Paul's rhetorical exuberance in this passage not be understood as legitimating verbal abuse of one's opponents. "We must beware lest any intemperance or excessive bitterness should creep in under the cloak of zeal," Calvin writes.[6]

In reading Paul's sharply worded warning in this passage, it is of crucial importance to recognize that Paul is not rampaging against all Jewish Christians. He has no quarrel with Jewish Christians "who as believers continued to circumcise their sons in accordance with the ancestral traditions."[7] Even less is Paul denigrating "Jews in general." Rather, he is denouncing certain Jewish Christian teachers who insist, in the church in Philippi and elsewhere, that circumcision is a necessary prerequisite for *all* members of God's covenant community and, accordingly, a necessary condition for Gentiles as well as Jews. Only in this way can they be in right relationship with

4. Peter T. O'Brien, *The Epistle to the Philippians* (Grand Rapids: Eerdmans, 1991), 354.
5. Bockmuehl, *Phillipians*, 177.
6. John Calvin, *Galatians, Ephesians, Philippians and Colossians*, CNTC, ed. David W. Torrance and Thomas F. Torrance (1965; repr., Grand Rapids: Eerdmans, 1979), 268.
7. O'Brien, *Philippians*, 357.

God. Paul's barbs are aimed at those particular Jewish Christians who think they must correct and improve Paul's gospel of the grace of God in Jesus Christ by adding the requirement that all heirs of God's covenant promises must be circumcised.

> Neither circumcision nor uncircumcision is anything, but a new creation is everything!
>
> (Gal. 6:15)

Paul counters by arguing that the practice of circumcision is not the necessary and exclusive sign of belonging to the covenant community. On the contrary, those who trust in Christ and refuse to boast about their achievements under the law are true heirs of the promise to Abraham. They too are circumcised—of the heart if not in the flesh (cf. Jer. 4:4). Paul pointedly exclaims: it is "we who are the circumcision, who worship in the Spirit of God and boast in Christ Jesus" (3:3). Christians, Paul argues, place their confidence not in a religious inheritance or a ritual practice but in the grace of God made known in Jesus Christ.

In view of the centuries-long disparagement of Jews by Christians and the reprehensible history of persecution of Jews climaxing in the horrendous event of the Holocaust, it must be emphasized that the outbursts of Paul in this passage do not represent the full sweep of his understanding of the place of the Jewish people in the economy of salvation. For that we have to consult above all Romans 9–11, where Paul is at great effort to say that Israel is and remains God's chosen people. Paul's missionary proclamation of the gospel aims not to exclude Jews but to include the Gentiles. The God of Israel has brought into being in Christ a new, enlarged covenant community composed of Jews and Gentiles. Far from canceling God's covenant with Israel, God's action in the faithfulness of Christ extends God's covenantal grace to the Gentiles. "I ask, then, has God rejected his people? By no means! I myself am an Israelite, a descendant of Abraham, a member of the tribe of Benjamin. God has not rejected his people whom he foreknew" (Rom. 11:1–2). The charge that Paul is overtly anti-Jewish, or at least harbors anti-Jewish biases, is simply mistaken.

Since the phrase "confidence in the flesh" appears three times in the opening verses of this passage, it is essential to clarify first what Paul does *not* mean by these words. His fight against such confidence has nothing to do with a gnostic dualism of body and spirit. There were, to be sure, many religious movements in the early centuries of the church that claimed secret knowledge (gnosis) to be the way of salvation. These movements postulated a radical opposition between the good world of the spirit and the evil world of matter and body. When Paul lambasts "confidence in the flesh," he is not equating "flesh" with "body" or saying that embodied life is evil while spiritual life apart from the body is good. In other words, Paul does not here, or anywhere else in his writings, reject a healthy affirmation of bodily existence as part of God's good creation.

Rather, in this section Paul uses the phrase "confidence in the flesh" in both a particular and a more comprehensive sense. Its particular reference is to trusting in being circumcised as guarantor of a right relationship with God. More comprehensively, "confidence in the flesh" includes every attitude that disregards humanity's radical and continuing dependence on the grace of God and instead places trust in one's "gifts and achievements."[8] All such confidence in the flesh gives rise to self-righteousness and boasting before God. Whatever form this boasting takes— *my* family lineage, *my* nation, *my* culture, *my* religion, *my* achievements—Paul says an unequivocal no to it. The embargo on all self-elevating "boasting" is a signature of his theology. "What do you have that you did not receive? And if you received it, why do you boast as if it were not a gift?" (1 Cor. 4:7; cf. Rom. 3:27; Eph. 2:8–9).

In sum, the point of Paul's critique of the Jewish Christian advocates of the necessity of physical circumcision is not to exalt "us Christians" over against "those Jews," as if Christians now possess a right to God's grace while others do not. In Paul's view, no one has a claim on God's grace. The smug attitude "God's grace belongs to us Christians, not to the Jews" would only be another form of "confidence in the flesh." No, the only basis of confidence, according to Paul, is the acknowledgment and reception of the sheer gift of God's

8. Gordon D. Fee, *Paul's Letter to the Philippians* (Grand Rapids: Eerdmans, 1995), 315.

new act of grace in Jesus Christ. The true heirs of Abraham put their trust not in themselves or their achievements or their cultural or religious heritage but in the Lord who has done a new thing in Christ to reconcile all people to himself, Jews and Gentiles alike.

3:4b–9
Letting Go of the Past

Paul now makes his case for the basis of true confidence by telling the story of the dramatic change that Christ has brought about in his life. As many expositors note, there is a striking similarity between the pattern of his story and the pattern of the Christ hymn of 2:5–11. Paul's own story bears the imprint of Christ's way of self-emptying and exaltation.[9] In both accounts there is first a movement to the depths—for Christ, a self-emptying or pouring out of himself; for Paul, a loss of all he previously considered valuable. Then there is a movement to the heights—for Christ, being highly exalted and given a name above every name (Lord); for Paul, being drawn forward toward "the goal for the prize of the heavenly call of God in Christ Jesus" (3:14). Paul's account of his journey of faith bears the marks of a fundamental reshaping of his identity and practice by Christ.[10]

Paul begins by describing his background and his pre-Christian life as a strict observer of the Jewish law (3:4b–9).[11] He says that if confidence were based on following the law, he would have many more reasons to be confident than his enemies have. After all, he was circumcised precisely as the law demands (on the eighth day, as Lev. 12:3 stipulates, not earlier, or days or years later); he was born into the Jewish community (not an outsider borrowing or stealing some of its practices); he belonged to the tribe of Benjamin (not one of the lesser tribes, but the leading tribe of the Jewish people); he was a Hebrew of the Hebrews (he spoke the language of the chosen people

---

9. Ibid., 314.
10. David G. Horrell, *Solidarity and Difference: A Contemporary Reading of Paul's Ethics* (London: T. & T. Clark, 2005), 242.
11. The following paragraph draws from Bockmuehl, *Philippians,* 194–203.

and knew the faith of Israel from the inside); he was a Pharisee (the school of strictest adherence to the law); he had earlier zealously persecuted the church (proof abundant of the utter seriousness of his Jewish allegiance); and to sum it all up, "as to righteousness under the law," he was completely "blameless" (he scrupulously kept all of its commandments).

This remarkable self-description of Paul shows conclusively that his experience as a law-observant Jew did not cast him into a pit of despair. He does not say that his life under the law drove him into a spiritual crisis. He does not say that it left him with a guilt-stricken conscience. He does not say that the law consigned him to impotence because he was unable to fulfill its demands. All of these are standard ways in which many later Christians, especially Protestant theologians, described the futility of the efforts of Paul to obey all the commands of the law and in that way to find salvation. No, Paul claims that he strictly adhered to the law, and by its standards he was "blameless." Not, of course, blameless in the sense of perfect—for how could Paul think of anyone but Christ as the perfectly obedient one?—but blameless in the sense of commendable or at least beyond reproach. Life under the law for Paul was not a miserable failure but, seen apart from Christ, a remarkable success.

As Joseph Hellerman has shown, Paul's remarkable summary of his elite Jewish pedigree and his outstanding moral credentials follows "the typical structure of honor inscriptions" that archaeologists have found in ancient Philippi.[12] Like these ancient Roman inscriptions, the first four items in Paul's honor list describe his distinguished family background (his "acquired honor") and the last three items his notable personal achievements (his "achieved honor").[13] Concern for social standing, not least among retired Roman military in the colony, was a marked feature of life in Philippi. Paul's list of his impressive Jewish honors would have spoken directly to the temptation of Philippian Christians to place their "confidence in the flesh" by mimicking the dominant ideas of pride and honor in their city and the social stratification that accompanied it.

---

12. Joseph H. Hellerman, *Reconstructing Honor in Roman Philippi* (New York: Cambridge University Press, 2005), 125.

13. Ibid.

Having presented his own list of high honors, acquired and achieved, Paul now counts all of them as "loss" (3:7) because of the "surpassing value of knowing Christ Jesus my Lord" (3:8). He has willingly given up all his birth privileges and personal achievements in order to "gain" Christ and "be found in him." What he "lost" was "a righteousness of my own" (3:9), a righteousness that was his in part as an heir of God's chosen people and in part by virtue of his blameless moral life. He goes so far as to say that he now considers this sort of righteousness sheer "rubbish" or dung (3:8). What he has gained—or more precisely what he has been given—is the "righteousness from God" that comes "through the faith [or the faithfulness] of Christ" and is "based on faith" (3:9). Since this rich sentence summarizes all that Paul affirms in this passage, each of its parts deserves some comment.

Consider first Paul's contrast of "a righteousness of my own" and "the righteousness from God." Looking back on his earlier life in the light of Christ, Paul now calls what once seemed to prove he was in the right before God a "righteousness of my own that comes from the law." Over against this understanding of a righteousness partly inherited and partly achieved, Paul sets "the righteousness from God." True righteousness is not something we inherit or achieve but a gift from God, something that God graciously does on our behalf to make right what is awry.

In addition, "the righteousness from God"—what God does to make things right—markedly differs from "a righteousness of my own" because its benefits extend to Gentiles as well as Jews. Through Jesus Christ, God acts to justify—"rectify"[14]— the ungodly who trust in God (Rom. 4:5), whether Jew or Gentile. A number of NT scholars today agree that many traditional ways of thinking of God's "righteousness" or "right-making"—here and in Paul's letters generally—fail to recognize the profoundly corporate nature of his understanding of what God is up to in the world. Individualistic ways of thinking are alien to the apostle. His question is not reducible to the question of a solitary individual asking, How do I find a gracious

14. J. Louis Martyn translates the verb *diakaio* as "rectifies" rather than "justifies" to underscore the connection between righteousness and rectification or making right. See Martyn, *Galatians*, Anchor Bible 33A (New York: Doubleday, 1997), 249–50.

God? How am *I* to be saved? For Paul, the individual does not stand before God in a vacuum. Certainly there is a personal dimension to the right-making activity of God. However, Paul does not assume, as do many Christians today, that the spheres of personal and communal renewal are separable. As a Jew immersed in and formed by the faith of Israel, Paul understands God's "righteousness" or right-making activity as God's election of and faithfulness to a people who are called to worship and serve God.

Thus when Paul speaks of God's righteousness, he does not refer in the first place to God's moral perfection in contrast to the imperfection of frail and sinful creatures. Nor is he referring primarily to God as supreme judge who rewards the good and punishes the wicked. Instead, God's righteousness for Paul is God's own free and gracious activity on behalf of ungodly humanity. In Jesus Christ, God "justifies the ungodly" (Rom. 4:5; cf. Phil. 3:9) by grace alone, apart from merits or works, Jew and Gentile alike. God's righteousness "is not a moral attribute that unites him with the good and separates him from the evil."[15] Rather, the righteousness of God has to do centrally with God's right-making activity on behalf of sinners and the outcast that, by grace, has happened once for all in the event of Christ crucified and risen and that by his Spirit continues to create and sustain a holy people elected for God's service in the world. The righteousness of God shatters all moral pretensions and breaks down the once-impregnable wall between Jew and Gentile.

A second and closely related element in Paul's understanding of "the righteousness from God" is its mediation "through the faith of Christ." The Greek phrase here is *dia pisteos Christou,* which the NRSV translates "through faith in Christ," while also offering an alternate translation in a footnote, "through the faith of Christ." I follow a number of scholars who favor this alternate translation.[16] The

---

15. Ernst Käsemann, *On Being a Disciple of the Crucified Nazarene* (Grand Rapids: Eerdmans, 2010), 16.

16. See especially R. B. Hays, "Pistis and Pauline Theology," and the responses by J. Dunn, "Once More: Pistis Christou," and P. Achtemeier, "Apropos the Faith of/in Christ," in *Pauline Theology,* vol. 4, ed. E. Elizabeth Johnson and David M. Hay (Atlanta: Scholars Press, 1997), 35–92. Scholars in agreement with Hays include N. T. Wright, *Paul: In Fresh Perspective* (Minneapolis: Fortress, 2009), 112; O'Brien, *Philippians,* 398–99; Bockmuehl, *Philippians,* 211–12; J. Louis Martyn, *Theological Issues in the Letters of Paul* (Edinburgh: T. & T. Clark, 1997), 150.

reasoning is that "through the faith [or faithfulness] *of* Christ" rather than "through faith *in* Christ" better honors Paul's thinking not only here but elsewhere as consistently christocentric (focused primarily on what Christ does) rather than anthropocentric (focused on what we do). In other words, it is not *our* faith in Christ that mediates God's righteousness but what *Christ* does on our behalf. Christ has already acted for us before we ever respond in faith. For us he emptied himself, humbled himself, and became obedient even to death on a cross.

> *Pistis Christou* is an expression by which Paul speaks of Christ's atoning faithfulness, as, on the cross, he died faithfully for human beings while looking faithfully to God.
>
> J. Louis Martyn, *Theological Issues in the Letters of Paul* (Edinburgh: T. & T. Clark, 1997), 151.

We are neither the source nor the mediator of righteousness to ourselves, whether by our distinguished heritage, our good deeds, or our acts of faith. Righteousness comes "from God" and "through the faithfulness of Christ."

Paul does not tell his readers how "the faithfulness of Christ" both decisively reveals and mediates "the righteousness of God" to us. As noted earlier, there is no developed theory of the atonement in Paul's Letter to the Philippians. Still, if God was decisively at work making things right through Christ, this must entail some understanding of his atoning work in the cross and resurrection, even if in Philippians Paul does not say that "Christ died for our sins" (1 Cor. 15:3) or that because of Christ we have been freed from the dominion of sin and death (Rom. 8:2). While a classic text of Pauline atonement doctrine like Romans 3:21–26 is better known than Philippians 3:7–11 because of the epochal role it played in the sixteenth-century Reformation debates, there are important agreements between the two passages.[17] Both emphasize that what makes for righteousness is not our inherited privileges or our moral accomplishments but instead the gracious gift of God received by faith. Both imply that there can be no boasting before God. Both emphasize the centrality of Christ's saving work. While the Romans passage is more explicit about the saving significance of the cross of Christ (it is called "a

17. See Bockmuehl, *Philippians,* 211.

sacrifice of atonement by his blood," Rom. 3:25), the Philippians passage speaks of "the faithfulness of Christ" and has in mind the saving act of Christ, whose self-emptying, self-humbling, and obedience even to "death on a cross" has been described earlier in the Christ hymn (2:5–8) and whose "sufferings" are recalled in 3:10.

There is a third factor in Paul's description of "the righteousness from God" that comes "through the faithfulness of Christ": what Christ has done for us calls for our appropriate response. Paul has this response in mind when he speaks of the righteousness from God through the faithfulness of Christ as "based on faith." Our act of faith is not ignored or trivialized. God's grace does not make us into puppets; God wants our free and glad response. For Paul, however, our faith is not the primary or initiating factor. Our response follows what God in Christ has done to set things right and to bring about a new creation. As J. Louis Martyn states, "God's rectifying act . . . is no more God's response to human faith in Christ than it is God's response to human observance of the Law. God's rectification is not God's response at all. It is the *first move;* it is God's initiative, carried out by him in Christ's faithful death."[18] Thinking of God's right-making activity as set in motion or made possible by our act of faith seriously distorts Pauline doctrine. The Reformation slogan "justification by faith" is often misunderstood in this way. Justification by faith, however, does not mean that our faith makes everything right in our relationship with God and others. Rather, the phrase is shorthand for the affirmation "justification by the grace of God received by faith."

In summary, in contrasting "a righteousness of my own" with "the righteousness from God" that comes "through the faithfulness of Christ" and is "based on faith" (3:9), Paul is saying several crucially important things. First, he is saying that prior to receiving Christ's self-revelation on the road to Damascus, he considered himself "blameless" in fulfilling his covenant responsibilities as a member of God's chosen people. However, in the light of the revelation of God in the crucifixion and resurrection of Christ, Paul came to see everything differently. Whereas the "righteousness of my own" is based on

---

18. Martyn, *Theological Issues*, 151.

a distinguished pedigree or notable achievements, "the righteousness from God" comes to us as sheer gift.

Second and no less important, for Paul the right-making activity
of God that comes through the faithfulness of Christ and is received
by faith brings into being not just new persons but a new creation, a
people of God inclusive of Jews and Gentiles.[19] What God has done
through Christ not only shatters all boasting in human achievements, it also radically redefines the boundaries of the covenant
community created by God's grace. It is highly probable that Paul
formerly thought of the people of Israel as the sole recipients of the
grace and righteousness from God; the Gentiles were considered
beyond the bounds of God's favor. In the light of the revelation of
Christ, however, Paul now proclaims that God's right-making grace
through the faithfulness of Christ has opened the covenant community to Gentiles as well as Jews. The "new creation" in Christ of
which Paul speaks in 2 Corinthians 5:17 is not simply a collection
of new individuals but "a new social reality" that includes both Gentiles and Jews.[20] Being "in Christ" means membership in the people
of God that transcends the boundaries of Jew and Greek, slave and
free person, male and female (Gal. 3:28).

Third, if the Gentiles too are now recipients by faith of the gift of
the righteousness of God through Christ, if Jews and Gentiles are
now becoming one new humanity in Christ, then indeed the work
of Christ has inaugurated the completion of God's redemptive purposes and the renewal of all things. The cross and resurrection of
Christ are nothing less than cosmos-altering events for Paul.

Worth noting are the several arresting metaphors that Paul uses
to describe how he now thinks of his former life as a law-observing
Jew in comparison with his new life in Christ.[21] One metaphor is
monetary or financial. Paul says he counts as "loss" what he earlier

---

19. This is one of the important emphases of the so-called new perspective on Paul.
"Righteousness, *dikaiosynē*, ... means 'covenant status,' or 'covenant membership'. ... The
doctrine of justification by faith was born into the world as the key doctrine underlying the
unity of God's renewed people" (Wright, *Paul,* 113). See also N. T. Wright, *Paul for Everyone:
The Prison Letters* (Louisville, KY: Westminster John Knox Press, 2004), 121.

20. John Howard Yoder, *The Politics of Jesus: Vicit Agnus Noster* (Grand Rapids: Eerdmans,
1994), 222.

21. My summary of Paul's use of metaphors in this passage draws on Stephen E. Fowl,
Philippians, 152-54.

considered "gains" and now values knowing Christ as Lord as his supreme "gain" (3:7–8). While the metaphor of loss and gain is clear and effective, it has its limitations when taken too literally, especially in the modern American economy driven by Wall Street investors. As Fowl observes, "Christ is not . . . some blue chip stock that Paul has added to his portfolio."[22] The prosperity gospel popular in some church quarters today— come to Christ and financial rewards will quickly follow—runs in a very different direction from Paul's call to a life conformed to the crucified Lord.

Even more striking is a second metaphor Paul uses to describe his former life under the law. He calls it "rubbish" or dung, and contrasts it with "the surpassing value of knowing Christ Jesus my Lord" (3:8). How are we to understand this? Barth's comment on the strong language is perceptive: "To repent—one surely turns here involuntarily to this concept—does not mean to be liberalized, to become indifferent to what we formerly were, to the former objects of our devotion and the former conduct of our lives, but to be horrified by it all."[23] But does this then mean Paul wants to trash the law given by God to the covenant people? Not at all. What Paul is saying is that the way he earlier *perceived* and *used* the law of God had to be entirely given up as worthless and replaced by a new way of perceiving the purpose of the law and the scope of the righteousness of God. Paul does not trash the law of God. He understands its purpose now in a completely different light.[24]

If we are not to misunderstand Paul, we have to distinguish between the intrinsic goodness of the law of God and how it is appropriately or inappropriately used. As a Jew, Paul highly esteems the law as God's precious gift to the covenant people of Israel (Rom. 7:7–12). However, the law is abused when it is turned into an engine of self-righteousness, boasting, and denigration of others. According to Paul, God has done something radically new in Christ. God has acted for the salvation of all people apart from any merit or achievement of their own. Paul affirms, as does Calvin in a much

---

22. Fowl, *Philippians*, 153.
23. Barth, *Philippians*, 97.
24. See Paul W. Meyer, "Romans 10:4 and the 'End' of the Law," in *The Divine Helmsman*, ed. J. L. Crenshaw and J. S. Sandmal (New York: KTAV, 1980); Fowl, *Philippians*, 161.

> Originally the law is not
> demonic. The apostle rejects
> this idea as blasphemy. It is
> a helpful guide toward a life
> according to the will of God,
> but as all other gifts, it is
> misused when one's own piety
> is made the meaning
> and goal of the divine mercy.
>
> Ernst Käsemann, *On Being a Disciple
> of the Crucified Nazarene* (Grand Rapids:
> Eerdmans, 2010), 190.

later time, that those who recognize God's new and decisive action in Christ and put their trust in him do not dishonor but rightly honor the law of God. Indeed, for Paul, Christ is the "end" (*telos*) of the law (Rom. 10:4), in the double sense of "canceled" and "fulfilled"—canceled, because its misuse as a means of gaining salvation or as a vehicle of boasting before God has been exposed as useless; fulfilled, because the law finds its true end or goal in the gift of grace in Christ and the new life in him. By the life-giving Spirit of Christ, believers are now called and empowered to obey the "law of Christ" (Gal. 6:2). To repeat: Paul does not trash the law; he trashes the misperception and distortion of the law by the spirit of self-righteousness and the exclusion of others whom God has now included in the covenant promises by God's new and astonishing work of free grace in Christ.

Paul also uses a third metaphor to contrast his former life and his new life in Christ. He says he now wants to "be found in Christ" (3:9). In other words, Christ is not a commodity to be gained or possessed but "a home where the lost Paul is found."[25] Christ is the location, the home, of Paul's new identity. Moreover, Paul's use of the passive mode ("being found") in this passage is significant. It expresses the idea that Christ, not Paul, is the primary actor in his dramatic turnaround. It is not Paul who has found Christ, but Christ who has found Paul, and it is "in Christ" that Paul finds himself. Apart from Christ, we think we must and are able to construct our own identity, to make something of ourselves, to become our own persons, to find ourselves. But Paul insists that a new identity—his true identity—has been given to him by Christ. He wants to "be found in Christ" because "Christ Jesus has made me his own" (3:12). As Paul says elsewhere, our lives are "hidden with Christ in God" (Col.

25. Fowl, *Philippians*, 153.

3:3). In faith we acknowledge that Christ has first found us, and on this basis we are enabled to find ourselves, our true identity, in him.

From the preceding comments, it should be clear that, according to Paul, to be "found in Christ" goes beyond even when it includes what is sometimes called a personal conversion. Being found in Christ for Paul also means being found in the new community of Christ that includes Jews and Gentiles. Recall that the story of Paul's own faith journey was triggered by those who claimed that to be included in God's chosen people one must be circumcised. When to this claim Paul retorts: "It is we who are the circumcision" (3:3), by "we" he means both Jewish and Gentile Christians in Philippi and elsewhere who together make up the new social reality created by God's gracious act in Jesus Christ. Even if Paul uses a number of first-person singular pronouns in his narrative, the aim of his story is not simply to testify about his own personal relationship with Christ but instead to describe the radical transformation that coming to know Christ makes in the understanding of the righteousness that comes from God. And this change has much to do with the new communal reality ("new creation," as Paul calls it in 2 Cor. 5:17) created by God through the faithfulness of Christ and received by faith. The view of "a righteousness of my own" that Paul gave up was not only based on pride rather than on the saving love and faithfulness of Christ; it was also tied to the assumption that God's election of Israel excluded Gentiles from membership in God's covenant community unless they became law-observant Jews and were physically circumcised.

FURTHER REFLECTIONS
Righteousness from God

The phrase "righteousness from God" (3:9) and the closely related phrase "justification by faith alone" (*sola fide*) are of great importance in Paul's theology. As noted in the introduction of this commentary ("Central Themes of the Letter"), they also continue to be a storm center in the interpretation of his thought. Paul clearly wants his readers to look to Christ rather than to their own religious and moral achievements or their social standing as the source of true righteousness. In the Reformation period, Luther and Calvin made this a cardinal point in their recovery of Paul's teaching. Luther speaks of the "righteousness from God" as an "alien" righteousness. He means that it is not something inherent in our nature or something that we earn by our works. Rather it is the free gift of God embodied in all that Christ has done for us, and it is received by faith alone. Calvin agrees: The righteousness from God comes from outside us. It "does not belong to man"; rather, "it resides in faith in Christ."[26]

Once again we note that this doctrine of Paul, central to the sixteenth-century Reformation, is often misunderstood and distorted. It is a serious misreading of Paul's teaching to think that our act of faith in Christ is the basis of the righteousness from God or God's justification of us rather than what God in Christ has done for us. In effect, this flawed understanding turns upside down all that Paul wants to say.[27] Paul never makes the mistake of giving priority to our act of faith over God's act in Christ. The righteousness from God is God's gracious act of rectifying or justifying the ungodly in the life, death, and resurrection of Christ on our behalf. Our act of receiving God's gift neither causes nor prompts nor supplements God's giving. It simply accepts the gift given.

How does this Pauline teaching of righteousness from God, or justification by grace received by faith, bear on the life and witness of the church today? First, it counters the common human inclination to see one's own piety and morality as deserving of acclamation in contrast to the life and practices of others. What invariably flows from this attitude is what Reinhold Niebuhr called "the fury of self-righteousness."[28] We see this fury often at work in disputes among family members, in ecclesiastical controversies, in battles in the halls of Congress, in struggles between advocates of social change and those defending the status quo, in hot or cold wars between nations. "The righteousness from God" that centers on the

26. See Martin Luther, "Two Kinds of Righteousness," in *Career of the Reformer*, LW 31, ed. Harold J. Grimm (Philadelphia: Muhlenberg, 1957), 297–306, and John Calvin, *Galatians, Ephesians, Philippians, and Colossians,* 274.
27. Barth, *Philippians,* 101.
28. Reinhold Niebuhr, *An Interpretation of Christian Ethics* (New York: Harper & Brothers, 1935), 230. See further Philip G. Ziegler, "Justification and Justice," in *Justification: What's at Stake in the Current Debates,* ed. Mark Husbands and Daniel J. Treier (Downers Grove, IL: InterVarsity, 2004).

saving activity of Jesus Christ is a sheer gift, but at the same time it places under judgment all human claims of being absolutely in the right, claims that brook no criticism and give no quarter, offspring of what Paul calls "a righteousness of my own."

Second, Paul's message of the righteousness from God announced in the gospel relieves those who receive it of the burden of proving their human worth and dignity to God, to others, and to themselves. The dignity of countless human beings is often under attack because of their race, ethnicity, gender, personal history, or social position. Against such assaults is not only the biblical declaration that we are all created in the image of God but also the Pauline doctrine of the righteousness from God. Assurance of the inalienable truth of our human worth and dignity comes not from any value society may grant to us or from the value we may assign to ourselves but from the forgiving love and astonishing mercy of God in Christ.

Third, according to Paul, God's free gift of righteousness through Christ received by faith builds new community. It does not aim simply at the salvation of individuals but also at the breaking down of barriers and the creation of a new community, a new people of God that includes Jews and Gentiles and indeed all manner of people. Once again, however, a misunderstanding may easily intrude. If we say that Paul understands the right-making activity of God to aim at new community in God's service rather than at the rescue of isolated individuals, this does not mean that communities of faith, including Christian communities, are any less immune to the temptation to claim a righteousness of their own. The arrogance of self-righteousness afflicts communities as well as individuals. Over against any such claim, Paul declares that the righteousness from God is a gift that never becomes our possession such that we can claim it as belonging exclusively to us. We can only give thanks to God for God's unbounded love that justifies the ungodly. Paul's doctrine of righteousness from God stands opposed to every tendency to sacralize a particular race, nation, or church and every effort to demonize all who are outside the precincts of our sacred group.

Finally, we follow in the trajectory of Paul's theology if we say that the righteousness from God through Christ, which is received by faith alone, draws the believing community into activity that participates in and corresponds to God's right making. Just as it is true that "God's gift makes givers" (Rowan Williams), it is also true that God's right-making activity in Christ calls forth a people who in their common life and witness to the world cultivate and practice right making that bears some likeness to God's right-making activity. Rather than accommodating to the present order of things, God's activity of setting things right "is contentious and contested."[29] Properly understood, the doctrine of God's righteousness, God's justification of the ungodly, draws the church into the struggle for greater justice and reconciliation in the world, always of course with the recognition that only God can and will bring God's purposes to completion at the coming "day of Christ" (1:6, 10). God in Christ has brought about a radically new beginning for humanity and for the whole creation.

With God's right-making activity in Christ, a new world has dawned but is not yet fully formed. The eschatological and cosmic context of Paul's thought must always be kept in view in our interpretation of Paul's understanding of the righteousness of God that comes as a gracious gift through Christ rather than from our own efforts. The right-making activity of God, centered in Christ, comes to its astonishing goal in the universal recognition of the lordship of Christ (2:9–11), the resurrection from the dead (3:11), and the transformation of the body (3:21). Explicitly in Romans 8, Ephesians 1, and Colossians 1, but implicitly also here in Philippians, Paul is speaking of "the entire renewal of the cosmos in which the Christian is invited to be a participant."[30]

3:10–14

Pressing On toward Christ

As Paul's personal narrative shifts from past to present and future, the way of Christ described in the Christ hymn again shapes his account. Earlier we noted the resemblance between, on the one

29. Käsemann, *On Being a Disciple*, 182.
30. Wright, *Paul*, 114.

hand, the hymn's description of Christ's emptying and humbling himself and becoming obedient even to death on a cross (2:5–8) and, on the other hand, Paul's giving up every reliance on his distinguished heritage and outstanding achievements. He willingly suffered "the loss of all [these] things," surrendering his "confidence in the flesh," his ability to boast about his belonging to God's elect people, and his blamelessness under the law (3:4b–9).

Now we find a further resemblance between the hymn's account of God's exaltation of Christ (2:9–11) and Paul's description of his new life in Christ. He wants "to know Christ and the power [*dynamin*] of his resurrection," to share in "his sufferings by becoming like him in his death," in order to come at last to "the resurrection from the dead" (3:10–11). Paul's life is now a kind of strenuous race "straining forward to what lies ahead" (3:10–14). Putting the past behind him, his eyes are on "the prize of the heavenly call of God in Christ Jesus" (3:14). Clearly, reception of the righteousness that comes from God through the faithfulness of Christ does not bring an end to Paul's striving. It does not render him passive. On the contrary, he moves relentlessly forward in hope and service.

This arresting passage calls for several comments. First, note that Paul binds together a life of knowing "the power of his [Christ's] resurrection" and "the sharing of his sufferings" (3:10). Sharing in the sufferings of Christ is, as we have seen, a motif that runs throughout the letter. It is what Paul experiences continuously in his apostolic mission, and it is what has landed him in prison more than once. It is also what Paul exhorts the Philippians to continue to do as they face the difficulties of Christian life and witness in a hostile environment. From the very first words of this letter in which Paul identifies himself not with the honorific designation of "apostle" but with the lowly title of "slave" of Jesus Christ, Paul is defining the true meaning of participation in Christ and the mission of the gospel. In brief, "The apostolate is carried out in the weakness and poverty of Christ, not through force or the strategies of force."[31]

As previously noted, so prominent is the theme of suffering in the Letter to the Philippians that some commentators have made

---

31. Jürgen Moltmann, *The Church in the Power of the Spirit* (New York: Harper, 1977), 361.

suffering and martyrdom the all-controlling theme of the letter. This is, however, an overstatement. Suffering by and for itself is not for Paul the rule governing Christian life or the way by which its goal is attained. Sharing the suffering of Christ would not even be possible apart from experiencing something of "the power of his resurrection" here and now. Notice that in this passage, Paul even places wanting to know "the power of his [Christ's] resurrection" *before* the "sharing of his sufferings." As Bockmuehl states, "The 'fellowship of his sufferings' is always in the light of his past triumphant victory and our common glorious future."[32] This ordering emphasizes that it is only because Paul—and indeed Christians in every era—have already experienced a measure of the power of the resurrection of Christ in their lives that they have the will, the stamina, and the hope to "keep on keeping on" in the midst of great adversity. Paul and all Christians live not only *under* the cross but also *after* Easter. That the crucified Christ is the living Lord is for them both the first and the last word.

Thus when Paul says he wants "to know Christ and the power of his resurrection" (3:10), this cannot mean that he does not now know Christ at all or that he does not participate at all here and now in the power of his resurrection. Rather, he is saying that he does not know Christ and the power of his resurrection fully at present. In another letter, Paul makes explicit this distinction between knowing now in part and knowing fully only later (1 Cor. 13:12). While the "already/not yet" distinction is only implicit in Philippians 3:9–11, it is fundamental to a proper understanding of Paul's faith and theology. He strains forward not from a state of emptiness to one of fullness, but from partial to fuller knowledge and participation in Christ's resurrection power. He is on the way to the goal of resurrection from the dead when Christ's resurrection power will be manifest to all creation. Christ's resurrection has inaugurated the coming of the new age, but his resurrection power has yet to be fully seen. Thus Paul neither limits Christian life in the present to a participation in the sufferings of Christ nor restricts Christ's resurrection power to a distant future. On the contrary, by the power of the Spirit

---

32. Bockmuehl, *Philippians,* 214.

there are beginnings and provisional realizations of the new life in the present (Rom. 5:1–5). It is because there is already a real if partial knowing of Christ, and a real if partial participation in the power of his resurrection by the Spirit, that Paul calls Christians to rejoice in the midst of suffering and to hope confidently for the fulfillment of what is present now only in part.

Paul is clear, however, that the power of the resurrection of Christ cannot be experienced apart from a genuine sharing in his sufferings. Creation still groans (Rom. 8:22). Christ has been raised from the dead, but we still await the redemption of our bodies (3:21; cf. Rom. 8:23). In the meantime, we are called by Christ to take up our cross and follow him (Mark 8:34). What could ignoring or denying this mean, other than transforming the gospel into "another gospel"

> With the raising of Jesus all has not yet been done. The end of death's domination is still outstanding.
>
> Jürgen Moltmann, *Theology of Hope* (New York: Harper & Row, 1967), 163.

(Gal. 1:7) of self-indulgence and illusory disregard of the continuing forces of sin and death at work in oneself and in the world? The slogan of this other gospel would then be: "Everything has been accomplished! Since we already fully enjoy the resurrection power of Christ, why should we get involved in the messiness of the world?" Something like this view was evidently popular in certain quarters of the church in Corinth, and Paul fought it tooth and nail. Even if there is no reason to think that this "resurrection sans cross" had taken root in Philippi, Paul cautions against it. He warns against the "enemies of the cross" whose god is their belly and whose minds are set on earthly things (3:18–19).

The equivalent of this one-sided triumphalist version of the gospel in our own time would be the preachers of a prosperity gospel, or what Bonhoeffer called "cheap grace." Soft-pedaling the call to costly discipleship, the message becomes: if you become a Christian, you will find yourself on the highway to success and prosperity!

Second, since for Paul, Christians know Christ's resurrection power at present only in part, he views life in Christ as unfinished. Living in the shadow of the cross of Christ, Paul is in constant movement toward God's promised future. His picture of Christian life, far from closed and stationary, is open and dynamic. Paul is on the way. Indeed, he is not strolling but running. "Straining forward" (3:13), he continues to "press on toward the goal for the prize of the heavenly call of God in Christ Jesus" (3:14). The metaphor of "the prize" is linked to the race metaphor in Paul's mind, and it should not be pressed too hard. Paul does not think of our service to Christ as something meritorious and deserving of a prize or reward. It is the "call" (*klesis*) of God in Christ that draws Paul forward. Christ "called" him to be an apostle (Rom. 1:1; 1 Cor. 1:1), and in particular, to be an apostle to the Gentiles (Gal. 1:15–16). Driven by this call, Paul presses on in his ministry, emphasizing that he has not yet "reached the goal" (3:12) and is not "already perfect" (RSV). Paul does not get discouraged by his past failures or become complacent on account of some successes he may have experienced. He is drawn on by the call of Christ and the "prize" of resurrection from the dead and fuller union with Christ.

Paul's image of Christian life and ministry as being constantly on the move and running toward a goal not yet reached is far different from perennial tendencies in the church to shut down the dynamism of Christian faith. The image of running contrasts sharply with the idea of having already arrived, being already perfect, and no longer being propelled forward by the love of Christ and the call to share his love with others (cf. 2 Cor. 5:14). Paul's way of describing Christian life implies that there is no greater temptation to the life of faith than to allow the passion for Christ and his coming kingdom to wither away; no greater temptation to theology than to become a deadly scholasticism where all questions are fully answered and no fresh insights or needed corrections are possible; no greater temptation to the church than to think it has already arrived at its goal or no longer thinks it is even necessary to have a goal, with the result that the missionary church becomes a mausoleum church.[33] For Paul, while God has indeed already won a great victory over sin, evil, and death by raising the crucified Christ from the dead, and while we are truly reconciled to God by virtue of Christ's victory, Paul hastens to the

---

33. Citing this passage of Philippians, Luther writes that even the Saints "become pleased with themselves . . . and stop right there and are unwilling to go forward." *Lectures on Romans,* LW 25, ed. Hilton C. Oswald (St. Louis: Concordia, 1972), 246.

consummation and final revelation of this victory that is still to come. Christians are thus called to engage in the ministry of reconciliation in countless new times and circumstances (cf. 2 Cor. 5:17–20). The reconciling work of God in Christ goes on in the power of the Spirit, and the Christian vocation is to take part in it.

Paul's metaphor of the life of faith as a race toward the goal line is one of his favorites. He asks the Galatians: You were running a good race. Who cut in on you and kept you from obeying the truth? (Gal. 5:7). Writing to the Corinthians, he describes the race of faith as requiring discipline and self-control; keeping on the track rather than getting sidetracked; and running straight for the prize (in Greek games, usually a garland or wreath) at the finish line (1 Cor. 9:24–27). In the Corinthian passage, Paul says that in a race "only one receives the prize" (1 Cor. 9: 24). This is to underscore the importance of keeping on the move. Worth noting is that in his Letter to the Philippians Paul does not say that only one of the runners in a race can be the winner. Such an emphasis would present too competitive and too individualistic a picture of the Christian life. This would go against the grain of the call to solidarity and regard for others that permeates the Letter to the Philippians.

Paul does not tell the story of his running in faith as hard as he can to brag that he is outrunning all others. Rather, he tells the story to invite others to run with him, to show them the kind of single-mindedness and persistence that belongs to life in Christ. As a runner for and toward Christ, Paul is no solitary individual. He wants the Philippians to "join in imitating" him (3:17). He has no desire to run alone. He is eager to have them running alongside him.

Third, we should take special notice that the "goal" (3:12) of Paul's hastening forward is described as "the resurrection from the dead" (3:11). As Paul uses the phrase, "resurrection from the dead" is an apocalyptic image of the completion of God's redemptive purposes. Paul is the theologian of a "new creation" in Christ (2 Cor. 5:17), of the beginning of "the resurrection of the dead" (1 Cor. 15:21) in him. When he speaks of the righteousness of God revealed in the crucifixion and resurrection of Christ, he is proclaiming the inauguration of a new era, the beginning of the new life in Christ, the commencement of a new vocation in him, and a new hope of renewal that embraces the entire cosmos. The power of the resurrection of the crucified Lord, while known in part now, will be fully known only in the future. It is to that consummation that Paul moves, indeed hastens like an Olympian sprinter.

There can be no question that for Paul the power of resurrection, like the power of creation out of nothing (*ex nihilo*), belongs exclusively to the living and gracious God. Whoever says "resurrection" speaks of the God "who gives life to the dead and calls into existence the things that do not exist" (Rom. 4:17). Moreover, as Paul will soon make explicit, resurrection from the dead is, in his view, inseparable from resurrection of the body (3:21). Paul refuses to abandon embodied existence in his hope for participation in the glory of God.

Closely related to its embodied nature, "resurrection from the dead" is for Paul a communal rather than an individualistic hope. When Christ comes again, he will transform "the body of *our* humiliation" and conform it to "the body of his glory" (3:21, emphasis added). Of course, Paul can use the first person singular in confessing his faith and hope. He can speak of "*my* God (1:3), of "Christ Jesus *my* Lord" (3:8), of honoring Christ "in *my* body" (1:20), and of hoping that "*I* may attain the resurrection from the dead" (3:11). However, he would never think of his God as his private deity, or of his Lord as other than "*the* Lord Jesus Christ," or of his body as separate from "the body of *our* humiliation" (3:21). Paul does not envision himself as being all alone at the goal toward which he strives. He is a member of God's people, part of a great multitude. If we speak of Paul's spirituality, it is no bodiless or individualistic spirituality. It would have to be called an "embodied spirituality" and a "communal spirituality."[34]

Paul is certainly aware that expectation of the resurrection from the dead can be intoxicating, which is why he does not want to bypass "the sharing of [Christ's] sufferings" on his way to "the resurrection from the dead" (3:10, 11). Paul is realistic about the seriousness of the human condition and the costliness of Christian discipleship even as he is unshakably confident in the promises of God. Refusing to separate resurrection hope from embodied life and its "excruciating realities,"[35] he harbors no illusions that he could earn or achieve

34. See Jürgen Moltmann, *The Spirit of Life* (Minneapolis: Fortress, 1992), 94.
35. Bockmuehl, *Philippians*, 217.

resurrection by his own efforts. Thus when he says he hopes he may "attain" the resurrection from the dead (3:11), attain does not mean "acquire" or "earn." That would suggest that Paul thinks he will win the right to participate in the resurrection from the dead by his present suffering and his life of faithful obedience to the way of Christ. Thinking in this way would defeat all that he has said previously about the difference between a righteousness that is from God and a righteousness that is acquired and owned by us. No, the word translated "attain" has here the contextual meaning of "reach" or "arrive at," not the sense of "acquire" or "achieve."

3:15–17
Exhortation Not to Uniformity but to Unity

Having depicted his own unfinished journey of faith in Christ, Paul now returns to exhortation (3:15–4:1). We have seen how Paul's use of the Christ hymn recalling the way of the self-humbling Christ, obedient even to death on a cross, provided the theological basis for urging the Philippians to make Christ's cruciform life their own. Similarly, Paul's account of his surrender of his past honors in order to gain Christ and his pressing forward toward the goal of resurrection has the aim of helping to form the faith and life of the Philippian Christians. Just as the exhortation "Let the same mind be in you that was in Christ Jesus" introduced the Christ hymn (2:5), so the exhortation "Brothers and sisters, join in imitating me, and observe those who live according to the example you have in us" concludes Paul's description of his journey of faith (3:17).

At the commencement of this new round of exhortations, Paul explains that his appeal for unity of heart and mind among the Philippians is not an appeal for absolute uniformity. In Christ there is a deep unity of those who are "mature" in Christ (3:15), but such unity does not come by way of coercion or threat. Let us "be of the same mind," Paul urges, "and if you think differently about anything, this too God will reveal to you" (3:15). In other words, Paul trusts that God will reveal the truth of the way he has commended to those who at present are unable to follow his

reasoning.[36] This is a remarkable statement. It explodes the myth
that Paul is a doctrinaire know-it-all who imperiously demands
immediate submission to his authority in all matters in the churches
he has founded.

What Paul is saying here can be understood as having two aspects.
First, he allows that differences in judgment will arise in the church
and that it must learn to live with these differences until more light
is received from the Word and Spirit of God. Simply suppressing disagreements or silencing dissident voices is not the way of waiting on
illumination from God that Paul counsels in this passage. Second,
Paul's advice to the Philippians when they "think differently about
anything" suggests that he acknowledges that there are secondary
matters, "minor issues,"[37] about which Christians may and will differ.
Calvin would later call these "matters of indifference" (*adiaphora*).[38]
While Paul does not give any examples of such disputes about less
important matters, he evidently knows that there are such differences among members of the Philippian community. He is confident that the Spirit of God will guide the community to a good
resolution of their disagreements on these matters or will enable it
to accept these differences with humility and thanksgiving because
they need not be divisive and may even be enriching.

At the same time, Paul wants the Philippians to be united, to
be of the same mind, and to "hold fast to what we have attained"
(3:16). What they and Paul have attained in their understanding
and practice of the gospel—what holds them together in the midst
of their differences—is their solidarity in Christ and the cruciform
way of life that this entails. In other words, their unity in Christ
is expressed in their common adherence to him as their crucified
and risen Lord. Attending this adherence are a common foundational narrative and common affirmations of faith, attitudes, and
practices that are in conformity with the way of Christ. What are
these core affirmations and practices? Judging from the Letter of

---

36. A. Katherine Grieb helpfully distinguishes "being of the same mind," when it is used to
signify orthodoxy as opposed to heresy, from Paul's meaning of "a pattern of life to be
imitated." "Philippians and the Politics of God," *Interpretation* 61 (2007): 263.
37. O'Brien, *Philippians*, 437.
38. John Calvin, *Institutes of the Christian Religion* 4.17.43; ed. John T. McNeill, trans. Ford Lewis
Battles, LCC (Philadelphia: Westminster, 1960).

Philippians as a whole, we can say they include the lordship of Jesus Christ; his incarnation, servant ministry, crucifixion, and resurrection; the worship of God in the power of the Spirit of Christ; a life of humble service and love of others that bears likeness to the way of Christ; a readiness to suffer for the sake of the gospel; joy in the Lord in all circumstances; and the hope in the coming of the Savior in glory to make all things subject to him. These are matters that the "mature" have attained and agree on, and Paul wants the Philippians to hold fast to them.

3:17 *Imitation of Paul?*

As he has stated early in the letter, Paul's rationale for continuing his ministry with the Philippians despite his strong yearnings to "depart and be with Christ" (1:23) is for the sake of their "progress and joy in faith" (1:25). To this end he has urged them to have the mind of Christ, to be of one accord, and to put the interests of others above their own. He has exhorted them to honor people like Timothy, who puts the interests of Jesus Christ first, and like Epaphroditus, who even risked death for the work of Christ. He has told them of his own loss of everything in order to gain Christ and has described his life and ministry now as a "straining forward" to the goal of the heavenly call of God in Christ Jesus. Now he urges the Philippians: Move forward with me in your Christian life and service. "Join in imitating me" (3:17). "Live according to the example you have in us," he continues, meaning himself and his helpers like Timothy and Epaphroditus.

A nagging question will arise for many readers at this point. Is this a step too far? Is there danger in Paul's exhortation to imitate him? If Christ is our Lord and our singular model of the shape and direction of the new life to be lived in him, why do we need to look to Paul as an example? Will not his "imitate me" inevitably become competitive with the mind of Christ? Does Paul's christocentrism here run the danger of being trumped by "Paulocentrism"? There are critics of Paul who see his "imitate me" as evidence corroborating the charge that he represents an authoritarian mind-set, that he espouses a "subordinating chain of models" to be followed and "casts the community [in Philippi] in the dependent, subordinate role of a hierarchical system."[39]

We could rephrase the question and apply it to congregational life today. Are not preachers who call attention to themselves—their charm, their charismatic personality, their rhetorical skills, their ability to use their own life story to dramatic effect—in danger of obscuring Christ as the true content of the gospel and the model of Christian life? The answer must surely be: yes, such a danger exists. But that is not to say this is what Paul is doing, nor is it to say there can be no valid role in Christian community life for the exemplary witness of an apostle or for the special witness in word and life of other faithful disciples.

Some commentators suggest that in calling the Philippians to imitate him, Paul is reminding them of his apostleship. This is unlikely. Paul does not begin the letter with his usual self-description of "apostle," and there is little reason to think that he is pulling rank at this point. Indeed, Paul's opening description of himself and Timothy as slaves of Jesus Christ, his frequent reference to his readers as brothers and sisters, and, above all, his centerpiece Christ hymn with its depiction of the self-emptying of Christ all demonstrate that the Letter to the Philippians as a whole subverts the customary ideas of rank and hierarchy. Its message works to transform the meaning of *power* as that term is commonly understood. So when Paul says, "imitate me," this cannot be a power play.

Nor should there be any suspicion that in telling the story of what he had surrendered in order to be found in Christ, to participate in his suffering and in the power of his resurrection, and to strain forward to what lies ahead, Paul wants his readers to think of his example as in any way competing with or even replacing that of Christ. Note that Paul says not simply "imitate me," but "join in imitating me." The meaning is clear: join in imitating me as I imitate Christ (1 Cor. 11:1). As Walter Hansen writes, "The entire letter conveys Paul's sense of mutuality and equality with his friends in Philippi. When he calls them to follow his example, he is urging them to join

---

39. Joseph A. Marchal, "Imperial Intersections and Initial Inquiries: Toward a Feminist, Postcolonial Analysis of Philippians," *Journal of Feminist Studies in Religion* 22 (Fall 2006): 30.

with him in his own journey to know Christ."[40] It should be added that Paul quickly changes from the singular to the plural in this exhortation: "Join in imitating *me* . . . and . . . live according to the example you have in *us*" (3:17, italics added). Paul does not isolate his witness from that of his coworkers in the service of Christ like Timothy and Epaphroditus. Also note that, far from describing himself as having already attained perfection, Paul acknowledges that he is still very much on the way. Paul's is "no arrogant claim which demands that his readers should follow in his magnificent steps!"[41] Paul the servant of Christ does not want to become his competitor.

But the broader question remains: Is there a place and a need in Christian life for concrete examples of the mind of Christ as it finds expression in the lives of faithful Christians? The simple answer is yes. Not that proclamation of the person and way of Christ is insufficient. He is and remains the central and unsubstitutable power and paradigm of Christian life. But God has honored the adopted children of God with the privilege and freedom of bearing witness with their own voice and in their own life.

Today a celebrity culture mediated by film, videos, smartphones, TV, and the Internet casts its spell far and wide. Young people especially are bombarded with vivid images of the supposedly exciting worlds inhabited by movie stars, popular musicians, professional athletes, business executives, and glamorous politicians. The idea that Christians have no need for concrete examples of life in Christ is entirely out of touch with the essentials of spiritual and moral development. If, according to an African proverb, it takes a village to raise a child, Christian wisdom says it takes a faithful community, living by the Word and Spirit of God, to nurture a Christian. People are not formed in Christian faith and life by pulling themselves up by their bootstraps. They do not gain the capacity to discern "what is best" apart from the witness of prophets and apostles to the living Christ or apart from the help of a worshiping and serving community that looks to Christ as Lord and finds in his way the pattern and direction for life in his service.

---

40. G. Walter Hansen, *The Letter to the Philippians* (Grand Rapids: Eerdmans, 2009), 261.
41. O'Brien, *Philippians,* 447.

3:18–19
Another Warning

Now as before (3:2–4), Paul's appeal for unity and a life in the likeness of Christ is accompanied by a warning. The warning is that there are "enemies of the cross" (3:18) who do not live in conformity with the way of Christ or by the example of Paul and his fellow workers. They live for themselves. They are pleasure seekers. Their minds are set not on Christ, his humility, and his service of others, but on sensual gratifications and earthly possessions. Who are these "enemies of the cross"? Are they the same people whom Paul has earlier called "dogs" and "evil workers" because they want to seduce the Philippians into thinking that circumcision is a necessary rite for all, Jews and Gentiles alike, who wish to follow Christ? While we cannot be certain, it seems more likely that the "enemies of the cross" Paul has in mind are a different group of people who pose rather different temptations to the Philippian church. If Paul earlier combated those who thought they could achieve perfection by adopting religious rules and rituals, he now seems to have in mind people who wallow in self-indulgence ("their god is the belly") and crave social approval and material goods ("their minds are set on earthly things"). With moral perfectionists on one side and moral libertarians on the other, Paul is indeed walking a moral "tightrope" with his warnings in this letter.[42]

It is possible that the attitude and behavior of those whom Paul calls "enemies of the cross" may be the same as those in Corinth who denied the resurrection: "Let us eat and drink, for tomorrow we die" (1 Cor. 15:32). Or to paraphrase: "Enjoy life as much as you can, like our Roman friends who are happy if they have their bread and circuses." On the other hand, instead of thinking of such out-and-out hedonists, he may have in mind those who all too easily conform to the ways of the dominant culture in Philippi. These cultural conformists, as they may be called, swim with the reigning

---

42. Richard Hays, *The Moral Vision of the New Testament: Community, Cross, New Creation* (San Francisco: Harper, 1996), 27.

social and cultural stream and offer little or no resistance to its values. If such people represent the kind of mentality Paul is warning against, it is entirely clear why he calls them "enemies of the cross." They know nothing of a cruciform life of service to others. They have no interest in taking risks for the cause of the reign of Christ that is far greater than themselves. They could not care less about the mind of Christ. They are content to follow the customs and rituals of their city and to find whatever enjoyment they can in the privileges of Roman citizenship. The road they are traveling, Paul says, ends in "destruction" (3:19).

In opposition to all such cultural and political accommodation of Christian life, Paul tells the Philippians to remember that "our citizenship is in heaven" (3:20). Paul's use of the word "citizenship" (*politeuma*) here "would have explosive theological and political potency" in the Philippian context.[43] We are citizens of the kingdom where Christ reigns, Paul claims. Christ is our Lord, not Caesar. Our allegiance is to Christ, and our way of life is set not by what is expected and popular among the citizens of a colony of Rome but by the mind of Christ. In making this claim, Paul is not urging Christians to become apolitical and just ignore their worldly responsibilities. That is not at all the meaning of his declaring that our citizenship is "in heaven," as though heaven is a place of escape and has no earthly significance.[44] On the contrary, Paul's point is that Christians are to be clear about their deepest loyalties and are called to follow the way of Christ in their daily lives here and now. They refuse to give their ultimate allegiance to the powers that be. They are summoned to live *in* but not *of* the world. Their standards and models of what constitutes fully human life are not set by the prevailing culture and its social, economic, and political institutions but by what might be called "the politics of God in Christ" and the new life together that God's politics creates and sustains.[45]

---

43. Bockmuehl, *Philippians*, 233.
44. See Christopher Morse, *The Difference Heaven Makes: Rehearing the Gospel as News* (New York: T. & T. Clark, 2010).
45. See Paul Lehmann, *Ethics in a Christian Context* (New York: Harper & Row, 1963), 81–105; Grieb, "Philippians and the Politics of God."

3:20–4:1

Expecting a Savior

As citizens of God's reign, Christians are to embody the hope that
is directed toward a coming "Savior, the Lord Jesus Christ" (3:20).
Living in expectation of the coming of the Lord sets the whole of
one's life in a new and different framework. It is not the same as
withdrawing from the world. Instead it means a radical reordering
of one's priorities and a relativizing of things previously considered
essential (cf. 1 Cor. 7:29–31).

Neither in Philippians nor in his other letters does Paul write
as a modern social activist or as an unperturbed quietist. He does
not call us to bring in the kingdom of God by our energetic efforts,
but neither does he instruct us to sit still and twiddle our thumbs.
When Paul in this passage reminds the Philippians that "our citizenship is in heaven" (3:20), this is not a call to withdraw from the
world. Rather, it is a summons to comport ourselves in this world as
responsible citizens of a different reign. All that we do here and now
stands under the reminder that we "are expecting a Savior, the Lord
Jesus Christ" (3:20). That is to say, Christians expect not the coming
of a benevolent successor to Caesar, or a world that we make safe for
democracy by whatever means we deem necessary, or the coming of
a utopia of freedom and justice constructed by us. We await "a Savior" who rules his commonwealth in an altogether different manner
from the powers of this world. Christians await a Savior, not a new
ideology, not a new social program, not a new set of ideals. All that
would be no more than a reflection of ourselves, and if this is all our
activity amounts to, do we really need a Savior?[46]

But if Christ reigns and we are called to bear responsible Christian witness in word and in deed to his reign here and now, why do
we still await a Savior? Has Christ not already come? Has he not
already been crucified and raised from the dead for our salvation?
Yes, Paul would reply, he has come, and he has accomplished our
reconciliation with God. But the work of our redemption and the
redemption of the world is not yet complete. Evil is not yet fully

---

46. Barth, *Philippians*, 115–16.

conquered. Sin, suffering, and death, "the last enemy," are still present in the world (cf. 1 Cor. 15:25–26). Resurrection is for us still a future reality. The transformation of all things has not yet occurred. The new heaven and the new earth have not yet appeared (Rev. 21:1). All this awaits the "day of Jesus Christ" (1:6), his expected arrival in judgment and glory. So in the present, Christians run; they press on toward the goal. But this

> How to speak of resurrection requires artfulness. The mark of theological wisdom is knowing when and how to speak of such matters in a way that avoids an escape from the reality of death.
>
> Donald H. Juel, "Christian Hope and the Denial of Death," in *The End of the World and the Ends of God,* ed. John Polkinghorne and Michael Welker (Harrisburg, PA: Trinity Press International, 2000), 181.

does not mean that they try to run ahead of Christ. They pray and wait for his coming even as they hasten to follow him in all of their decisions and actions.

When Christ comes, Paul declares, he will "make all things subject to himself" (3:21). Augustine calls attention to the discrepancy between 3:21 and 2:9–11. Whereas in 3:21 Christ subjects all things to himself, in 2:9–11 (and in 1 Cor. 15:27) it is the Father who subjects all things to Christ. Augustine resolves this apparent difference in the acting subject by insisting that "the working of the Father and of the Son is indivisible."[47]

As noted previously, Paul's use of the phrase "resurrection from the dead" emphasizes the embodied and corporate dimensions of God's redemptive purposes. This is now made explicit in Paul's affirmation that the expected Savior "will transform the body of our humiliation" and conform it to "the body of his glory" (3:21). Paul's hope in the resurrection power of the expected Lord is very different from belief in the immortality of the soul. That way of thinking belongs to ancient Greek philosophy, which

> A bodiless soul is not a human being, and reincarnation would never be able to redeem us from entrapment in death.
>
> Hans Urs von Balthasar, *Credo: Meditations on the Apostles' Creed* (New York: Crossroad, 1990), 95.

47. Augustine, *On the Trinity* 8.15 (*NPNF¹* 3:25).

assumes a separation of body and soul. In a Platonic context, the idea of immortality of the soul means a sloughing off of the body and an eternal continuation of that part of us that is called "soul." While this may be the hope of ancient Platonic philosophy and its modern philosophical and spiritual descendants, it is contrary to what Paul means by the resurrection from the dead. In this passage Paul connects "resurrection from the dead" with Christ's transformation (not discarding) of "the body of our humiliation."

> [God] wills to form relationships with humankind, and wills that humans should relate to one another. Why should we imagine that this relationality will not characterize the resurrection state?
>
> Anthony C. Thiselton, *Life After Death: A New Approach to the Last Things* (Grand Rapids: Eerdmans, 2012), 112.

Paul's hope in the coming of the Lord embraces not only the body but also our essentially relational nature as God's creatures. We belong to God's commonwealth, and in that commonwealth there is community with God and others. Reconciled community and liberated cosmos belong to the ends of God. Paul's resurrection hope is stunningly comprehensive.[48]

At the conclusion of this section, Paul can exhort his beloved brothers and sisters of Philippi to stand firm in the Lord "in this way" (4:1) He means in "the way" of the humble, self-giving Christ who has been exalted to God's side (2:5–11) and whose coming as our Savior we eagerly await (3:20). The way of Christ is also the way Paul and his fellow workers try to exemplify and the way the Philippians too are urged to follow (3:17).

FURTHER REFLECTIONS
Hope

Paul's letters have a "thoroughgoing eschatological orientation."[49] Best known for his emphasis on faith or for his description of love as

---

48. The most influential modern text on this topic is Jürgen Moltmann, *Theology of Hope* (New York: Harper & Row, 1967). See also Daniel L. Migliore, *Faith Seeking Understanding*, 2nd ed. (Grand Rapids: Eerdmans, 2004), 330–53.
49. Fee, *Philippians*, 150.

the most excellent of ways (1 Cor. 13), Paul is less well known as the earliest Christian theologian of hope. Yet it is Paul who tells us that the instruction and encouragement of Scriptures are given that "we might have hope" (Rom. 15:4); that Abraham believed God's promise, "hoping against hope" (Rom. 4:18); that God is "the God of hope" (Rom. 15:13); that we were saved "in hope" (Rom. 8:24); that if our hope in Christ were restricted to the present life only, we would be "of all people most to be pitied" (1 Cor. 15:19).

Even if the word *hope* is not found in Philippians, the reality of hope in Christ, as we have seen, suffuses the letter. Paul "awaits" a coming "day of Christ" (1:6, 10); together with the Philippians he expects a Savior from heaven, the Lord Jesus Christ, who will conform "the body of our humiliation" to his body of glory (3:20–21); he is confident that in God's good time Christ's lordship will be universally confessed (2:10–11); he describes his life as like a runner straining to reach "the goal for the prize of the heavenly call of God in Christ Jesus" (3:14); and he exhorts the Philippian community to rejoice with him always because "the Lord is near" (4:5).

This robust Pauline orientation of Christian life to the hope that is given in Christ has either been largely lost in many churches today or appears in badly distorted form. On the one hand, many Christians retain only a vague hope for some form of personal survival after death. Beyond this, their hope is mostly concentrated on the health and success of their own children and grandchildren. On the other hand, some Christian groups reduce hope in Christ to the expectation of a coming "rapture" of true believers that will remove them from all the turmoil and conflict of a doomed world. Seriously marginalized in this depiction of the end time is the central NT witness to the ministry, cross, and resurrection of Jesus Christ.[50] What can the church today learn from Paul's understanding and practice of hope as expressed in the Letter to the Philippians?

A central feature of Paul's hope is that it is centered on Christ. Paul's hope is far from empty or baseless. It is far more than mere wishing. Wishing is often done with crossed fingers because the outcome is completely uncertain. Paul hopes not with crossed

---

50. See Migliore, *Faith Seeking Understanding*, 334–37.

fingers but with confidence because his hope is based on what God has accomplished in Christ and on the renewing work of the Spirit here and now (see Rom. 5:5).

Another feature of Paul's hope is its indissolubly communal character. It is not reduced to "pie in the sky by and by" for individual believers. This is not to say, of course, that Paul dismisses the hope for personal fulfillment in Christ. He clearly states: "*I* want to know Christ and the power of this resurrection" (3:10); "*I* press on toward the goal of the prize of the heavenly call of God in Christ Jesus" (3:14). The explicit or implied use of the first-person pronouns in such affirmations shows that Paul does not think that Christian hope excludes personal fulfillment. Yet Paul's hope is far from being purely private in nature. He does not summon Christians away from "selfish ambition" and "conceit" (2:3) and to the unity and harmony of life in Christ only to throw community to the winds when he hopes for "resurrection from the dead" (3:11) and participation in the "commonwealth" of Christ (3:20 RSV). The language of resurrection, as found in Paul and in the New Testament generally, is a thoroughly communal hope.

Furthermore, Christian hope, for Paul, is inseparably bound to responsible Christian practice. Hope in Christ funds activity in his service; it does not lead to passivity or quiescence. Jürgen Moltmann captures well Paul's understanding of hope when he writes, "Those who hope in Christ can no longer put up with reality as it is, but begin to suffer under it, to contradict it." God's promised future "stabs inexorably into the flesh of every unfulfilled present."[51] This does not mean that Christian hope encourages utopian fantasies or revolutionary violence in order to realize the hoped-for future. Paul's hope is, in Karl Barth's words, both a "hastening" and a "waiting." The hopeful Christian neither

> **The difference between the Christian hope of resurrection and the mythological hope is that the former sends a man back to his life on earth in a wholly new way.**
>
> Dietrich Bonhoeffer, *Letters and Papers from Prison* (New York: Macmillan, 1972), 336–37.

---

51. Moltmann, *Theology of Hope,* 21.

hastens to act without also waiting on God nor waits on God and does nothing. In hope we hasten to love and serve God and neighbor, but we continue to pray and wait on God and do not think we can bring in God's kingdom by our actions.[52]

Equally striking, hope has a cosmic dimension for Paul. The cosmic sweep of his hope comes to expression most fully in Philippians in the Christ hymn (2:5–11). According to the second stanza of the hymn, Christ will be confessed as Lord and worshiped by all creatures, whether in heaven or on earth or under the earth. This cosmos-embracing expression of hope is reminiscent of Romans 8, where Paul speaks of the whole creation groaning to obtain the freedom of the glory of the children of God and of the passages in Colossians and Ephesians affirming that God through Christ has reconciled "all things" (*ta panta*) to himself (Col. 1:20) and has planned to gather up in him "all things" in heaven and on earth (Eph. 1:10).

Paul's talk of hope is Christ-centered, communal, practical, and cosmic. While it would be anachronistic to read an explicit and developed ethic of ecological responsibility into Paul's letters, it is nevertheless the case that Paul believes that God is creator of all, that Christ is Lord of all, and that therefore the scope of Christian hope, worship, and service in the Spirit of Christ reaches far beyond the limits of our imagination. Hope in Christ includes a reconciled humanity and a liberated creation.

---

52. Karl Barth, *The Christian Life: Church Dogmatics IV, 4; Lecture Fragments* (Grand Rapids: Eerdmans, 1981), 205–13. See also Nigel Biggar, *The Hastening That Waits: Karl Barth's Ethics* (New York: Oxford University Press, 1993), 74–78.

4:2–9

Personal Appeals and Final Exhortations

In this section, Paul reprises one of the major themes running through the letter—"Be of the same mind" (4:2; cf. 2:2; 2:5). This time his urging is addressed specifically to Euodia and Syntyche, two women in the Philippian congregation who are at odds with each other. After asking another member of the congregation for help in bringing about the reconciliation of these women (4:2–3), Paul repeats his call to rejoice, to be diligent in prayer (4:4–7), to affirm all that is excellent and worthy of praise (4:8), and to keep following his teaching and his life example (4:8–9).

4:2–3
Euodia and Syntyche

We do not know the nature of the dispute between Euodia and Syntyche. It is possible that their disagreement was one of the reasons prompting Paul to write in the first place. If so, he may have postponed making direct mention of it until a clear and strong theological basis for his appeal has been offered in the letter. There is certainly no reason to suppose, as some commentators have conjectured, that the quarrel of Euodia and Syntyche was about Paul and his allegedly high-handed ways. Mention of these women by name underscores again that women had a prominent role in the Philippian community from its inception. Paul acknowledges their valuable contribution to his ministry: "They have struggled beside me in the work of the gospel" (4:3).

Note that Paul does not assume he can resolve the dispute by simply saying, "Stop it!" If his understanding of his apostleship and of the nature of leadership in the community were of an authoritarian sort, no doubt this is how he would have reacted. But as we have argued throughout the commentary, Paul approaches his friends in Philippi as a pastor and a brother in the faith, not as an autocrat. All who are in Christ belong to a community marked by mutual care and shared responsibility. Recall that Paul is glad the Philippians pray for him (1:19) even as he prays for them (1:9–11). Recall too that he urges them to "join in imitating me" (3:17), which properly understood means "join me in imitating Christ." Paul clearly views Christian discipleship and Christian ministry not as a lonely, private matter but as life and service in community. It comes as no surprise, then, when he asks his "loyal companion" (the Greek word Syzygus could also be a personal name) to "help these women" (4:3) who are disagreeing with each other. This appeal for help is significant. For Paul, ministry in a local congregation is a shared responsibility rather than a solo affair. Everyone has some gift to offer for the welfare of the whole. Whatever the name of the trusted companion, he or she was apparently gifted in handling conflict and resolving disputes. Paul is not afraid to say he needs help, and he calls on others to do their part.

Although just what was going on in the dispute between Euodia and Syntyche is unknown, we have to assume that it had the potential of injuring and perhaps even dividing the community. We can also assume that if Paul thought that the dispute had to do with what he considered the very heart of the gospel, he would have said so. As we have seen, he did not hesitate to take a firm stand in one instance against the Jewish Christians who were insisting on the necessity of circumcision for Gentile Christians and in another instance against the "enemies of the cross." When the gospel is placed in jeopardy, Paul is adamant. So in the dispute between Euodia and Syntyche we likely have a case of a disagreement that, in Paul's view, was within the scope of acceptable differences of opinions or proposals that should be tolerated and patiently worked through under the guidance of the Spirit rather than allowing the matter to lead to schism in the church. Remember what Paul said earlier: be of the same mind, and hold fast to what we have attained, "and if you think differently about anything [not about the essentials but about relatively secondary matters], this too God will reveal to you" (3:15).

Paul shows a fine sense of the need for patience and forbearance when disagreements arise in the community. Then and today, the well-being of Christian communities depends on a sincere desire for reconciliation when disputes arise, an ability to listen carefully to others, and, above all, a prayerful reliance on the continuing work of the Holy Spirit among the faithful.

4:4-7

Rejoice!

In this penultimate section of the letter, Paul repeats his appeal for joy. "Rejoice in the Lord always; again I will say, Rejoice" (4:4). As he has made clear throughout the letter, the spirit of joy characterizes life in Christ: not rancor, weariness, or fear, but sheer joy. This is not an appeal for Christians to be happy-go-lucky, always smiling, slapping one another on the back, and finding everything to be just fine. Superficial optimism has nothing to do with what Paul calls joy. "Joy in Philippians," Barth observes, "is a defiant Nevertheless."[1]

Note especially that Paul says not simply, "Rejoice," but "Rejoice *in the Lord*." The qualifying phrase is crucial. Joy in the Lord is altogether different from a happy mood we may be in for a time because things seem to be going our way. Christian joy is deeper and more lasting than that. We rejoice in the Lord because of the grace of God freely given to us in Jesus Christ, because of the forgiveness of sins and reconciliation of ruptured relations with God and others that he has accomplished, because of the new life and new community that have been created by the power of his Spirit, and because of the great hope of the consummation of God's purposes and our participation in the eternal life and glory of God that we have in Christ.

Moreover, Paul says, we rejoice because "the Lord is near" (4:5). It is not clear whether we are to understand the nearness of the Lord

---

1. Karl Barth, *The Epistle to the Philippians* (Louisville, KY: Westminster John Knox Press, 2002), 120.

in a spatial or a temporal sense. The spatial meaning would be: the Lord is near to us in our prayer, worship, and service, so near that Paul can say that he and his fellow believers live "in Christ." Therefore, rejoice! The temporal meaning would be: the Lord is coming very soon. The time is short. Lift up your heads, take heart, and rejoice! Rather than choosing between the spatial and temporal ways of understanding the nearness of the Lord, it is consistent with Paul's theology overall to hold them together in dialectical tension. Paul knows of a real presence here and now of the crucified and risen Christ (cf. Gal. 2:20; Col. 1:27), and he also expects the risen Christ to come soon in glory. As other letters of Paul explain more fully, it is the Spirit who enables us to hold together the already and the not yet of God's purposes in Christ. The presence of the risen Lord in the power of his Spirit is the "first fruits" of the resurrection of all who belong to Christ (Rom. 8:23; 1 Cor. 15:23).

For Paul, joy in the Lord is appropriately accompanied by "gentleness" (NRSV) or "forbearance" (RSV) that should be shown to all people (4:5). The Greek word *epieikes* offers a number of possibilities of translation: "gentleness" suggests relating to others without harshness or coercion; "forbearance" implies accepting others in all their differences and shortcomings, and being prepared to forgive them; "kindness" connotes a show of concern and mercy toward others; "patience" describes a self-control that gives others time and refuses to force matters to a rapid and often premature resolution.[2] All these marks of the new life in Christ rule out the spirit of retaliation, vengeance, and violence. Furthermore, Paul emphasizes that these ways of acting should extend beyond a few of our favorite friends in the congregation and even beyond the Christian community. They are to be made known and practiced in relation to all people (4:5). To all, gentleness, forbearance, kindness, and patience are to be extended. This way of interpreting Paul is fully consonant with his teaching elsewhere: "If it is possible, so far as it depends on you, live peaceably with all" (Rom. 12:18). As Horrell states, for Paul, "the way in which Christians are to act toward outsiders is an

---

2. As Barth notes, Luther translates *epieikes* with *Lindigkeit*, "leniency," or "mild-mannered disposition," the opposite of being bristly or uptight. Barth, *Philippians*, 121.

extension of the way they are to treat one another: with love, goodness, and forbearance."[3]

Here again is an instance of Paul's urging that the life of Christians should be guided and governed by the way of Christ. The gentleness and forbearance of those in Christ toward all others constitutes a likeness to and a participation in the humility and graciousness of Christ (2:5–8; 2 Cor. 10:1). Even as the self-lowering of Christ is a mark of his lordliness rather than a contradiction of it, so the gentleness and forbearance of Christians in their relationships with all others are signs of moral strength rather than of lack of conviction or the desire to please.

In view of the fact that Paul's reminder that "the Lord is at hand" follows quickly on his exhortation to show "gentleness" to others, a good case can be made for underscoring the importance of patience as one of the virtues of life in Christ. Our joy in the Lord and our gentleness in dealing with others are at risk when we become impatient, tired of waiting, insistent that everyone and everything should change this instant. When things do not go exactly as we had planned and we find we are no longer in control, we are apt to become impatient, and this can easily turn into abuse of others. Patience, Barth explains, is one of the attributes or perfections of God. "Patience exists where space and time are given with a definite intention, where freedom is allowed in expectation of a response. God acts in this way."[4] Impatience often goes hand in hand with anxiety. Joy in the Lord and forbearance toward others are accompanied by a freedom from haughty impatience and life-suffocating anxiety or "worry" (4:6).

In admonishing his friends not to worry, Paul echoes the words of Jesus in the Sermon on the Mount: "Do not worry about tomorrow" (Matt. 6:34). Neither Jesus nor Paul holds the naive belief that there will never be cause for concern about the future. But our

3. David G. Horrell, *Solidarity and Difference: A Contemporary Reading of Paul's Ethics* (London: T. & T. Clark, 2005), 268. James Davison Hunter aptly comments, "If Christians cannot extend grace and love through faithful presence within the body of believers, they certainly will not be able to extend grace to those outside." Hunter, *To Change the World: The Irony, Tragedy, and Possibility of Christianity in the Late Modern World* (New York: Oxford University Press, 2010), 281.
4. Karl Barth, *CD* II/1:408.

concerns are to be taken to God in prayer. We are to give thanks to God even as we pray honestly and fervently for others and ourselves. Paul's assurance is that the "peace of God"—not just any peace, but God's peace that comes from the knowledge of God's right-making and reconciling activity in Jesus Christ and that "surpasses all understanding"—will "guard" our hearts and minds (4:7). At least two commentators suggest that Paul may use the word "guard" here to contrast the basis of Christian confidence and security with what the garrison in Philippi who guard the interests of the empire can provide.[5]

FURTHER REFLECTIONS
Joy

From beginning to end, Paul's Letter to the Philippians is etched with joy and filled with the summons to rejoice (1:4, 18, 19, 25; 2:2, 17, 18, 29; 3:1; 4:4). The exhortation reaches its crescendo in 4:4: "Rejoice in the Lord always; again I will say, Rejoice." Paul's urging here is probably best rendered not in words alone but in words accompanied by soaring music: Handel's "Hallelujah Chorus," or the lines of the familiar hymn set to the final movement of Beethoven's Ninth Symphony: "Joyful, joyful, we adore Thee, God of glory, Lord of love. . . ."

> The joy of the gospel fills the hearts and lives of all who encounter Jesus.
>
> Pope Francis, *The Joy of the Gospel: Evangelii Gaudium* (Frederick, MD: Word among Us Press, 2013), 4.

What is the source of Paul's rejoicing? The answer is clear: he rejoices "in the Lord." The lordship of Jesus Christ is good news, the best news possible. Christ is the servant Lord, the Lord who though equal with God has come to us in humility (he "emptied himself," 2:7). He is the Lord who was crucified for our sake, was raised from the dead, and is with us now, giving new meaning and purpose to our lives ("For to me, living is Christ," 1:21). He is the one whose imminent coming ("The Lord is near," 4:5) will mean the consummation

5. Markus Bockmuehl, *The Epistle to the Philippians* (London: Hendrickson, 1998), 248; Stephen E. Fowl, *Philippians* (Grand Rapids: Eerdmans, 2005), 184.

of all things and the offering of endless praise to God by all creatures ("Every tongue should confess that Jesus Christ is Lord, to the
glory of God the Father," 2:11). Captivated by the gift of God in Jesus
Christ, Paul cannot help but rejoice, and he urges his fellow Christians to join him in rejoicing, just as Mary sang at the annunciation
of the coming birth of Christ, "My spirit rejoices in God my Savior"
(Luke 1:47) and just as Jesus counseled his disciples, "Be of good
cheer, I have overcome the world" (John 16:33 RSV).

Human life stagnates and withers when joy is absent. The desire
for joy and delight in life belongs to all human beings. The philosopher Friedrich Nietzsche thought that the "death of God" at last
released humans to be free, creative, and joyful in their exercise of
"the will to power." Having great power and unrestricted freedom,
however, does not guarantee joy. It often results in misery and
emptiness. Human life flourishes not when it has unlimited power
or possesses complete autonomy, but when it is gifted with the joy
of life in communion with God and our fellow creatures. All human
beings long to rejoice. "Even the most objective man of action, the
strictest scholar, the most serious theologian burning perhaps with
asceticism or philanthropy, does not really want only this, not to
speak of artists who are usually the sincerest in this matter. No, in
and with all these things, or side by side with them . . . [the Christian]
also wants to have a little, and perhaps more than a little, enjoyment. It is hypocrisy to hide this from oneself."[6]

In the spirit of Paul's "rejoice in the Lord," Augustine speaks of
enjoyment of God as the goal of human life. For Augustine, God is
the supreme good (*summum bonum*) and the source and object of
true joy. "The happy life is this—to rejoice to thee, in thee, and for
thee."[7]

In the spirit of Paul's "rejoice in the Lord," Jonathan Edwards,
preaching on the excellencies of God, contends that God is no
killjoy. On the contrary, God wills that human life flourish. Indeed,
God wants us to enjoy the fullness of life that God eternally possesses. The question is only what makes for true and lasting joy. In

6. Barth, *CD* III/4:375.
7. Augustine, *Confessions* 10.22.32, LCC 7, ed. Albert C. Outler (Philadelphia: Westminster, 1955), 221.

Edwards's words: "How great must be the happiness of the enjoyment of him? The happiness of soci-ety, and the enjoyment of entire friends, is one of the highest sort of pleasures, next to the pleasures of religion; if that be so sweet, how inexpressibly sweet and delightful

> **Our chief end is to glorify God and to enjoy him forever.**
>
> Westminster Shorter Catechism, answer 1, *The Constitution of the Presbyterian Church (U.S.A.), Part I, Book of Confessions,* 7.001.

must it be to enjoy this excellent being."[8] Edwards envisions heaven as the ever-expanding joy of the saints, whose knowledge and love of God, and of all things in God, increases to all eternity.[9]

Also in the spirit of Paul's "rejoice in the Lord," Karl Barth, meditat-ing on the uniqueness of rejoicing in the God of the gospel, writes, "About the other gods one may reflect, may bow to fate with a dark face, and with self-made comfort may pursue their ideas fanatically. But where is the joy in that? Joy is the rarest and most infrequent thing in the world. We already have enough fanatical seriousness, enthusiasm, and humorless zeal in the world. But joy? This shows us that the perception of the living God is rare. When we have found God our Savior—or when he has found us—we will rejoice in him."[10]

Paul's summons to Christians to rejoice, Augustine's description of God as the supreme good who is the source and object of deep and lasting joy, Edwards's depiction of the sweetness and delight to be found in God revealed in Christ, and Barth's words about the rarity of true joy make us aware of the extent to which Christian life today, in both its personal and corporate expressions, often suf-fers a deficit of joy. Do the lives of Christians today radiate joy, or is their witness to the world better described as sullen and weary? Nor is it only Christian congregations and their pastors who some-times seem bereft of joy. Often the work of many theologians also appears more laborious and burdened than joyful. In view of the

8. Jonathan Edwards, *Sermons and Discourses, 1720–1723,* WJE 10, ed. Wilson H. Kimnack (New Haven, CT: Yale University Press, 1992), 428–29.
9. See Steven M. Studebaker and Robert W. Caldwell III, *The Trinitarian Theology of Jonathan Edwards: Text, Context, and Application* (Burlington, VT: Ashgate, 2012), 213–28; Amy Plantinga Pauw, "'Heaven is a World of Love': Edwards on Heaven and the Trinity," *Calvin Theological Journal* 30 (1995): 392–401.
10. Karl Barth, *Insights* (Louisville, KY: Westminster John Knox Press, 2009), 13.

> Generations of "good" people in the West have had their Christianity made dull and impotent by moralism. How many have even suspected that the God of joy is at the heart of it all?
>
> Daniel W. Hardy and David F. Ford, *Jubilate: Theology in Praise* (London: Darton, Longman & Todd, 1984), 143.

overwhelming reality of suffering, injustice, and evil in the world, lament and protest undoubtedly have their place in Christian life and theology. Nevertheless, is it possible to be an ambassador of the good news of God with and for us, and even perhaps to devote one's entire life to exploring the riches of this message and laboring to put it into practice—and yet, to lack joy? Barth's judgment has a sting but it rings true: "The theologian who has no joy in his work is not a theologian at all."[11]

Note that Paul *urges* us to rejoice; he does not think that joy can come as the result of a command. In his letter Paul tells us of ways in which our joy "in the Lord" can be awakened, strengthened, and shared. Above all, look to Christ and what he has done for us and for the whole world. Find enjoyment in the company and love of fellow Christians. Give thanks to God as you bring your petitions to God in prayer. Show patience and gentleness to all people. Let the peace of God dwell in your hearts. Attend to all excellent things. Live a life of generous service to God and others. Be of good cheer: the Lord is near.

4:8–9

Virtuous Things

In the memorable paragraph that follows, Paul exhorts the Philippians to "think about" (*logizesthe*) things that are true, honorable, just, pure, pleasing, commendable, excellent, and praiseworthy. Many commentators point out that such virtue lists were common among Greek moralists of Paul's time. In particular, the Greek word *arete* ("virtue, excellence") is often found among the philosophical

11. Barth, *CD* II/1:656.

schools of ancient Greek culture. It referred to the best and the highest form of moral life and character human beings could achieve. New Testament scholars suggest that some of the items in Paul's list, such as just and praiseworthy, would be familiar to the Philippians who were proud citizens of the Roman Empire.[12]

So what was Paul trying to achieve by offering such a list, and what can we learn from it? First, Paul exhorts the Philippians not to close their eyes and ears to the world around them on the assumption that everything out there is evil. Paul is no Manichean. He is no despiser of the finer elements of human culture. "*Whatever* is true . . . ," Paul writes (4:8). That is to say, there are words worth listening to and deeds worth honoring outside the proclamation and life of the church. The wisdom tradition of the Old Testament is a striking example of the openness of the faith of Israel to the wisdom of other peoples and cultures. For Paul, of course, Christ is the fullness of the "wisdom of God" (1 Cor. 1:24), but this does not mean that Paul sees Christ and human culture in absolute opposition. "The apostle lifts up good and positive factors in the heritage of Philippian Christians and their non-Christian neighbors."[13]

Second, Paul's exhortation to his readers to be open to the true and the just wherever they appear is not the same thing as encouraging Christians to search for a convenient "point of contact" to facilitate acceptance of the gospel. Even further off target would be the idea that he is cultivating an easy conscience for Christians who incline to accommodate the gospel of Jesus

> We are called neither to a simple affirmation of human culture nor to a simple rejection of it. . . . We have to say both "God accepts human culture" and also "God judges human culture."
>
> Lesslie Newbigin, *The Gospel in a Pluralist Society* (Grand Rapids: Eerdmans, 1989), 195.

Christ to the prevailing cultural ethos. Rather, Paul's call to attend to all excellent and praiseworthy things acknowledges that God is at work not only in the church but in the whole creation. There are, to be sure, times and places when the church is called to stand firmly, unambiguously, and even relentlessly against the society and culture

---

12. See John Reumann, *Philippians* (New Haven, CT: Yale University Press, 2008), 640.
13. Ibid., 639.

in which it finds itself. But the (often embarrassing) fact is that those outside the church sometimes speak words and exhibit attitudes and behaviors that are what one should expect to hear and see from Christians. They may even serve to shame the church, which all too often lags behind the world in zeal for excellence in its labors. Christians are to be "open to the ways and works of God whenever and wherever they appear,"[14] and, we may add, whether or not they bear the name "Christian."

Also important to note is that when Paul urges the Philippians to "think about these things," he is not referring to an abstract, "ivory tower" kind of thinking. He is not recommending mere passive contemplation of things praiseworthy. He is speaking about a way of thinking and judging that is indivisible from willing and doing. In other words, "The excellencies of Phil. 4:8 are to be made manifest in one's life."[15] Here in Philippians and in Paul's letters generally, theology and ethics, thinking and doing, are inseparably linked. God has created and redeemed us as embodied, active creatures, not as bodiless spirits. If Paul is far removed from a materialist philosopher like Ludwig Feuerbach who claims that we are what we eat,[16] he is equally far removed from an idealist philosopher like Plato for whom the truly real is to be found in the disembodied realm of ideas and ideals.

Still, some readers might want to ask further: Does not Paul's list of virtuous things to think about in 4:8 weaken the Christ-centered focus of his letter? As a Tertullian might wonder, "What indeed has Athens to do with Jerusalem? What concord is there between the Academy and the Church?"[17] Such anxieties, however, are misplaced. Paul has no intention of writing as an ancient Greek moralist in the closing paragraphs of his letter. He is not all of a sudden substituting Aristotle for Christ.

In fact, the list of things Paul urges the Philippians to think about in 4:8 gains Christian specificity in the context of the letter as a whole. For Paul, Christ is the central reality of the Christian life and

14. Fred B. Craddock, *Philippians* (Atlanta: John Knox, 1985), 73.
15. V. P. Furnish, *Theology and Ethics in Paul* (Nashville: Abingdon, 1968), 89.
16. Ludwig Feuerbach, *The Essence of Christianity* (New York: Harper & Row, 1957).
17. Tertullian, *Prescription against Heresies* 7 (ANF 3:246).

"the prototype and measure of all Christian discipleship."[18] Note that in the verse that immediately follows, Paul hastens to identify the criteria that are to guide the Christian community in discerning what is true, honorable, and just: "Keep on *doing* [not just thinking about] the things that you have learned and received and heard and seen in me" (4:9). At its core, what the Philippians have "learned and received and heard and seen" in Paul is the gospel of the crucified and exalted Lord proclaimed and exhibited. By his words and actions, Paul witnesses to Jesus Christ, who is the source and standard of all that is excellent and praiseworthy.

FURTHER REFLECTIONS
Excellence

As numerous scholars have noted, most of the excellent and praiseworthy things mentioned in Philippians 4:8 are familiar to Hellenistic writers of that time. Far from this being a problem, however, it shows that Paul values the good that is present even in a fallen world. While not allowing themselves to be absorbed *by* the world, Christians nevertheless are to live *in* it, with appreciation for all that uplifts rather than demeans human life. Have respect for *"everything that is humanly true and good,"* as Barth paraphrases Paul.[19]

What constitutes virtue and the virtuous human life has differed widely in different cultures and eras. For Homer, the paradigm of virtue was the strong and brave warrior. For Aristotle, the exemplar of virtue was the man of practical wisdom, justice, temperance, and fortitude. Neither Homer nor Aristotle would have included humility in his list of virtues or considered faith, hope, and love the highest of virtues, as does the New Testament. Alasdair MacIntyre puts the point sharply: "Aristotle would certainly not have admired Jesus Christ and he would have been horrified by St. Paul."[20] Medieval Christian theology, and Thomas Aquinas in particular, adopted the

---

18. Bockmuehl, *Philippians,* 254.
19. Karl Barth, *The Epistle to the Philippians* (Louisville, KY: Westminster John Knox Press, 2002), 124.
20. Alasdair MacIntyre, *After Virtue: A Study in Moral Theory* (Notre Dame, IN: University of Notre Dame Press, 1981), 172.

Aristotelian catalog of cardinal virtues (justice, prudence, courage, self-control), adding to them the higher theological virtues (faith, hope, and love). It has sometimes been thought that the two sets of virtues, the Aristotelian and the specifically Christian, are related like two stories of a building, one standing on top of the other, with the bottom level largely independent and uninfluenced by the upper. However, it is doubtful that this view properly represents the thinking of either Thomas or Paul.

Can this remarkable verse of Philippians provide a clue to what might be called Paul's "theology of culture"? If so, his position is perhaps best described as dialectical. Paul neither uncritically blesses every aspect of human culture nor teaches that Christians should reject *tout court* everything about it. He calls for resistance to all powers and forces of this world that challenge the lordship of Christ (recall what he says about intimidation in 1:28 and standing "firm in the Lord" in 4:1) and yet urges respect for what is true, just, and praiseworthy wherever they are manifest.

This Pauline dialectic offers important guidance for the mission of the church and the task of theology today. While the proclamation of the gospel must always remain the primary responsibility of the church, effective proclamation will not be simply dismissive, let alone downright hostile, to the true, the just, and the good that are present in the life and culture of its hearers. Likewise, while the mission of the church on behalf of the poor and the unjustly treated will take its rationale and direction from the teachings and way of Jesus Christ, this in no way prohibits the church from joining with all people of goodwill in activities that serve the common good.

At the same time, Paul's call to the Philippians (and to all Christians) to attend to whatever is true, just, honorable, and praiseworthy by no means fosters an uncritical attitude toward whatever at any time might be assumed and broadcast as what is true, just, and honorable. In other words, truth, justice, beauty, goodness, and all other commendable things are not left simply untouched by the gospel. On the contrary, it is fair to say that for Paul all of the excellencies mentioned in 4:8 have been freshly minted by Christ. In other words, we should not sever 4:8 from 4:7, where Paul speaks of the "peace of God" that guards our "hearts and minds in Christ

Jesus," or from 4:9, where Paul exhorts the Philippians "to keep on doing the things that you have learned and received and heard and seen in me," an admonition that surely refers ultimately not to Paul himself but to Christ, who is the Lord whom Paul seeks to emulate (1 Cor. 11:1). Christ is, for Paul, the epitome, the fulfillment, of all the excellent things that Paul enumerates in his commendation. In "thinking about these things" as Christians, we are called also to think about how they are supremely embodied in Christ and to live our lives accordingly.

Stated somewhat differently: determining what is true, just, and praiseworthy is not for Paul a matter that can simply be read off the customs and practices of a particular society or culture. Nor is it resolved by popular vote. Rather, for Paul, Christ is the ultimate measure of what is true, just, and good. It is by thinking and living according to the "mind" of Christ (2:5) that Christians are to discern "what is best" (1:10) and live their lives in a way "worthy of the gospel of Christ" (1:27). Just as we can assume that when Paul writes his unforgettable description of "the more excellent way" of love (1 Cor. 13), his decisive model is the love of God in Jesus Christ, so when Paul speaks of excellent things in Philippians 4:8, we can assume that he finds the supreme instance of each of them in Christ.

In his celebrated essay "True Virtue," Jonathan Edwards acknowledges the presence of the admirable and the excellent in nature and in human life and culture. But like Paul, Edwards finds the fullness of what is excellent in Christ. As Edwards explains in a sermon titled "The Excellency of Christ," true divinity and true humanity are united in Christ. He combines the strength of a lion and the meekness of a lamb. He is higher than the highest angels of heaven, and yet there is none humbler than he. Thus infinite highness and infinite condescension meet in Jesus Christ, and this conjunction of excellencies is the basis of his beauty and his appeal.[21] Edwards's sermon stands in the line of Paul's Christ hymn and the accompanying exhortations to make our own the "mind" of Christ and to let our character, decisions, and actions be patterned after his.

---

21. Jonathan Edwards, *Sermons and Discourses, 1734–1738,* WJE 19, ed. M. X. Lesser (New Haven, CT: Yale University Press, 2001), 588–89.

As noted earlier, when Paul exhorts Christians to think about excellent things, he does not assume a separation of thought and practice, contemplation and action. Just as "Let the same mind be in you that was in Christ Jesus" (2:5) is not for Paul merely about thoughts and attitudes but also about practices and actions, so the exhortation to think about excellent and praiseworthy things is more than an encouragement to lofty thoughts and high-minded aspirations. It is about reforming and reshaping every aspect of our lives, including the thoughts we entertain, the desires we have, the goals we set, and the actions we take. Paul wants to cultivate among his readers faithful solidarity and moral maturity in Christ.

Paul's call to Christians to attend to all that is excellent and praiseworthy is a reminder that the process of attaining to maturity in Christ is affected, for good or ill, by the figures we admire, the values we espouse, the hopes we cherish, and the foundational stories we tell and retell. The lives of Christians, and indeed all human beings, are moved and shaped by what we admire, desire, and choose to imitate. We eventually become like what we most love. We are pulled to and fro, up and down by our strongest attachments. Tell me what you love, Augustine said, and I will tell you who you are. "My weight is my love. By it I am carried wherever I am carried."[22] Christians will respect and value those "excellent things" to which all people have access. At the same time, they will rejoice above all in the excellence of Jesus Christ, who deepens, reforms, and perfects all that is commendable in human life.

Paul concludes this section with the assurance that if the Philippians remain faithful to what they have heard from and seen in him, "the God of peace" will be with them (4:9). Paul has earlier spoken of "the peace of God" that passes all understanding (4:7); he now speaks of "the God of peace." We might gloss these two phrases by suggesting that they respectively describe God from the point of view of God's relation to us ("the peace of God") and from the point of view of God's own eternal life ("the God of peace"). In other words, just as God not only *acts* lovingly toward us, humbling God's

22. Augustine, *Confessions* 13.9.10.

self in Christ for our salvation, he also *is* loving in God's own triune reality from and to all eternity, so God not only graciously *grants* peace to us ("the peace of God") but *is* at peace in God's own eternal life (the "God of peace"). In the eternal life of God there is no competition, no conflict, no alienation, only eternal peace, harmony, and the mutual sharing of love. The God of peace is altogether different from all the gods of war and violence. The judgment of Richard Hays is deeply unsettling but accurate: "One reason that the world finds the New Testament's message of peacemaking and love of enemies incredible is that the church is so massively faithless."[23]

The Philippians knew well that Rome and the great and intimidating empire it had built also offered "peace," the peace and security of the Pax Romana. But such peace is ultimately based on fear, violence, and conquest. The peace of God of which Paul speaks and which is made known in Jesus Christ is altogether different. It is the peace built on God's surprising gift of righteousness and new life in Christ that is extended to all, the peace incarnated in one who humbled himself and took the form of a servant, the peace achieved not by coercion but by the unconquerable love of the crucified and risen Christ. "The peace of God which surpasses all understanding" is not Pax Romana but Pax Christi.

---

23. Richard Hays, *The Moral Vision of the New Testament: Community, Cross, New Creation* (San Francisco: Harper, 1996), 343.

4:10–20

Concluding Thanks and Doxology

In this penultimate section of the letter, Paul thanks the Philippians for their gifts. He kindly tells them that they probably wanted to send something earlier to him but did not have the opportunity to do so (4:10). He then adds that he is not in dire need and that he has learned to make do with whatever he has. He can live contentedly with little or with plenty because he finds his strength to carry on his ministry from Christ, whatever the outer circumstances (4:11–14). As a final expression of his gratitude, Paul commends the Philippian church as a leader among all the churches in sharing with him "in the matter of giving and receiving" (4:15–20).

4:10

At Last

Some commentators view the fact that only toward the very end of the letter in its canonical form does Paul thank the Philippians for the gift they have sent him as evidence that this section is part of a separate letter. Would it not have been unusual, not to say discourteous, they ask, if Paul had postponed his thanks to the concluding section of the letter rather than mentioning it much earlier? In favor of the integrity of the letter in its present form, however, one might respond that Paul had other concerns that he thought important to address first. Alternatively, one might ask whether what comes last must necessarily be of least importance. Why might not a word of thanks be a fitting conclusion rather than an anticlimax? In any case, little of interpretative significance seems to hang on the question of whether this section is part of another letter of Paul to the Philippians.

Here as throughout the letter, Paul's special bond with the Philippians is evident. Even though it has been some time since his friends have shown concern for him, he does not scold. He does not reprimand them for forgetting about him. If their delay has disappointed him, he does not make an issue of it. Instead, he gently makes allowance for the long interval ("at last") since they last showed their support (4:10). We might paraphrase: "I know your love and concern for me is constant; you just did not have the opportunity to show it until now." Paul's graciousness and "gentleness" (4:5) as a church leader is evident here. He is not quick to accuse his brothers and sisters in Christ of faithlessness when they seem not to be living up to his expectations. He assumes the best of their intentions and allows that there were no doubt good reasons why they had not been able until now to show their continued support of his gospel ministry. He is grateful for their kindness in wanting to share in his present "distress" (4:14).

Paul is walking a delicate line here. On the one hand, he does not want the Philippians to think he is interested only in their gifts, not in their "progress and joy in faith" (1:25). Bockmuehl wisely observes that Paul places his thanks at the end of the letter to indicate that "the gift from the Philippians is not the main purpose of Paul's writing, but secondary in importance to their own concord and adoption of the mind of Christ."[1] Moreover, while Paul wants to express hearty thanks for the gifts he has received, he does not want to do so in a way that suggests that he is overly dependent on his supporters. He does not want to be a burden. Although he believes that he deserves financial support for his ministry from the churches he has founded (1 Cor. 9:3–18), he is a tent maker and prefers to support himself. Furthermore, he knows from experience with some of his churches that financial relationships can easily become matters of contention. He does not want his missionary endeavors to be compromised by suspicion of his motives. Evidently, only with the

---

1. Markus Bockmuehl, *The Epistle to the Philippians* (London: Hendrickson, 1998), 258.

Philippian community does Paul feel relatively at ease in accepting gifts. But even here he wants to avoid giving the impression either that they are obligated to support him or that he is totally dependent on them. Paul thinks theologically about all aspects of his life and relationships. For him, participation in the proclamation of the gospel is understood as a privilege rather than a heavy obligation or unpleasant duty. He wants it to be clear that his proclamation of the gospel is "free of charge" (1 Cor. 9:18). All is grace.

The complexity of the financial relationship between pastor and congregation in many churches today as well as in Paul's day is well known. Does a preacher remain in the good graces of her congregation if she speaks about controversial issues and takes public stands that are offensive to some members? Should a preacher feel free to ask for a raise in salary if he is in need, or can better carry out his responsibilities with the additional funds, or has helped the church to flourish? Unfortunately, these questions are sometimes dealt with in the strict cost-analysis calculations that govern a secular business rather than, as Paul surely would encourage, in terms of partnership in the gospel.

4:11–14

Contentment

Mention of his distress gives Paul an occasion once again to confess his complete dependence on the grace of God. In the final analysis, he has no real "need" (4:11) other than this. While he welcomes gifts from his friends because this is evidence of their love and concern for him, he has learned to be "content with whatever I have," whether it is little or plenty. Do the words "little" and "plenty" recall the way of Christ as described in the Christ hymn of chapter 2? Do we have here further evidence that Paul understands his own life and ministry as a participation in and correspondence to the way of Christ? Just as Christ took the form of a servant and humbled himself for our sake, so Paul is determined to proclaim the gospel even when, like a slave, he has "little" and even goes hungry. Likewise, just as Christ's exaltation by God and being given the name that is above every name is all to the glory of God the Father, so Paul remains confident of God's faithfulness and trusts that his times of poverty ("going hungry") and times of plenty ("being well-fed") will be used to the magnifying of the name of Christ and to the glory of God. That is, he does not view having plenty as proof of the gospel any more than he sees times of having little as disconfirmation of the gospel. Rather, he says he has "learned to be content" with whatever he has (4:11).

Where did Paul learn this "secret" (4:12) of contentment? While it is possible that Paul was influenced by the Stoic philosophy that was popular in his time,[2] it is both unnecessary and misleading to look to Stoicism as the *source* of his ability to be content. It is true that Stoicism teaches the wisdom of being content regardless of one's circumstances. The Stoic sages urge the cultivation of a certain kind of dispassion (*apatheia*) that will guard one against the devastating times of depression and the all-too-short times of elation caused by life's alternating successes and failures. For the Stoic, the best way to cope with the vicissitudes of life and to be free and strong is to keep one's emotions under the control of one's reason and to avoid expecting too much or loving too much.

Paul's wisdom, however, is not the wisdom of Stoicism. Whereas for Stoicism, the strength to be content whatever the circumstances comes from within oneself, from the power of one's reason to control desires, for Paul it comes from outside, from Christ who strengthens him.[3] It is the wisdom of Christ crucified and risen, the wisdom of knowing "Christ and the power of his resurrection and the sharing of his sufferings" (3:10), that is the source of Paul's contentment. Here again—this time in his meditation on the ups and downs of his ministry—we encounter Paul's theology of the cross. The crucified and risen Christ, a scandal to Jews and foolishness to Gentiles (1 Cor. 1:23), is the one from whom he has learned to be content whether he has "little" or "plenty."

Further evidence that Paul's secret of contentment comes from a source other than Stoicism is his passionate engagement in the

2. See Troels Engberg-Pedersen, *Paul and the Stoics* (Edinburgh: T. & T. Clark, 2000).
3. Gerald W. Peterman, *Paul's Gift from Philippi: Contemporary Conventions of Gift-Exchange and Christian Giving* (New York: Cambridge University Press, 1997), 135.

ministry of the gospel. Far from a lack of passion and exuberance being a virtue for Paul, as it is for the Stoic, Paul gives himself whole-heartedly to the proclamation of the good news and to the praise of Christ to the glory of God. He is not cautious and restrained about his life in Christ and his proclamation of the gospel but is continu-ally "straining forward" (3:13) to what lies ahead, to the coming of Christ the Savior, the resurrection from the dead, and the transfor-mation of "the body of our humiliation" and its conformation to "the body of his glory" (3:21). Contentment for Paul means he will not allow outward circumstances to derail his passion for and joy in Christ. "Rejoice in the Lord always" is hardly advice that Paul has gleaned from Stoic philosophy.

Pauline contentment is not a conspicuous virtue in contempo-rary American culture or in American church life today. The main character of Richard Ford's novel *Canada* aptly complains of "the nervous American intensity for something else."[4] In some church quarters the gospel of success is preached to great acclaim. In this version of the gospel, contentment is supposedly found when one is able to buy the McMansion of one's dreams or when parents get their children into the best day-care center and eventually into an Ivy League university. The equation of contentment with the real-ization of every conceivable fantasy is just as foreign to Paul as is the Stoic version of contentment.

As I write, many dreams of uninterrupted growth in the Ameri-can economy have sharply diminished. This is surely a time for the church to lead the way in a reassessment of what makes for true con-tentment and real happiness. Does the church, in its message and practice, bear witness to a way of life together that is truly helpful because of knowing the secret of contentment? For Paul, in any case, the secret of contentment is abiding in the love of God in Jesus Christ and finding the purpose of life in responding to his call to share God's love in concrete ways with all others.

It is in the context of speaking of his contentment in both little and plenty that Paul writes one of his best-known affirmations: "I can do all things through him who strengthens me" (4:13). The "him" is, of

---

4. Richard Ford, *Canada* (New York: HarperCollins, 2012), 407.

course, the crucified and risen Christ present now in the power of the Holy Spirit. Chrysostom paraphrases Paul: "The success is not my own, but his who has given me strength."[5] Paul's great affirmation should not be taken out of context. It does not mean, "I can do anything whatever—whether handling dangerous snakes, jumping from the top of the Empire State Building without injury, or working my way up to the position of CEO of my company—as long as I invoke Christ as the source of my strength." Rather, it means that Christ empowers us for, and sustains us in, a life of service and witness to the gospel, whatever obstacles we may face. Is this empowerment from Christ always received directly, or is it often mediated through others? Note that Paul follows his affirmation that he can do all things through Christ who strengthens him with his thanks to his Philippian friends who kindly "share" his "distress" (4:14). We may infer from this particular expression of gratitude that Paul thinks of the solidarity of Christians in the service of the gospel as one of the ways in which Christ strengthens us to do "all things."

4:15–20

Except You Alone!

Continuing his words of thanks, Paul now gives a special compliment to the church in Philippi. Earlier he has called them "beloved" (1:12; 2:12), "brothers and sisters" (3:1; 3:17; 4:1), "my joy and crown" (4:1) whom he yearns for "with the compassion of Christ Jesus" (1:8). Now he tells them that "no church shared with me in the matter of giving and receiving, except you alone" (4:15). Some of the churches Paul founded were larger, richer, and probably more prominent. But the church at Philippi alone excelled in "the matter of giving and receiving."

In the Greco-Roman world of Paul's time, "giving and receiving" often referred to a form of business transaction in which, by giving something to someone, credits were gained, and by receiving the gift, debts were incurred. In addition to being a description of

---

5. Chrysostom, *Homilies on Philippians* 15 (*NPNF*[1] 13:250).

commercial transactions, "giving and receiving" was "the primary expression of friendship in Greco-Roman antiquity."[6] In other words, the phrase was part of the common vocabulary to describe conventions governing social relationships of that time.

Clearly as Paul uses the phrase he is not thinking in terms of a commercial exchange, of credits accrued and debits owed. He is not literally adding up the benefits he and the Philippians have given to and received from each other and declaring that they are now even. Giving and receiving, as Paul speaks of it in this letter, is altogether different from a commercial transaction. Indeed, Paul deepens and transforms the meaning of the phrase as used in both commercial and friendship relationships of his time. As Gerald Peterman notes, "Paul has elevated [the phrase "giving and receiving"] to a Christian appellation for missionary involvement."[7] Consequently, this simple Pauline phrase is "the key to much, not only in the present passage, but also to the letter as a whole."[8] Paul rejoices that the Philippians have been generous in their financial and other means of support for his ministry even as he has been as generous as possible in passing on the gift of the gospel and offering his apostolic encouragement and guidance to them. But he does not see their mutual giving and receiving as a transaction in which a gift incurs obligations, either their obligation to him for the gift of the gospel that he proclaimed to them (for his proclamation is "free of charge"; 1 Cor. 9:18) or his obligation to them for supporting his ministry (because their gift is not really to him but to Christ and the work of the gospel). Rather, Paul rejoices when he sees in his and their mutual giving and receiving a confirmation of his understanding of new community in Christ. Life in Christ does not follow the logic of commercial exchange or even the standard rules governing friendship in the ancient Greco-Roman world; instead it follows the logic of God's grace and the transformation of human life and relationships that it creates and sustains.

The dynamic of mutual giving and receiving is the heartbeat of the new life in Christ. As has been frequently emphasized in this

6. Gordon D. Fee, *Paul's Letter to the Philippians* (Grand Rapids: Eerdmans, 1995), 439.
7. Peterman, *Paul's Gift*, 199.
8. Fee, *Philippians*, 442.

commentary, faith is not in the first place a creative act on our part. Rather, it is first of all a receptive act, an acknowledgment of God's free and unconditional gift in Christ. That is why Luther, nearing death, could write, "We are all beggars. That is true."[9] He meant that in relation to God we are always on the receiving end of a gift that we do not earn or deserve. Yet as Rowan Williams rightly states, "God's gift makes givers."[10] In other words, God's giving empowers our giving as well as our receiving. If we have truly received God's gift, we become givers in return, givers of loving praise to God and loving assistance to our neighbor. Our gifts do not, of course, ever duplicate or complement God's gift of Christ to us as if that singular gift were somehow less than complete and sufficient. Nevertheless, God's superabundant grace does not stultify human response but activates it. The Spirit empowers us to receive the incomparable gift of God, to bear witness to it, and to live in correspondence to it in our daily lives and relationships to others.

Paul tells the Philippian church that they alone have excelled in the knowledge and practice of the truth that in receiving God's gift, we are called and enabled to give, and in giving, we find ourselves also receiving. Elsewhere Paul elaborates on the gifts that are given by the Spirit to all members of Christ's body and that are to be used in turn for the welfare of the whole body (1 Cor. 12). He emphasizes that all have gifts to contribute and none can be considered unimportant or inferior. In their giving and receiving, all contribute to the health and well-being of the entire community.

The interplay of the giving and receiving of love constitutes one of the important differences between Christian love and what commonly goes under the name of "charity." The act of charity is often thought to be a one-way street. The so-called benefactor gives but does not receive anything from those benefited. Thus does charity easily slip into patronage. According to many liberation theologians, the most serious flaw of attempts by affluent nations to assist the less commercially developed nations is the assumption that the affluent are exclusively the givers in the relationship and the poor exclusively the receivers. This is an

9. Martin Luther, *Table Talk*, LW 54, trans. Theodore G. Tappert (Philadelphia: Fortress, 1967), 476.
10. Rowan Williams, *Tokens of Trust* (Louisville, KY: Westminster John Knox Press, 2007), 107.

assumption that demeans the poor and devalues the special gifts they have and would like to share with others. The matter of giving and receiving thus not only goes to the heart of our relationship to God and our neighbors within and outside the community of faith, but it also sheds light on what makes for the health of human community generally and even the well-being of international relationships.

Concluding his reflections on giving and receiving, Paul describes the gifts the Philippian church has sent to him through Epaphroditus as "a fragrant offering, a sacrifice acceptable and pleasing to God" (4:18). Recall that Paul spoke earlier of his apostolic ministry and the sufferings that accompany it as a "libation" or offering poured over "the sacrifice and the offering" of the faith of the Philippians (2:17). When he now describes their gifts to him as a "fragrant offering" acceptable and pleasing to God, he expresses confidence that God's riches of grace in Jesus Christ will satisfy all their needs (4:18–19). Paul and the Philippians, each in their own way of giving and receiving, are doing what the apostle in another of his letters urges all who have been recipients of the grace of God to do: "Present your bodies [yourselves] as a living sacrifice, holy and acceptable to God, which is your spiritual worship" (Rom. 12:1).

Paul appropriately concludes his thanks for the gifts of the Philippians with a doxology: "To our God and Father be glory forever and ever. Amen" (4:20). The church in later centuries will expand this doxology, but the expansion stands in unmistakable continuity with the faith and theology of Paul's letter to the church at Philippi:

> All praise and thanks to God, who reigns in highest heaven,
> To Father and to Son and Spirit now be given,
> The One eternal God, whom heaven and earth adore,
> The God who was, and is, and shall be evermore.[11]

---

11. Martin Rinkart, trans. Catherine Winkworth, "Now Thank We All Our God," *Glory to God: The Presbyterian Hymnal* (Louisville, KY: Westminster John Knox Press, 2013), 643, stanza 3.

FURTHER REFLECTIONS
Giving and Receiving

The "matter of giving and receiving" is at the center of the worship of the church. When we hear the Word read and proclaimed, are renewed in the baptismal water, and receive the bread and wine at the Table of the Lord who gave his life for us, we are first and foremost sheer recipients of the astonishing generosity of God. We respond in wonder and thanksgiving, lift our voices in praise and blessing, and trust in God, who graciously hears our prayers and calls us to share what we have been given with our neighbors near and far.

> Love so amazing, so divine, demands my soul, my life, my all.
>
> Isaac Watts, "When I Survey the Wondrous Cross"

Giving and receiving is an integral element not only of Christian worship but of the whole of Christian life and Christian ethics. When Christians pray the Lord's Prayer, they ask God for forgiveness and promise in turn to forgive others. This receiving of God's forgiveness and the new freedom and constraint to forgive others defines Christian existence. God's giving and forgiving does not come to an end with our thankful reception but multiplies itself in our giving the gospel message and our love and compassion to others in need. Life in Christ is not based on an "economy of exchange" in which a gift places the receiver under obligation to respond with a benefit of equal value. Rather, life in Christ is marked by an "economy of grace."[12] Where God's grace abounds, praise of God and the gifts of God's children to one another and to all others increase as well.

The practice of giving and receiving, so constitutive for Christian worship and service, does not have its foundation there. It is a correspondence to and participation in the supreme expression of that love in the gift of Jesus Christ for the redemption and renewal of the world. Recall once again the twofold movement described in the Christ hymn (2:5–11): Christ who is equal with God gives of himself in humility and self-expending love and service even to death on a

---

12. Kathryn Tanner, *Economy of Grace* (Minneapolis: Fortress, 2005).

cross. Then the crucified Christ is exalted by God and given a name above every name to the universal praise of Christ and to the glory of God the Father. The Christ hymn speaks of God as wondrously free both to give and to receive. In our giving and receiving, we are gathered into Christ and take part in the rhythm of God's own eternal life of love.

That in God's own life it is a "matter of giving and receiving," albeit in an utterly singular manner, is one way of pointing to the incomprehensible truth of the church's doctrine of the Trinity. As has been noted throughout this study, Paul did not express his understanding of God rooted in the work of Christ and the activity of the Spirit in the conceptuality employed in the later church doctrine of the Trinity. The important point, however, is that in Paul's prayer and proclamation, in his hymn describing the way of the crucified and risen Christ, and in his participation in the transforming and promising power of the Spirit, Paul is already bearing witness to the fact that God's self-revelation and activity in Jesus Christ by the power of the Spirit is ultimately grounded in the reality of God as an unfathomable communion in love that has been opened to us. To have the mind of Christ is to participate in and correspond to God's own life of mutually shared love, God's own "threefold rhythm of love."[13]

According to classical Trinitarian doctrine, God does not live in solitude but in communion. God exists in this way not only in relation to us but in God's own eternal life. There is a mutual giving and receiving of love in the eternal triune life of God. The Father loves the Son and the Son loves the Father in the uniting love of the Spirit. The reality of the Trinity, alive in mutual love and communion, is the mysterious background of the Christ event and the pouring out of God's love to the world. In contrast to every form of deism, the God of the gospel is the God who in Jesus Christ becomes one of us and by the power of the Spirit works among us, uniting us to Christ and empowering us for the new life in him, all to the glory of God (4:19). The God identified by the action of Jesus Christ and the Spirit is freely and graciously active in "the matter of giving and receiving" both in relationship to us and in all eternity.

13. Williams, *Tokens of Trust*, 136.

"One alone cannot be excellent," declares Jonathan Edwards in defense of the Trinitarian understanding of God.[14] Edwards's point can be restated to say that one alone cannot engage in the giving and receiving of love. Barth similarly affirms that from all eternity, "God seeks and creates fellowship."[15] No matter how many majestic attributes may be ascribed to a god who wills to be eternally alone (*deus solitarius*), such a god is infinitely inferior to the God who abides in love and wills to share that life in love with us. Edwards and Barth speak for the entire classic theological tradition in affirming that from all eternity God's very life is in the mutual sharing of love, in the singular giving and receiving of love by Father, Son, and Holy Spirit. In Jesus Christ this glorious love of God has been poured out to the world, even to death on a cross. To have the mind of Christ and to live "in Christ" is to take part in God's cruciform, life-giving love and to have our attitudes, decisions, relationships, and practices continually reformed by and conformed to that love.

14. Jonathan Edwards, *"Miscellanies," a–500,* WJE 13, trans. Thomas A. Schafer (New Haven, CT: Yale University Press, 1994), 284. For an excellent study of Edwards on the Trinity, see Amy Plantinga Pauw, *The Supreme Harmony of All: The Trinitarian Theology of Jonathan Edwards* (Grand Rapids: Eerdmans, 2002).
15. Barth, CD II/1:274–75.

4:21–23

Final Greetings and Benediction

Paul now comes full circle in these final greetings and blessing. Recalling the beginning of the letter, where he sends greetings to "all the saints in Christ Jesus" (1:1), we are not surprised that in these concluding lines he sends greetings to "every saint" in Philippi (4:21). Paul will not play favorites at the beginning or the end. He knows well the damage favoritism can do in a congregation. He remembers how in Corinth one faction said, "I belong to Paul," another "I belong to Apollo," another "I belong to Cephas," and still another "I belong to Christ" (1 Cor. 1:11–13). Paul insists that Christ is not divided. Whatever disagreements may have arisen in Philippi, he does not want them to lead to serious divisions such as he earlier confronted in Corinth. "Greet every saint in Christ Jesus" (4:21). The call to unity, present throughout the letter, is clear: you are all one in Christ.

Note too that both in the opening greetings and here in the closing benediction, Paul speaks of the saints as persons "in Christ Jesus." Christian identity, belonging to the community of saints, is not a matter of ethnic background, racial heritage, national citizenship, denominational affiliation, subscription to creeds, or practice of prescribed religious rituals. It is a matter of being "in Christ Jesus," receiving God's gracious gift in him and sharing with others his life of humility and self-giving love. According to Gerd Theissen, there are two basic values of the primitive Christian ethic: renunciation of status and love of neighbor.[1] In his

---

1. Gerd Theissen, *The Religion of the Earliest Churches* (Minneapolis: Fortress, 1999), cited by Joseph H. Hellerman, *Reconstructing Honor in Roman Philippi* (New York: Cambridge University Press, 2005), 157, 211 n. 1.

Letter to the Philippians, Paul has focused on these prominent features of early Christian ethics and emphatically grounded them in the person and work of Jesus Christ.

Nor are we surprised that Paul now sends not only his own greetings but also the greetings of all the brothers and sisters who are with him (4:21). As we have often had occasion to note, Paul has an exceedingly strong sense of the solidarity of believers in Christ. He is not alone in his faith journey or in his gospel ministry. There are others with him, and their word of greeting to those in Philippi is as important as his. It is important to add, as David Horrell contends, that Paul's theme of solidarity in Christ does not lead to narrowness of spirit. It includes "expressions of concern for others," indeed for *all* others (4:5), and encourages generous acknowledgment of the manifestations of truth, justice, and excellence wherever they may appear (4:8).[2]

Among those who are with him and who send greetings are members of "the emperor's household" (4:22). The reference may well be to members of Caesar's court in Rome, but since it could also refer to members of the imperial service in other parts of the empire, it does not settle the question of the city in which the letter was written. In any case, some of Caesar's own servants have evidently come to faith in Christ through Paul's ministry. Paul's mention at the beginning of the letter that the gospel is being made known "throughout the whole imperial guard" as a result of his imprisonment is now matched at the end of the letter with a reference to those in "the emperor's household" who send along their greetings to the brothers and sisters in Philippi. Paul obviously intends these references to fortify the beloved community of believers in Philippi who dwell in a city proud of imperial Roman power, are under threat of reprisals for their beliefs, and must at times be tempted to wonder whether the lordship of Christ will ultimately prevail.

The last word of the letter is also the first: "the grace of the Lord Jesus Christ be with your spirit" (4:23). The grace of God in Jesus Christ is indeed the first and last word not only of Paul's Letter to the Philippians but of the proclamation of the gospel in every time and place.

2. David G. Horrell, *Solidarity and Difference: A Contemporary Reading of Paul's Ethics* (London: T. & T. Clark International, 2005), 269.

Selected Bibliography

Barth, Karl. *Church Dogmatics.* Edited by G. W. Bromiley and T. F.
    Torrance. 4 vols. in 13. Edinburgh: T. & T. Clark, 1936–1977.
———. *The Epistle to the Philippians.* Translated by James W. Leitch.
    Louisville, KY: Westminster John Knox Press, 2002.
Bauckham, Richard J. *God Crucified: Monotheism and Christology in
    the New Testament.* Carlisle, Cumbria: Paternoster, 1998.
Bockmuehl, Markus. *The Epistle to the Philippians.* Peabody, MA:
    Hendrickson, 1998.
Calvin, John. *Galatians, Ephesians, Philippians and Colossians.*
    CNTC. Edited by David W. Torrance and Thomas F.
    Torrance. Reprint, Grand Rapids: Eerdmans, 1979.
Craddock, Fred B. *Philippians.* Interpretation. Atlanta: John Knox,
    1985.
Dunn, James D. G. *The Theology of Paul the Apostle.* Grand Rapids:
    Eerdmans, 1998.
Fee, Gordon D. *Paul's Letter to the Philippians.* Grand Rapids:
    Eerdmans, 1995.
Fowl, Stephen E. *Philippians.* The Two Horizons New Testament
    Commentary. Grand Rapids: Eerdmans, 2005.
Hansen, G. Walter. *The Letter to the Philippians.* The Pillar New
    Testament Commentary. Grand Rapids: Eerdmans, 2009.
Hays, Richard B. *The Moral Vision of the New Testament: A
    Contemporary Introduction to New Testament Ethics.* New
    York: HarperSanFrancisco, 1996.
Horrell, David G. *Solidarity and Difference: A Contemporary Reading
    of Paul's Ethics.* London: T. & T. Clark, 2005.

Hurtado, Larry W. *Lord Jesus Christ: Devotion to Jesus in Earliest Christianity.* Grand Rapids: Eerdmans, 2003.

Martyn, J. Louis. *Theological Issues in the Letters of Paul.* Edinburgh: T. & T. Clark, 1997.

O'Brien, Peter T. *The Epistle to the Philippians.* Grand Rapids: Eerdmans, 1991.

Wright, N. T. *Paul: In Fresh Perspective.* Minneapolis: Fortress, 2009.

PHILEMON

Introduction:
Why Philemon? Why Now?

Containing only 25 verses and totaling roughly 335 words in the Greek text, Philemon is the shortest of Paul's letters and one of the shortest books of the New Testament. Yet its importance is greater than its size or the infrequency with which it is included among the church's lectionary readings or as a text for church study groups. Attention to this brief letter can enrich our understanding of the fullness of the gospel that Paul proclaims and its bearing on both our personal life and our life in community. A few commentators even advance such provocative claims that the Letter to Philemon "represents Paul at his theological best"[1] or provides "the key to the whole of Paul's thinking."[2]

In the early centuries of the church, some theologians thought it was a mistake to have included the letter in the biblical canon. They viewed it as a strictly personal letter of Paul to a friend that dealt with only minor matters, was theologically thin, and lacked significance for the universal church. Patristic theologian John Chrysostom (347–407), however, vigorously defended the letter against its critics. He contended that everything the apostles said and did can be of profit to us and saw the letter as an exemplar of Paul's graciousness and humility in dealing with slaves.[3] At a much later time but in somewhat the same vein, John Calvin

---

1. John G. Nordling, "The Gospel in Philemon," *Concordia Theological Quarterly* 71 (2007): 82.
2. Markus Barth and Helmut Blanke, *The Letter to Philemon* (Grand Rapids: Eerdmans, 2000), 214, summarizing the view of N. R. Petersen, *Rediscovering Paul: Philemon and the Sociology of Paul's Narrative World* (Philadelphia: Fortress, 1985).
3. John Chrysostom, *Homilies on Philemon* (NPNF[1] 13:545–46).

found the letter of value because it showed "the sublime quality of Paul's spirit."[4]

In the modern era, the letter has enjoyed something of a renaissance, at least among biblical scholars. Contemporary interest is due primarily to three factors: the letter's display of Paul's remarkable pastoral and rhetorical skills; the light it sheds on the attitude of the NT church and of Paul in particular to the institution of slavery in the Greco-Roman world of the first century; and the case study it offers for rethinking the proper use of Scripture in the life of the church. In response to the questions, Why study Philemon, and why study it now? this commentary is written in the conviction that Paul's brief letter shows him as a skillful practitioner as well as a consummate theologian of reconciliation; that it contains an indispensable first word, if admittedly not the last word, about the incompatibility of the Christian gospel with the ownership or exploitation of fellow human beings; and that it makes unavoidable our wrestling with the question of how Scripture functions for Christians today as the living word of God. More pointedly, the commentary asks to what extent we can understand the Letter to Philemon as an integral part of the gospel of God's work of reconciliation and transformation through Jesus Christ and as instructive to the church of every age in its confrontation with issues of human dignity and social justice.

Historical Background

Although we know that Paul wrote the letter while in prison, the precise place and date of the writing are uncertain. The traditional view is that it was composed in Rome, where Paul was imprisoned at the end of his life. However, given the considerable distance between Rome and Colossae—the probable destination of the letter—some scholars think that Ephesus, where Paul was also imprisoned for a time, is a more likely place of origin. The date of writing is usually set between 55 and 65 CE. Wherever and whenever the letter was

---

4. John Calvin, *The Second Epistle of Paul to the Corinthians, and the Epistles to Timothy, Titus and Philemon*, CNTC 10, ed. David W. Torrance and Thomas F. Torrance (1964; repr., Grand Rapids: Eerdmans, 1979), 393.

written, Paul's imprisonment must have been of such a nature as to allow friends to visit him, provide him with the essentials of life, and act as couriers for his letters.

While the primary addressee of the letter is Philemon, the host of a house church in Colossae, it is not what we would call a private piece of correspondence. Among the addressees are not only two other persons (Apphia, Archippus) but also "the church in your house" (v. 2). There is good reason, therefore, to think that the letter was intended to be read aloud to all members of the house church and that its contents would have been openly discussed by them.

The central issue of the letter concerns a young slave by the name of Onesimus who has either run away from his master Philemon or gotten in some other kind of trouble with him. Seeking help from Paul, Onesimus has been converted to the gospel (v. 10) and has even become one of Paul's assistants (vv. 11, 13). In the letter we learn that Paul is sending Onesimus back to Philemon with a written appeal on his behalf.

Slavery was a deeply embedded institution in the Roman Empire of the first century, with slaves comprising as many as one-third of the inhabitants of cities. Scholars caution against simple equations of slavery in the Roman Empire with the practice of slavery in North America in the eighteenth and nineteenth centuries. Among the important differences: slavery in the Greco-Roman world was not racially based; the education of slaves was often encouraged; and, most important, many urban slaves could expect to be emancipated by the age of thirty. Still, depending on the character and mood of their owners, the treatment of slaves could be brutal. As their owner's property, they could be severely punished or sexually exploited.[5]

The situation of a runaway slave in the Roman Empire was especially precarious. According to Peter Stuhlmacher, a runaway had five alternatives: (1) join a band of outlaws, (2) disappear in the subculture of a large city, (3) flee to the hinterlands, (4) be hired by a farmer or craftsman, or (5) seek asylum in a temple and hope to be

---

5. See S. Scott Bartchy, "Slavery: Greco-Roman," in *Anchor Bible Dictionary,* ed. David Noel Freedman (Garden City, NY: Doubleday, 1992), 6:65–73; Jennifer A. Glancy, *Slavery in Early Christianity* (Minneapolis: Fortress, 1966), and *Slavery as Moral Problem in the Early Church and Today* (Minneapolis: Fortress, 2011).

taken as a slave by a more humane owner. Stuhlmacher comments, "Astonishingly, Onesimus chooses none of these ways. Instead he turns to Paul for help, presumably having heard of him in his master's house."[6]

As a Roman citizen, Paul would be fully aware that Roman law required that a runaway slave be returned to his owner. Roman law also provided that someone might act as intercessor for a slave in some kind of trouble with the owner and plead for a measure of restraint or even leniency.[7] Paul's awareness of the legal complexities surrounding slaves separated from their owners may help to explain his careful choice of words and his insistence that his appeal is based not on law but on love.

We would like to know far more than we do about the events leading up to Paul's letter. Much remains unknown. What was the underlying aim of Paul's intervention? How was the letter received by Philemon and the house church in Colossae to which it was sent? What was the history of the relationship between Philemon and Onesimus? Did Onesimus run away, as has been assumed traditionally, and if so, why? Had he committed some wrong, such as stealing, as many commentators have speculated, or might he have left his master simply because he yearned for his freedom? Why did Onesimus look to Paul for help? Did Philemon and the church in his house know that Onesimus was with Paul? Had they, as some commentators suggest, in fact sent him to assist Paul in his work?

While questions like these abound, the answers of biblical scholars are varied and inconclusive. The present commentary is primarily interested in the theological, pastoral, and ethical significance of the letter. Far from being a marginal piece of first-century correspondence of little abiding value, the Letter to Philemon is a noteworthy member of the Pauline literary corpus, a part of the Christian canon of Scripture, and a text with surprising relevance for Christian life and ministry today.

---

6. Peter Stuhlmacher, Der Brief an Philemon (Zurich: Benziger/Neukirchener Verlag, 1975), 22–23.
7. For the text of the often-cited example of the letter of Pliny the Younger to Sabinianus, see Joseph A. Fitzmyer, The Letter to Philemon (New York: Doubleday, 2000), 20–23.

Brief History of Interpretation

From Chrysostom to Calvin

At least since John Chrysostom, the dominant interpretation of the letter by theologians and preachers has been that Onesimus was a slave who had stolen money or goods from Philemon, his master, and then run away. After Onesimus met Paul, was converted, and then was allowed to serve the apostle for a time, Paul sent him back to his owner with an appeal that the runaway, now a Christian, be treated in a compassionate manner and welcomed home despite his earlier disobedience and thievery. From the perspective of the traditional reading of the letter, it is unthinkable that Paul would have even hinted at the manumission of Onesimus.

Since aiding or abetting runaway slaves was illegal in the Roman Empire, it is understandable that Chrysostom and other writers of the patristic era were concerned that Christians who sympathized with the runaways or encouraged their manumission were putting the reputation of Christianity at risk. As Chrysostom writes, "We ought not to withdraw slaves from the service of their masters. For if Paul, who had such confidence in Philemon, was unwilling to detain Onesimus, so useful and serviceable to minister to himself, without the consent of his master, much less ought we so to act."[8] Basil the Great (330–379) is still more explicit: "All bound slaves who flee to religious communities for refuge should be admonished and sent back to their masters in better dispositions, after the example of St. Paul who, although he had begotten Onesimus through the gospel, sent him back to Philemon."[9]

Readings of Philemon from this socially conservative perspective remained the standard not only for patristic and medieval theologians, but also for the sixteenth-century Reformers. Although Martin Luther movingly writes that "we are all his [Christ's] Onesimus's if we believe,"[10]

---

8. Chrysostom, *Homilies on Philemon*, 546.
9. Basil, *The Long Rules*, Q.2.R, cited in *Colossians, 1–2 Thessalonians,1–2 Timothy, Titus, Philemon*, ACCS, New Testament 9, ed. Peter Gorday (Downers Grove, IL: InterVarsity Press, 2000), 314.
10. Martin Luther, "Preface to the Epistle of St. Paul to Philemon," in *Word and Sacrament* 1, ed. E. Theodore Bachmann, LW 35 (Philadelphia: Fortress, 1960), 390.

he also contends that Onesimus is an example of the misuse of freedom, of refusing to do the duty of a slave in the calling that God has assigned to him. Not surprisingly, the Letter to Philemon became for Luther a "trump card" in his battle against the revolutionary spiritualists of the Reformation period.[11] Although John Calvin's theology is on the whole more socially progressive than Luther's, he is equally explicit in rejecting any interpretation of Paul's letter that might encourage Christians to challenge established social institutions such as slavery. "The faith of the Gospel," Calvin says, "does not overthrow civil order or cancel the rights of masters over their slaves."[12]

In Antebellum America

The question of the proper interpretation of the Letter to Philemon became part of the great slavery controversy in mid-nineteenth-century America. Defenders of slavery found in the letter explicit biblical support of the legitimacy of the institution. They saw it as particularly relevant to the controversial Fugitive Slave Act of 1850 mandating that runaway slaves be returned to their legal owners. Critics of slavery, on the contrary, argued that this reading of the letter contravened both its spirit and the spirit of the gospel.

The Southerner James Thornwell and the Northerner Charles Hodge, two of the most highly respected theologians of the period, agreed that although the abuse of slaves was deplorable and contrary to biblical teachings, the Bible nowhere unconditionally condemns the institution of slavery. Both were sharply critical of what they considered the illegitimate demands of the abolitionists. Both endorsed the Fugitive Slave Act as the law of the land that must be obeyed. As late as 1861, Joseph Ruggles Wilson, a pastor in Augusta, Georgia, and father of the future president Woodrow Wilson wrote that Paul "did not hesitate to urge Onesimus to go at once to his master, confess at his feet the grievous fault he had committed, and beg to be received once more among the number

11. Barth and Blanke, *Philemon,* 206.
12. Calvin, *Philemon,* 400–401.

of his slaves."[13] In the eyes of the pro-slavery lobby in the antebellum South, Paul's Letter to Philemon was sometimes referred to as "the Pauline Mandate."

Anti-slavery writers also tried to find support for their cause in the letter because it was potentially "the most dangerous book in the entire Bible."[14] Their arguments, however, frequently lacked the exegetical rigor of their opponents. They contended that the Bible should be read for the timeless truths it contains, such as the Golden Rule, or that Paul had planted the seed of the gospel with the confidence that it would grow secretly and eventually destroy the institution of slavery. Defenders of slavery called such arguments specious attempts to circumvent what the biblical text actually says. Increasingly forced to cede the field of a literal reading of the Bible to the pro-slavery camp, a number of abolitionists eventually found it necessary to rest their opposition to slavery not on the Bible but on what they considered self-evident moral truths.

On the eve of the Civil War, the positions of the two camps were clearly irreconcilable. As historian Mark Noll has argued, the crisis that led to the Civil War was more than a social and political crisis; it was also a theological crisis, a crisis in the interpretation of the Bible and its authority in American public life. From the founding of the nation, it was assumed that the Bible provided authoritative religious guidance for the American experiment. In the decades leading to the war, this assumption was profoundly shaken. Biblical scholars and pastors could not agree whether the Bible condoned or condemned the institution of slavery. According to Noll, it was the force of arms, not a consensus about the teachings of the Bible, that finally decided the matter.[15]

13. Larry J. Kreitzer, *Philemon* (Sheffield: Sheffield Phoenix Press, 2008), 103.
14. J. Albert Harrill, *Slaves in the New Testament: Literary, Social, and Moral Dimensions* (Minneapolis: Fortress, 2006), 168.
15. Mark A. Noll, *The Civil War as a Theological Crisis* (Chapel Hill: University of North Carolina Press, 2006). For the persistence of forms of neoslavery in the Southern states after the Civil War, see Douglas A. Blackmon, *Slavery by Another Name: The Re-Enslavement of Black Americans from the Civil War to World War II* (New York: Anchor, 2009).

In the Modern Era

While the advance of historical and literary studies of the Bible in the modern period has shed new light on the context and significance of Paul's Letter to Philemon, a wide spectrum of interpretations remains.

At one pole of the spectrum are interpreters who contend that the freedom of which Paul speaks is "spiritual and eschatological" and does not bear directly on worldly institutions like slavery. Paul makes no bid for the manumission of Onesimus in the Letter to Philemon. Those in Christ are already free, whether their temporal condition is that of master or slave.[16]

At the opposite pole of the spectrum are commentators who read the letter as having an unmistakably liberationist intent. They contend that Paul goes well beyond seeking leniency for Onesimus or simply venturing faint hints at manumission. According to these scholars, the central purpose of the letter is to secure the freedom of Onesimus and arrange his return to Paul as an assistant in the work of the gospel. A basic claim of this liberationist reading is its congruence with the passionate declarations of freedom in Christ that pervade Paul's theology (e.g., "There is no longer Jew or Greek, there is no longer slave or free, there is no longer male and female; for all of you are one in Christ Jesus," Gal. 3:28; cf. Gal. 5:1; 1 Cor. 7:21).[17]

Most modern biblical scholars stand somewhere between the traditionalist and the liberationist readings of the letter. They cautiously entertain the *possibility* that Paul wanted Philemon to set Onesimus free. Even if Paul does not explicitly ask Philemon to set Onesimus free and leaves open the question of how Philemon should deal with Onesimus in the near future, the apostle clearly hopes that Philemon will freely decide out of love to do "more" than Paul has asked for.[18]

---

16. John Nordling, *Philemon* (St. Louis: Concordia, 2004), offers an extensive defense of this more traditional view of the letter with the assistance of Luther's theology of the two realms (worldly and spiritual) in which Christians exist.
17. Richard Horsley surveys efforts to read the letter to Philemon as a call to free Onesimus. "Paul and Slavery: A Critical Alternative to Recent Readings," *Semeia* 83–84 (1998): 153–200.
18. Joseph Fitzmyer, I. H. Marshall, N. T. Wright, and Peter Stuhlmacher are among NT scholars who think it possible, though far from certain, that Paul hints at manumission of Onesimus.

Many scholars judge that preoccupation with the issue of slavery can obscure the deeper meaning and perennial significance of the letter. In their view, what the letter is primarily about is "the difference the transforming power of the gospel can make in the lives and relationships of believers, regardless of class or other distinctions."[19] This is not to say, however, that nothing can be gathered from the letter about Paul's attitude toward the institution of slavery. Even if Paul is an evangelist rather than a social reformer in the modern sense, the import of his message in this, as in his other letters, is incompatible with the enslavement of some human beings by others.[20]

For other interpreters, the argument about whether Paul is a budding liberationist or a staunch social conservative on the matter of slavery can easily miss the importance of *how* Paul goes about presenting his appeal. Paul is a skillful rhetorician who carefully chooses his language and strategy to achieve his encompassing purpose of reconciliation and liberation. To modern readers who understandably wish that Paul had given a more robust protest against unjust and inhuman institutions like slavery, Ben Witherington offers this reminder: "The letter to Philemon raises in an acute way the whole question of what sort of means can and will achieve great and good ends, and what sort will amount to raging against the machine without effect. The answer lies in part in the art of effective persuasion, and of course also in the grace of God."[21]

The Letter to Philemon Read as Scripture

As evident from the controversies swirling around its interpretation, the Letter to Philemon confronts its readers in an acute way with the question of the proper reading and interpretation of the Bible. What does it mean to live in accordance with the witness of Scripture? Does the Bible speak clearly and with one voice on all matters? Is it unanimous, for example, about how the church should order its life,

---

19. Cain Felder, "Philemon," in *New Interpreter's Bible* (Nashville: Abingdon, 2000), 11:885.
20. Ibid., 887.
21. Ben Witherington III, *The Letters to Philemon, the Colossians, and the Ephesians: A Socio-Rhetorical Commentary on the Captivity Epistles* (Grand Rapids: Eerdmans, 2007), 96.

or about what role the church should play in the struggles for justice and peace in the wider society?

Modern historical-critical study contributes much to our understanding of the biblical writings. It illuminates the circumstances of the biblical writers, the richness of their witness, and the meaning their words carried in their own historical context. What historical scholarship cannot do, however, is give definitive answers to the question of the proper interpretation and use of the Bible as the word of God for our own time. This becomes especially evident when the controversy centers on social or political issues that the biblical writers did not and could not themselves have addressed. The Bible is for the church the living word of God. Reading the Bible as Scripture means reading it not only with literary care and historical understanding but also with expectancy, trust, and imagination as bearer of the living word of God for us today.[22]

What assumptions are appropriate to bring to a theological reading of the book of Philemon? If reading it merely as a historical document is rejected, should we read it as an infallible text that can be understood without historical sensitivity or imaginative reappropriation? Is a theological interpretation of Scripture as living word of God a matter of simple transference of particular biblical texts to our own time? Shall we assume, for example, that since neither Jesus nor Paul explicitly condemns the institution of slavery, we should not condemn it either? We must say a clear no to all of these questions. Responsible biblical interpretation will take into account the changing contexts in which the church conveys the gospel message and engages in its mission. While Paul did not directly challenge the institution of slavery in the secular domain, he preached a message of reconciliation that calls for a new social order in the life of the church—a new way of being human in community by the grace of God—that bears concrete corporate witness to God's coming reign of peace, justice, and freedom throughout the earth.

In the Letter to Philemon we find the brief account of an estrangement and a call to reconciliation. The story that this letter tells, however, cannot be rightly grasped unless it is seen in the light of the

---

22. Ellen F. Davis and Richard B. Hays, eds., *The Art of Reading Scripture* (Grand Rapids: Eerdmans, 2003).

overarching biblical story of God's reconciliation of the world in the ministry, death, and resurrection of Jesus Christ.[23] A study of the Letter to Philemon thus highlights the fact that the Bible characteristically provides us with neither a set of abstract doctrines nor an exhaustive system of ethical rules to be

> Reading Scripture in faith is reading it as moving towards or around a unifying narrative moment, the story of the work of Jesus.
>
> Rowan Williams, *On Christian Theology* (London: Blackwell, 2000), 56.

mechanically followed. Instead, its witness directs us to the living God decisively revealed in Jesus Christ and still at work through the power of the Word and Spirit for the renewal and transformation of all things. In our reading of Scripture, as in all things, we are summoned to trust in Christ, to have what Paul calls in Philippians the mind of Christ (Phil. 2:5), and to follow him in new times and situations of Christian discipleship.

Some scholars speak repeatedly of the ambiguity of the Letter to Philemon. I would speak instead of the intriguing openness of the appeal that comprises the heart of this remarkable text. By *openness* I mean something altogether different from moral relativism or guarded neutrality on great moral issues like slavery. Rather, the Letter to Philemon remains open in the disturbing way that the ending of the Gospel of Mark remains open to its readers' response and decision. As many scholars have noted, the ending of Mark's Gospel does not provide a neat closure to his story.[24] Absent an appearance of the risen Jesus on Easter morning and given instead a promise of meeting him in Galilee, readers must decide whether they will take up their cross and follow the crucified and risen Jesus with fear and amazement but also in faith and hope. For the evangelist Mark, God alone can ultimately bring closure to the story. In the meantime, we are called to discipleship.[25]

23. See Richard Bauckham, "Reading Scripture as a Coherent Story," in Davis and Hays, *Art of Reading Scripture,* 38–53.
24. See especially Donald H. Juel, *The Gospel of Mark* (Nashville: Abingdon, 1999). "Endings are important because they do something to readers" (171).
25. See Brian K. Blount, "Is the Joke on Us? Mark's Irony, Mark's God, and Mark's Ending," in *The Ending of Mark and the Ends of God: Essays in Memory of Donald Harrisville Juel,* ed. Beverly Roberts Gaventa and Patrick Miller (Louisville, KY: Westminster John Knox Press, 2005), 15–32.

In a similar way, Paul's brief letter finally confronts not only Philemon and the church in his house but also members of the church today with the question of how *we* will bring Paul's appeal on behalf of Onesimus to an appropriate ending in our own attitudes and actions on matters of human dignity and social justice in the light of the gospel of Jesus Christ. Human slavery of numerous sorts—one need only think of the worldwide sex trade or child labor practices in many lands—is still very much with us. Just as the Gospel of Mark leaves us with the disturbing question of how *we* will respond to the open mystery of the crucified and risen Jesus of Nazareth narrated by the evangelist, so Paul's Letter to Philemon continues to unsettle and provoke us by asking how *we* will respond to Paul's passionate appeal to Philemon and to all the people of God then and now to welcome Onesimus—and all of our brothers and sisters—and to share with them "all the good" that we have in Christ, gladly doing "even more" than what Paul explicitly requested. In the final analysis, this is why the church should wrestle with the Letter to Philemon and why it should do so now.

1–3

Greetings

Verse 1. As in his other correspondence, Paul follows the formal pattern of salutations of his time by first identifying himself, naming the person or community to whom he is writing, and then extending greetings to them (which in Paul's case takes the form of offering "grace ... and peace from God our Father and the Lord Jesus Christ").

In this letter Paul describes himself not as an "apostle" (*apostolos*), as in the opening of many of his letters, nor as a "slave" (*doulos*), as in the salutations in Romans and Philippians, but as a "prisoner [*desmios*] of Christ Jesus." Use of the word "prisoner" is not aimed at awakening pity in his readers. On the contrary, Paul considers his sufferings a mark of honor rather than a cause for remorse or pity. Indeed, his multiple sufferings for Christ were the one thing about which he was prepared to "boast" when he encountered folk who insisted on boasting according to human standards (2 Cor. 11:16–30). As used here, *prisoner* has a double meaning: Paul is of course a prisoner in the sense of physical confinement; more important, however, he is a captive of Christ Jesus and belongs to him, body and soul. Hence the self-description can be translated either "prisoner *of* Christ Jesus" (expressing Paul's view of himself as a captive of Christ) or "prisoner *for* Christ Jesus" (meaning that Paul's imprisonment is due to his labor on behalf of the gospel). The two translations express the personal and vocational aspects of Paul's total dedication to Christ. Moreover, it is possible that in calling himself a prisoner, Paul is expressing his solidarity with the vulnerable person on whose behalf he is writing. As Markus Barth and Helmut Blanke note, "In brief, his state as a captive places Paul at the side of the slave rather than of the master."[1]

To his own name as sender, Paul adds the name of Timothy "our brother." As in Philippians, where the name of Timothy is also set alongside Paul's, the point is not that Timothy is coauthor of the letter but that Paul is not alone in his ministry. He has beloved and respected coworkers and assistants beside him. Ministry for Paul is a team effort rather than an endeavor undertaken by a solitary individual.

Verse 2. The addressees of the letter are Philemon "our dear friend and co-worker," Apphia "our sister," Archippus "our fellow soldier," and "the church in your house." Whether Apphia is Philemon's wife and Archippus their son, as some commentators speculate, is uncertain. Equally uncertain is the suggestion that the terms "co-worker," "sister," and "fellow soldier" might represent different church functions.[2] In any case, far more important is Paul's friendly and grateful description of his addressees. He knows them well and honors their friendship and their labors for the gospel.

Most noteworthy of all, however, is Paul's inclusion of "the church in your house" among those to whom he is writing. This is far more than a courtesy on Paul's part.[3] By including "the church in your house" as one of the addressees at the beginning of the letter, Paul signals that the matter of Onesimus, about which the letter is primarily concerned, is not a purely private affair between Onesimus and Philemon and a few of his kin or close associates. Paul is also addressing all the members of the house church, with the implication that all are expected to be involved in the response that is given to the letter. In this way, Philemon is made accountable to the church, and the church is made to bear some responsibility for the action he takes. As Richard Hays states, "Paul insists on laying the decision-making process open to the community's scrutiny."[4] Paul's theological and moral concerns in this letter thus have a communal as well as a personal dimension.

1. Markus Barth and Helmut Blanke, *The Letter to Philemon* (Grand Rapids: Eerdmans, 2000), 244.
2. Sara Winter, "Paul's Letter to Philemon," *New Testament Studies* 33 (1987): 1.
3. Peter O'Brien, *Colossians, Philemon,* Word Biblical Commentary 44 (Waco, TX: Word Books, 1982), 274.
4. Richard B. Hays, *The Moral Vision of the New Testament: Community, Cross, New Creation; A Contemporary Introduction to New Testament Ethics* (San Francisco: Harper, 1996), 57 n. 45.

Verse 3. Paul now extends his blessing to the readers. It is a serious mistake to assume that the opening blessing in any of Paul's letters is a purely formal and thus largely empty routine. The mistake would be especially ruinous in the reading of this letter. At the deepest level, the letter is a matter of remembering the source of all "grace" and "peace" and what difference grace and peace make in our common life. The letter has as one of its major aims the achievement of genuine peace and reconciliation between those who are estranged not only from each other but to that extent also from the "God of peace" (Phil. 4:9) who works reconciliation through Christ (cf. 2 Cor. 5:18). In his opening blessing, Paul places the letter and its appeal on behalf of the slave Onesimus in the wider framework of the all-transforming gift of grace and peace "from God our Father and the Lord Jesus Christ." As this letter demonstrates, Paul is not only a stalwart proclaimer but also an exemplary practitioner of the gospel of reconciliation and new life in Christ.

FURTHER REFLECTIONS
House Churches

The original gatherings of Christians were not in picturesque white church buildings in the village square, in tall steepled churches in cities or suburbs, or in impressive stone or crystal cathedrals. When Christians were no longer welcome in temples and synagogues, they met in the homes of members able and willing to be host or hostess. Only after Constantine I embraced Christianity and ended state persecution of the new faith movement in 312 CE were church buildings erected.

Embedded in the phenomenon of early Christian house churches is a distinctive ecclesiology. Although belonging to different groups and classes of the larger society, including women, slaves, and the poor, members of these early Christian congregations were bound

> It was precisely the heterogeneity of status that characterized the Pauline Christian groups.
>
> Wayne A. Meeks, *The First Urban Christians: The Social World of the Apostle Paul* (New Haven, CT: Yale University Press, 1983), 79.

together by their faith in Christ. Whatever their background or status, all had received the gospel, all were baptized in the name of Jesus Christ, and all shared in the common meal their Lord had instructed them to observe on a regular basis. These practices could become matters of dispute in Paul's congregations (regarding baptism, see 1 Cor. 1:10–17; regarding the Lord's Supper, see 1 Cor. 11:17–22), but it is clear that Paul understood these practices as sealing the union of diverse believers with Christ and one another.

The meetings of first-century Christians in private homes no doubt raised the suspicions of other residents in the area. Unlike the Jewish community, the early Christian movement had no recognized status within the Roman Empire. Gathering to worship Jesus Christ as Lord made the early Christians deviants from the loyalties and practices of the recognized religious groupings and most emphatically from the official cult of the emperor.

As for organization, the early Christian house churches had no clear division between clergy and laity. Only later did this division come to characterize ecclesial organization. There were, of course, leaders of the church—Philemon being an obvious example—but their leadership was based on recognized gifts and special resources rather than on institutionalized roles.

Members of the house churches were clearly committed to sharing the gospel with others. As virtually all of Paul's letters indicate, these small congregations supported his missionary endeavors with money and helpers. Paul's suggestion to Philemon that Onesimus be allowed to return to continue to help him in his imprisonment is clearly part of a larger pattern of support that Paul received from many of the house churches.

As previously noted, Paul's inclusion of "the church in your house" among the addressees of his letter constitutes a call to common responsibility and lifts the letter out of the mistaken category of purely private correspondence. All members of Philemon's community are summoned to assume their part in the decision that Philemon faces even as he in turn is made accountable to them. In other words, "All those present are expected to hear the reading of the letter, to ponder its substance, and to assist one another in making decisions and taking actions."[5]

Paul's expectation of corporate as well as personal responsibility in congregational life poses challenging questions for churches today. Is the life of many twenty-first-century congregations characterized by an ethos of passivity and an absence of voice among its members? Is the pastor or church council or church session expected to take responsibility for most of the important decisions in the life of the church without any significant participation by a majority of its members? Even if there are opportunities for church members to meet for prayer, Scripture study, and fellowship, do such meetings also include opportunities for members to take their share of responsibility for deliberating on pressing social and ethical issues facing the church and the wider society and considering possible courses of faithful witness and action?

The gathering of small groups of Christians to pray, study Scripture, and assist one another in addressing both personal and wider social issues from the perspective of their common faith is often a mark of Christian life in countries where Christians remain a comparatively small minority or are the target of persecution. Such contemporary house churches have helped many of their members to find deeper friendships and a sense of belonging. Beyond this, they have learned that being a Christian is far more than being a mere consumer or observer of religious rites and practices. To be a Christian is to become a responsible participant of life in Christ, with all that this entails in mutual care and love of neighbor. It is this call to active participation in and common responsibility for the witness and service of the church that is the real theological significance of Paul's reference to "the church in your house" in his Letter to Philemon.

The prospects of friendliness and intimacy associated with small house churches may offer an appealing contrast to the impersonal and bureaucratic nature of many large, established churches. It is easy, however, to overstate the strengths of house churches and overlook their temptations. In modern urban or suburban settings

---

5. Barth and Blanke, *Philemon*, 263.

they can become the domain of a privatized version of Christian faith with only like-minded members.

The film *Higher Ground* portrays the experience of a woman of faith in a close-knit evangelical house church. For a period of time, her life is enriched in many ways by belonging to the group, but she gradually finds the rules and expectations of the group to be confining and to restrict her growth in the life of faith. A sensitive person, she is unable to express her questions and doubts freely when conflicts arise or tragedy strikes. As much as she wants to belong to the tightly knit group, she has a sense of being unwelcome unless she conforms to what is considered the only right way of experiencing and thinking about her relationship to God. As a result, she becomes a reluctant outsider to friends and family members.

Paul's real challenge to the church in Philemon's house and to churches today is not a call to comforting intimacy and group conformity. The challenge is of a totally different order. It has to do with the shared responsibility of all members of the community for the integrity of its own life in Christ and for the faithfulness of its witness to all people of God's work of reconciliation, justice, and freedom proclaimed in the gospel.

4–7

Thanksgiving

Verses 4–5. Before making his appeal on behalf of Onesimus, Paul begins by thanking God for Philemon's love for all the saints and for his faith in Christ. By beginning the letter in this way, Paul sets his relationship to his friend in its proper theological context. While the love and faith that Paul commends are undeniably Philemon's own, they derive ultimately from a source greater than Philemon. If Paul seems to boast a bit about Philemon's exemplary witness, the boasting here, as everywhere in Paul's letters, is ultimately a boasting about the grace of God in Christ Jesus (Phil. 3:3; Rom. 3:27; 5:1–2; 1 Cor. 1:28–31). Paul's thanksgiving to God thus reminds Philemon that all that we are and do as Christians is grounded in God's gift to us in Christ and God's continuing work in us by the power of the Holy Spirit. Hence by commending Philemon's love and generosity and his strong faith in Christ, Paul is not indulging in idle praise. He is giving thanks to God for the evidence of the transforming work of the Spirit of Christ in the life of Philemon.

Many commentators have noted that the order of love and faith in this verse is unusual for Paul. Customarily he speaks first of faith and then of love, as he does, for example, in the Letter to the Romans, where he attends first to the meaning and importance of faith in chapters 1–8, followed by his exhortations to the life of love in chapters 12–15. In the Letter to Philemon, Paul probably mentions Philemon's love first because his primary concern here is not a defense of the act of faith from misunderstandings. Rather, it is to commend Philemon's practice of love to all the "saints" (*hagioi,* "holy ones"), that is, all who have faith in Christ and have been called to

207

his service.[1] Knowing that Philemon's love for others is rooted in his faith in Christ, Paul's letter is written in the confidence that his love will be extended to Onesimus as well.

Paul's rhetorical strategy in this letter has been the topic of considerable scholarly investigation in recent years. It is not hard to understand why. Paul is clearly eager to establish good rapport with Philemon. He wants to recognize and honor Philemon's service of the gospel before launching into an appeal that is bound to pose major difficulties for a slave owner who undoubtedly feels betrayed by the actions of his slave. Moreover, as the letter proceeds, the apostle will carefully choose his words and phrases to avoid appearing harsh or disrespectful. While all of this is true, there is more at work here and throughout the letter than clever diplomacy and rhetorical strategy. Paul is rhetorically skillful, but he is not devious. His prayers of gratitude for Philemon's works of love serve to spur on his "dear friend and co-worker" (v. 1) and prepare him for a new opportunity to demonstrate his love for and generosity to the saints.[2] At the same time, they will remind Philemon that the witness and service of every Christian are ultimately rooted not in our own virtue but in the grace of God.

Verse 6. Paul's prayer of thanksgiving to God not only sets the letter in an appropriate doxological context; it also anticipates the content of the letter. As biblical scholars have noted, the opening thanksgivings and prayers of Paul's letters set the tone and announce the theme of what follows.[3] In other words, Paul's prayers of thanksgiving are not mere pious prefaces; they lay the groundwork for the messages and appeals that are to come. In the case of the Letter to Philemon, Paul's thanksgiving prayer prepares for the appeal that he will soon be making on behalf of Onesimus.

1. In a Christian understanding of the word, being a "saint" is not equivalent to being morally perfect. Rather, saints are people whose love for others is rooted in the love of God. "Sainthood is not sheer will power . . . striving to accomplish a boundless task, but goodness overflowing from a boundless source." Robert M. Adams, "Saints," *Journal of Philosophy* 81 (1984): 396.
2. See Ben Witherington III, *The Letters to Philemon, the Colossians, and the Ephesians: A Socio-Rhetorical Commentary on the Captivity Epistles* (Grand Rapids: Eerdmans, 2007), 58.
3. See Paul Schubert, *The Form and Function of the Pauline Thanksgiving* (Berlin: Töpelmann, 1939); Peter T. O'Brien, *Introductory Thanksgivings in the Letters of Paul,* Supplements to Novum Testamentum 49 (Leiden: Brill, 1977).

Special attention should be given to verse 6, where Paul prays *for* Philemon. He prays not for someone whose faith is shaky or who has failed to heed the call to aid others in need. Rather he is praying for someone who is widely recognized

> **Even the most perfect men who deserve the highest praise need to be prayed for.**
>
> John Calvin, *Philemon*, CNTC, 10:394.

as a person of strong faith and an esteemed leader in his community. Whether strong or weak, healthy or sick, leader or follower, all need the prayers of their brothers and sisters in the faith. As the familiar hymn expresses it:

> God of the coming years, through paths unknown,
> We follow Thee.
> … … … … … …..
> When we are strong, Lord, leave us not alone,
> Our refuge be.[4]

The Greek of Paul's prayer for Philemon in verse 6 is compact and complex, and it has been translated in a number of ways.[5] The RSV translates: "I pray that the sharing of your faith may promote the knowledge of all the good that is ours in Christ." The NRSV translates: "I pray that the sharing of your faith may become effective when you perceive all the good that we may do for Christ."

At least three things stand out in these two translations. First, both emphasize that Christian faith includes a particular knowledge. Paul prays that the sharing of Philemon's faith "may promote the *knowledge* of all the good that is ours in Christ" (RSV), or that Philemon's sharing of faith "may become effective when you *perceive* all the good that we may do for Christ" (NRSV). Faith for Paul, in this and his other letters, is not reducible to warm feelings or mere opinions. It is instead a knowledge based on the revelation of the

---

4. Hugh Thomson Kerr, "God of Our Life," *Glory to God: The Presbyterian Hymnal* (Louisville, KY: Westminster John Knox Press, 2013), 686, stanza 3.
5. A translation "as comprehensive and multicolored as the Greek text of Philemon 6 has yet to be found." Markus Barth and Helmut Blanke, *The Letter to Philemon* (Grand Rapids: Eerdmans, 2000), 283.

saving activity of God in Jesus Christ proclaimed in the gospel and illumined to our hearts and minds by the Holy Spirit. Paul tells us that when he preached to the Corinthians, his sole purpose was to make known "Jesus Christ, and him crucified" (1 Cor. 2:2). Writing to the church in Rome, Paul reminds his readers that all Christians share the knowledge that the crucified Christ has been raised from the dead (Rom. 6:9). To be sure, in the time before the end, faith is only a partial knowledge (1 Cor. 13:12). Nevertheless, it is a knowledge well grounded and reliable. John Calvin's famous definition of faith is close to Paul's understanding: faith is "a firm and certain knowledge of God's benevolence toward us, founded upon the truth of the freely given promise in Christ, both revealed to our minds and sealed upon our hearts through the Holy Spirit."[6]

Second, for Paul the knowledge of faith is more than abstract theory or mere information. It is a knowledge that renews and transforms life. Note that Paul prays for Philemon's sharing of his faith to become "effective" (NRSV). That the knowledge of God in Christ is an effective, life-changing knowledge is a prominent motif in Pauline theology. When Paul speaks of the knowledge of God that comes by revelation—as when he encountered the risen Christ (Gal. 1:11–12)—he has in mind a knowledge that is creative and life renewing, not abstract and unproductive. Authentic knowledge of God issues in a new mind and a new way of life. It makes a real difference.

Third, the knowledge of which Paul speaks in this verse is the capacity to perceive "all the good that we may do for Christ" (NRSV), or alternately, a knowledge of "all the good that is ours in Christ" (RSV). The phrase "all the good" (*pantos agathou*) suggests that the reality of Christ is rich beyond measure and that our knowledge of and witness to the gospel of God's astonishing generosity toward us in Christ can and should grow. We are to enter into this knowledge ever more fully and become mature witnesses to the riches in Christ. The same point is eloquently expressed in another NT prayer attributed to Paul: "I pray that you may have the power to comprehend, with all the saints, what is the breadth and

---

6. John Calvin, *Institutes of the Christian Religion*, ed. John T. McNeill, trans. Ford Lewis Battles, LCC (Philadelphia: Westminster, 1960), 1:551.

length and height and depth, and to know the love of Christ that surpasses knowledge, so that you may be filled with all the fullness of God" (Eph. 3:18–19). With his reminder of "all the good" there is in Christ, Paul is suggesting that while Philemon has done well, he should not think that further progress in Christian faith and life is unnecessary. As for the difference between the translation of verse 6 by the RSV ("knowledge of all the good that is ours *in* Christ") and the NRSV (perception of "all the good that we may do *for* Christ"), the two translations are not mutually exclusive. Indeed, they belong together. Being *in* Christ is inseparable from a life *for* Christ.

Verse 7. By refreshing or renewing the hearts of the saints, Philemon's love has given Paul "joy and encouragement." Paul rejoices that Philemon's love has deeply touched the lives of others—literally has penetrated to their bowels (*splanchna*) or to the very core of their being, reviving and strengthening their faith in the Lord. Here and everywhere in his writings, Paul's joy in the Lord is increased by the spreading of the gospel by coworkers like Philemon and by the transforming effect the gospel they are sharing is having in the lives of the saints. Note that there is no petty jealousy at work in Paul's reaction to the effects of Philemon's witness, no sly suggestion that if the apostle had been on the scene the result would have been even greater. Whenever the gospel is proclaimed and the works of love flourish, Paul rejoices. Before Paul makes his special appeal regarding Onesimus, he wants to honor and rejoice in Philemon's valuable service on behalf of the gospel.

As already suggested, the key phrase "all the good" in verse 6 deserves special attention. It arguably signals in advance the essence of the appeal that Paul will make in the remainder of the letter. In effect, he will appeal to Philemon not to limit his witness and work for the gospel to the good and commendable things he has already done. The appeal will be for continuing growth in Christian discipleship as Philemon learns to discern and seeks to practice "all the good" that is ours in Christ and that we can do for Christ.

Paul concludes his prayerful preface by calling Philemon "my brother." The position of these words at the very end of the sentence gives them added emphasis. "My brother" expresses the deep solidarity in Christ shared by Paul and Philemon. As we shall see, being

brothers in Christ will be important in Paul's exhortation to Philemon to receive also his slave Onesimus as a "beloved brother" (v. 16).

FURTHER REFLECTIONS
All the Good

Paul's prayer that the faith of his readers will become effective as they
discern "all the good" that is ours in Christ sets the bar high for Philemon and for us. Suppose Paul had limited the appeal he will make
to Philemon to his refraining from treating the returning slave Onesimus harshly, to refusing to punish him as was a master's right under
Roman law. There surely would have been some good in that, but "all
the good"? The apostle might have been content to urge Philemon
to forgive Onesimus of any wrong he may have done and welcome
him back into the household. Again, this would surely have counted
as a good deed. Paul, however, seems to pray for far more. He prays
that Philemon's faith and love might become effective as he discerns
"all the good" that we have in and may do for Christ. As Paul's later
comments in the letter suggest, "all the good" that Paul wanted Philemon to consider included sending Onesimus back to Paul to assist
him in his ministry. It may even have included giving Onesimus his
freedom. That Paul intended the latter continues to be debated, but
as we shall see, subtle hints in the letter and the way it is crafted
leave this possibility open. In any case, in our own time, Christians
must surely agree that "all the good" in and for Christ includes recognition of the dignity and freedom not only of Onesimus but of all
people created in God's image and redeemed by Christ.

Paul's opening prayer that points Philemon to all the good in
Christ underscores an important feature of Paul's theology. He is
the apostle best known for his doctrine of justification by faith, or
more precisely, justification by grace received by faith. This doctrine
is true and immensely important. However, God's gracious forgiveness of our sins and renewal of our communion with God and each
other is only part of Paul's gospel. For Paul, the message of justification has its goal in sanctification, in the renewal and transformation
of life, in participation in a new people of God, in a living faith that

through love issues in good works, in mature discipleship attentive to all the good that God has given to us in Jesus Christ.

Paul's references to what is "good" often occur in the form of exhortations: "Do not be conformed to this world, but be transformed by the renewing of your minds, so that you may discern what is the will of God—what is good and acceptable and perfect" (Rom. 12:2); "Do not be overcome by evil, but overcome evil with good" (Rom. 12:21). The good for Paul, however, is not in the first place a moral imperative or a task to be accomplished. Rather, it is primarily a description of the reality and work of God. All that is good has its source in God, who is the supreme good. "In all things God works for good for those who love God, who are called according to his purpose" (Rom. 8:28). Paul's conviction is that the goodness of God has been decisively revealed by the love of God in Jesus Christ (Rom. 8:31–39), by the pouring of this love into our hearts by the Holy Spirit (Rom. 5:5), and by the promise that the "good work" God has begun in us will be brought to completion by the day of Jesus Christ (Phil. 1:6).

All this is to say that what is supremely good for Paul is not a product of the human imagination or humanity's highest moral ideal; it is instead the living and acting God. In Paul's theology, God's boundless love become incarnate in Jesus Christ defines the supreme good. The love of God in Christ reveals that God *is* good, that what God *does* is good, and that God *wills* our participation in God's own overflowing goodness by living and acting in ways that correspond freely and gladly to that goodness. Clearly for Paul, it is in Jesus Christ that "all the good" is to be found.

Paul's remarkable prayer that Philemon may promote "all the good that is ours in Christ" (RSV) and perceive "all the good that we may do for Christ" (NRSV) is important for the proper understanding of Christian faith and life today. In the first place, it underscores that the God of the gospel that Paul proclaims is far greater than all our moral strivings or moral ideals. In God's own triune life and in God's relationship to the world, God is supremely good, freely sharing life and love with others.[7] The incomparable goodness of God finds

---

7. Karl Barth, *CD* IV/2:755: "The statements 'God is' and 'God loves' are synonymous."

expression in several core Christian doctrines: the triune reality of God; God's creation of the world out of nothing; the redemptive ministry and sacrificial death of Jesus Christ; and the outpouring of the Holy Spirit and the gifts of the Spirit to all members of the body of Christ. God is not a lonely nomad who dwells in utter solitariness. The true God lives and acts in the sharing of life and love.

Then, too, as has been emphasized, all the good we have been given in Christ is not something that Paul urges us only to *think* about or merely to make an object of sublime contemplation. For Paul the good we have as a gift in Christ is a reality that God intends for us to participate in and to share with others. It is a gift not to be hoarded but to be lived out. If our lives are to be a fitting response to God's "indescribable gift" (2 Cor. 9:15) in Jesus Christ, we will "bear fruit in every good work" (Col. 1:10). Christian faith is in the first place a receptive act; it is acknowledging and receiving the gracious gift of God in Christ. But genuine faith is not moribund; it is accompanied by love; it issues in doing as well as believing; it is "faith working through love" (Gal. 5:6).

Moreover, the singularity of all the good that is in Christ, the richness of the life that he is and offers, always surpasses what we know and do as his followers. All the good that is now ours in Christ is also always ahead of us. There is always more. Our participation in the love of God in Christ is always incomplete and flawed. Sanctification is a dynamic and continuing process. Honestly recognizing that we have not yet reached the goal of what God intends for us and for all God's children increases our readiness to bear witness to and serve Christ in new and risky ways.

> **The temptation today is not so much that humans want to play God. It is much more that they no longer have confidence in the humanity which God expects of them.**
>
> Jürgen Moltmann, *In the End—The Beginning* (Minneapolis: Fortress, 2004), 93.

One of the great temptations for Christians and for the church as a whole is complacency. This temptation may be distantly related to the sin of sloth, one of the traditional seven deadly sins. However, complacency may be the more apt way of describing what so often fights against robust Christian witness and service. It is not that we are lazy and inactive. It is that we quickly become satisfied that we have already progressed far enough in our Christian life, or perhaps that circumstances do not permit our witness for Christ and for the justice and peace of his reign to go any further. In our complacency we forget Paul's prayer to perceive "all the good" that is ours in Christ and that we may do for Christ.

Again, Paul's exhortation to discern and pursue all the good in and for Christ has the purpose of building up the church. Paul closely associates doing good with loving our neighbor and strengthening the body of Christ. When Paul speaks of the gifts of the Spirit, he emphasizes that each gift is given for "the common good" (1 Cor. 12:7). In another place he writes: "Each of us must please our neighbor for the good purpose of building up the neighbor" (Rom. 15:2). James Dunn is surely right in concluding that for Paul "the good is to be identified as the same as that which builds up the church."[8]

However, Paul goes still further. His understanding of all the good that is in Christ is not confined to the church. He extends his exhortation to act for the good of others to include all people—even if he adds "especially" to members of the church. "Whenever we have an opportunity, let us work for the good of all, and especially for those of the family of faith" (Gal. 6:10). Paul calls on the Thessalonians to "always seek to do good to one another and to all" (1 Thess. 5:15). If Christians are attentive to all the good that is in Christ, they will be in the vanguard of those who seek the good of the local church community, the worldwide church, and also the "common good" of

> The joys and hopes, the griefs and the anxieties of the [people] of this age, especially those who are poor or are in any way afflicted, these too are the joys and hopes, the griefs and anxieties of the followers of Christ.
>
> *Gaudium et Spes* (Pastoral Constitution on the Church in the Modern World), Vatican II.

humankind. Do churches today seek to further the good only of their own membership or of people of similar background and class? Or does their witness and service in the name of Christ embrace also strangers and the afflicted, especially the poor and the abused?

8. James D. G. Dunn, *The Theology of Paul the Apostle* (Grand Rapids: Eerdmans, 1998), 686.

In the preamble to the Constitution of the United States, an often-neglected clause declares that one of the great purposes of the formation of the new nation is to "promote the general welfare." Christians attuned to the biblical witness will recognize in such expressions of concern for the general welfare a welcome echo of the prophetic voices of Israel and of the teachings and ministry of Jesus. They will also discern that when Paul prays for Philemon— and all Christians—to bear witness in word and life to *all* the good that is ours in Christ and that we may do for him, this includes praying and working for the good of *all*.

8–14

Appeal for Onesimus

Verses 8–9. After giving thanks to God for Philemon's love and faith and praying for the continued effectiveness of his witness, Paul now states the reason for his letter. He explains that although he is "bold enough in Christ" to command Philemon to do what is right, he chooses instead to appeal to Philemon *dia ten agapen* ("on the basis of love" [NRSV] or "for love's sake" [RSV]). The love to which Paul refers here is not simply love in general. Just as his famous hymn of love in 1 Corinthians 13 has its basis in and takes its contours from the love of God manifest in Jesus

> Now faith, hope, and love abide, these three; and the greatest of these is love.
>
> (1 Cor. 13:13)

Christ, so also Paul's appeal to Philemon is rooted in and directed by Christ's own way of love. Because this great love of God in Christ empowers and takes form in shared human love, Paul's appeal out of love includes also Paul's own love for Philemon, the love binding together the new community that meets in Philemon's house, and Philemon's own love that he has shared with all the saints and that Paul now wants him to extend to Onesimus as well.

That Paul in this letter chooses to "appeal . . . on the basis of love" rather than simply issuing commands tells us that his characteristic pastoral demeanor is not arbitrary and dictatorial but encouraging and kind. To be sure, we know from his other letters that at times Paul had no hesitation in issuing commands to his readers (for example, in his instruction to the Corinthians regarding the relationships of husbands and wives, or the observance of the Lord's Supper, 1

Cor. 7:8–16; 11:17–22). Even in the Letter to Philemon, his appeal on the basis of love does not preclude his speaking in the imperative: "welcome him . . . charge that to my account . . . let me have this benefit . . . prepare a guest room for me" (vv. 17, 18, 20, 22).[1] Overall, however, Paul exercises pastoral leadership in the Letter to Philemon in a friendly and compassionate manner. As a pastor, he follows the way of Christ, who for our sake humbled himself (Phil. 2:5–8). Calvin comments: "By his example he teaches pastors to try to lead their pupils gently rather than drive them on."[2]

While Paul describes himself here with a word (*presbyteros*) that some translations render "old man" (NRSV), the word can also signify an "ambassador" (RSV) or elder, someone in a position of leadership in the church. Even if the translation "old man" is followed, the word should not suggest that Paul is playing on the heartstrings of Philemon by reminding him of his old age and the special respect he is owed on that account. Similarly, in calling himself for a second time a "prisoner" for Christ Jesus and in the next verse (10) alluding again to his imprisonment, Paul is not asking for sympathy. Rather, he is presenting himself, like the person for whom he will make his appeal, as in a vulnerable condition. Being vulnerable for the sake of the well-being of others, however, is precisely the kind of paradoxical lordship exercised by the crucified Christ and the fitting mark of an apostle. In other letters Paul refers to his many sufferings for Christ as confirmation of his apostolic calling and authority (cf. 2 Cor. 11:16–12:10).

Verse 10. Paul now presents the substance of his appeal for his "child," Onesimus. Up to this point he has wisely avoided naming Onesimus without first expressing his thanks for Philemon's labors for the gospel and then praying for the effectiveness of his future service. Now, however, he identifies Onesimus by name and speaks of him as a child he has fathered (literally, "whom I have begotten"). In this way, Paul discloses that Onesimus has become a Christian through Paul's own witness and instruction. Naturally, this does not

1. Markus Barth and Helmut Blanke, *The Letter to Philemon* (Grand Rapids: Eerdmans, 2000), 378.
2. John Calvin, *The Second Epistle of Paul to the Corinthians, and the Epistles to Timothy, Titus and Philemon,* CNTC 10, ed. David W. Torrance and Thomas F. Torrance (1964; repr., Grand Rapids: Eerdmans, 1979), 396.

mean that Paul is taking credit for converting Onesimus, any more than he takes credit for converting anyone else. He considers himself simply the agent of the work of God, who alone brings about conversion. As he writes elsewhere: "What then is Apollos? What is Paul? Servants through whom you came to believe, as the Lord assigned to each. I planted, Apollos watered, but God gave the growth" (1 Cor. 3:5–6). At the same time, as "father" of Onesimus in Christ, Paul willingly assumes responsibility for the future growth and well-being of his "child." With Onesimus, as with all his "children," Paul experiences the "pain of childbirth" until "Christ is formed" in him (Gal. 4:19).[3] In this tender language of child and parent, Paul shows his concern that not only Philemon but also Onesimus, now a Christian, may discern and bring to fruition all the good that they have in Christ and may do for him. Familial language is pervasive in this brief letter. In addition to "child" and "father," "brother" appears several times. Paul will later emphasize that Philemon and Onesimus are truly "brothers" in Christ.

Verse 11. The name *Onesimus* literally means "useful." Playing on this meaning, Paul says that because of Onesimus's period of separation he had become "useless" in Philemon's eyes. In other words, he was simply not around to perform the services expected of him. Now, however, having become a Christian and acted as a helper to Paul in his imprisonment, the behavior of Onesimus once again matches his name. He has now become "useful" to both Philemon and Paul. As Paul will soon explain, so useful has Onesimus become to him that he would like to keep him as his assistant. Philemon, too, would gain from this arrangement since Onesimus would be serving as Philemon's personal representative in Paul's gospel ministry.

This remarkable turnaround—that the "useless" Onesimus has become "useful" to both Paul and Philemon—would be no surprise to Paul, steeped as he was in the biblical tradition. God specializes in making good use of people considered by others or by themselves as useless. Was this not the case with Moses ("Who am I that I should go to Pharaoh?"); David ("When the Philistine looked and saw David, he disdained him, for he was only a youth"); Paul ("I am the

---

3. On the metaphors of child and father, see the discussion by John G. Nordling, *Philemon* (St. Louis: Concordia, 2004), 235.

least of the apostles, unfit to be called an apostle, because I persecuted the church of God"); Mary ("How can this be, since I am a
virgin?"); even and especially Jesus ("Can anything good come out
of Nazareth?").

Verse 12. Although Paul loves Onesimus and greatly values his
usefulness, the apostle recognizes that Philemon has legal rights over
the slave and so is sending him back. We have to assume that with
Paul's encouragement, Onesimus is willing and ready to go back to
Philemon's household, with all the risks this would likely entail. Paul
adds that in sending Onesimus back, he is sending his "very heart"
(RSV). This is one of the several occasions Paul expresses the depth
of his love for Onesimus. As noted previously, the word translated
"heart" (*splanchna*) refers literally to one's bowels or inward parts,
the seat of one's deepest passions, including compassion. Paul is saying that in sending Onesimus back to Philemon, he is sending part of
himself.[4] Karl Barth notes that the verb form of this word ("to have
compassion") is used in the Gospels to describe the depth of Jesus'
love and compassion for the leper (Mark 1:41), for the two blind
men at Jericho (Matt. 20:34), for the dead man and his mother at
Nain (Luke 7:13), for the hungry crowd in the wilderness (Mark
8:2), and for the Galilean masses with spiritual needs (Matt. 9:36).[5]
Paul's love for Onesimus corresponds to the compassion of Christ,
who for our sake humbled himself and assumed the condition of a
slave.

Verse 13. Scholars debate whether this verse contains, in indirect form, part of the request Paul is making of Philemon. He has
said earlier, "I, Paul . . . am appealing to you for my child, Onesimus" (v. 10). But what precisely is the content of Paul's request?
According to one commentator, "The letter is skillfully designed
to constrain Philemon to accept Paul's request, and yet at the same
time, it is extremely unclear what precisely Paul is requesting!"[6] But
is it "extremely unclear"? Without question, part of the appeal, as
we shall hear, is that Philemon should welcome Onesimus home

---

4. Joseph A. Fitzmyer, *The Letter to Philemon* (New York: Doubleday, 2000), 109.
5. Barth, *CD* III/2:211.
6. John M. G. Barclay, "Paul, Philemon and the Dilemma of Christian Slave-Ownership," *New
Testament Studies* 37 (1991): 170–71.

just as he would welcome Paul himself (v. 17). But there is more to Paul's appeal than this request. As previously noted, Onesimus has become so dear to Paul that he can be called "my own heart" (v. 12). Paul further adds that he really "wanted to keep him with me, so that he might be of service to me." Would it not be reasonable for a reader of these words to conclude that Paul is not only gently asking Philemon to treat Onesimus well and welcome him home but also asking that Onesimus be returned to him? When one makes a request of a friend, it is often done in an oblique way so as not to force the friend into compliance. This would be especially true if the request involved some circumvention of customary practices or expectations.

Philemon is further told that Onesimus could be of service to Paul in his imprisonment "in your place." Again, this sounds very much like Paul giving Philemon good reason to return Onesimus to him. Surely Philemon would want, if possible, to be with Paul, helping in any way he could. Paul then suggests that since that is not possible, Onesimus could act as Philemon's substitute, his personal representative, doing in Philemon's place what he himself would want to do for Paul if he had the opportunity. Note the idea of representation at work in Paul's suggestion here. Onesimus can act as representative of Philemon in the service of the gospel, and as we will later hear, Paul can stand in for Onesimus in repaying any financial debt he might have incurred.

Verse 14. Despite his express desire to have Onesimus by his side, Paul sends him back because he "preferred to do nothing" without Philemon's "consent." Consent means voluntary agreement or approval. Paul is convinced that in making his appeal to Philemon it is better to be patient and respect the Spirit of Christ at work in Philemon rather than using strong-arm tactics. That there are times when doing nothing can be creative and helpful, indeed an act of grace, is a wisdom that pragmatic Americans accustomed to getting problems resolved with dispatch find hard to accept. We are inclined to equate doing nothing with impotence, sloth, or cowardly neutrality. However, when it is an act of grace that respects the freedom of others and recognizes our own limitations in controlling the future, doing nothing is altogether different from a lack of concern or courage. Instead, it may signify a refusal to force oneself on another, a willingness to give the other time, a readiness to continue in prayer for the fresh guidance of the Spirit, and a pause to consider whether acting preemptively, even for an alleged good, may backfire and result in greater evil.

Paul "preferred to do nothing" so that Philemon's "good deed" would be voluntary rather than forced, an act of freedom rather than something Philemon would do because he felt obligated or compelled. The contours of this good deed are not described. We should recall, however, Paul's initial prayer that Philemon discern "all the good" we have in Christ and can do for him. Is the "good deed" (*agathon*) Paul speaks of here simply Philemon's forgiving Onesimus and welcoming him home? Is it freely returning Onesimus to Paul to continue his service with him? Might it even involve giving Onesimus his freedom? Is it all of the above? Although there is room for commentators to disagree, Paul has already hinted in the direction of what he would like Philemon to do, and further hints will follow. By leaving open the precise details of the good deed he expects of Philemon, Paul's appeal out of love is willing "to let love do its work, for love is resourceful enough to find the right way in accomplishing the good."[7]

FURTHER REFLECTIONS
Appeal Out of Love

Paul's ethics, in this and his other letters, is an ethics of "appeal on the basis of love," not an ethics of sheer "command" to do one's duty. In Romans, for example, Paul first proclaims the gospel, the message of what God has done for our justification and salvation (chaps. 1–8), and only on this basis calls his readers to do what is good, acceptable, and perfect, to love others, be patient, feed the hungry, give drink to the thirsty, and so forth (chaps. 12–15). Similarly, in Philippians, Paul sets forth the Christ hymn as the great paradigm of Christian life (2:5–8), and all the exhortations of the letter have their point of reference in this self-giving activity of Christ.

7. Eduard Lohse, *Colossians and Philemon* (Philadelphia: Fortress, 1971), 202.

The appeal that Paul makes in the Letter to Philemon follows this sequence of gospel first and law second. That is, he does not first accost Philemon with demands of what he must do. He does not rest his appeal on some universal categorical imperative, as might a Kantian moral philosopher. Instead, "it is characteristic of the ethics unfolded in Philemon that it can neither be understood nor implemented without recourse to the good news on which it relies and is to confirm."[8]

The proper relationship of law and gospel has long been a matter of dispute in Christian theology. Which comes first? Must sinners first be hammered by the reminder of how far short they fall of the law of God before their anguish is relieved by the message of God's grace and forgiveness to those who repent? Is proclamation and reception of the gospel to be quickly replaced by a set of commands that one follows out of a sense of obligation or even fear? Conversely, is the grace of God empty of all commands and the new life in Christ free of any divine directions? Or is it neither of these alternatives? Is not the reality of God's wondrous grace in creation and redemption what awakens in us an ever-widening sense of gratitude and responsibility to act and relate to others in a way that corresponds to the grace of God?

In modern theological ethics, the writings of Karl Barth and Paul Lehmann have been notable for accenting the priority of the gospel to the law.[9] When the love of God manifest in Jesus Christ is placed first, the point is in no way to diminish the law's importance. On the contrary, the motive and goal of obeying the law are now understood in proper perspective. As the writer of the First Letter of John declares, "We love because he first loved us" (1 John 4:19). The love of God casts out all fear that arises when we separate the law of God from the love of God proclaimed in the gospel.

Equally important, an ethics of appeal on the basis of love makes

---

8. Barth and Blanke, *Philemon,* 121.
9. Karl Barth, "Gospel and Law," in *Community, State, and Church,* ed. David Haddorff (Eugene, OR: Wipf & Stock, 1960), 71–100; Paul Lehmann, "The Foundation and Pattern of Christian Behavior," in *Christian Faith and Social Action,* ed. John A. Hutchison (New York: Charles Scribner's Sons, 1953), 93–116; also Lehmann, *Ethics in a Christian Context* (New York: Harper & Row, 1963).

room for consent; it looks for voluntary agreement, not a coerced response. But just what is the meaning of "consent," "voluntary agreement," and "free will" in this context? Surely these terms as used by Paul have nothing to do with the naked and absolutized human freedom celebrated by those who consider themselves to be, in the well-known declaration of William Ernest Henley, "the master of my fate, the captain of my soul." Rather, what Paul means by freedom and consent is the spontaneous and glad yes of a creature to the wondrous love of God the creator and redeemer. "For freedom Christ has set us free," Paul writes in Galatians 5:1. True human freedom is not a given but a gift. We need to be liberated by a power beyond ourselves from the many kinds of bondage that imprison human life.

An analogy might be suggested from aesthetic experience. When we find ourselves in the presence of a great work of art like van Gogh's *Sunflowers* or hear a special performance of a great musical composition like Brahms's *German Requiem,* it is not coercion we experience when we offer our thankful response. We freely and gladly say, "Yes, this moves me. This is indeed beautiful." Likewise, the grace of God is indeed "irresistible," as traditional Calvinist theologians have insisted, but not in the sense that we are compelled to comply with grace against our will. Rather, we are joyfully overwhelmed by God's benevolence and gladly give our consent to it. We freely choose to live in accordance with this gift as our good, fitting, and sensible response.

An ethics of appeal based on love unashamedly speaks to the emotional and affective as well as rational side of our humanity. In making his appeal, Paul is not afraid to speak from his heart to the heart of Philemon. To be sure, he advances reasons for his appeal. But powerfully at work in his appeal is the reason with which he begins and ends his letter: "grace . . . and peace from God our Father and the Lord Jesus Christ" (vv. 3, 25).

15–20

More Reasons for the Appeal

Verses 15-16. Having begun his appeal to Philemon by explaining that Onesimus has become a Christian and a valued assistant to Paul in his imprisonment, the apostle now gives additional reasons for the appeal. Note that Paul's readiness to give reasons for his request underscores the fact that he has no desire simply to issue commands like a military officer. Just as faith seeks understanding, responsible action goes hand in hand with deliberation. Paul wants to convince Philemon and the church in his house that the action he is requesting makes sense in the light of the gospel, that it is a good, fitting, and reasonable thing to do.

Prominent among the additional reasons Paul offers is the proposal that the separation of Onesimus from Philemon was according to God's plan. It was God's purpose to bring something good out of an event that seemed evil to Philemon. Paul presents the idea of God's agency not by explicitly naming God as the initiator of the flight of Onesimus but by using the passive voice to describe what happened: "he was separated" (v. 15). This is an example of what is called the divine passive, characteristic of the tendency in Scripture to avoid the use of the holy name of God by expressing the action of God in the passive voice. "Was separated," therefore, is not a crafty circumlocution for the statement "Onesimus ran away," as some commentators suggest. Rather the meaning is "Onesimus was separated from you according to God's will." To paraphrase: "My dear brother, ponder the likelihood that God has been secretly at work in Onesimus's separation from you."

If the widely accepted assumption that Onesimus had run away is correct, the notion that God was at work in this event can hardly have been Philemon's first thought when he learned that Onesimus had gone missing. By the time Philemon received Paul's letter, Onesimus would have been absent for some time. Philemon would understandably have been more than upset; he would likely have been angry and may have calculated the degree of severity with which he would discipline his slave when he returned or was captured. Paul, however, thought it was important for Philemon to consider the hand of God in the Onesimus affair.

When Paul says "perhaps" (*tacha*) God was at work in Onesimus's leaving Philemon's household, this is not because he is uncertain of God's purposeful activity in the life of individuals like Philemon and Onesimus or in the course of nature and history. Rather, we can best understand the use of "perhaps" here as both pastorally and theologically intended. Pastorally, it would serve as a gentle introduction to a way of viewing the events surrounding Onesimus that Philemon would at first have found jarring and irritating. Theologically, the "perhaps" is appropriate because Paul recognizes that God's ways are deeply mysterious and God's working unfathomable. This is the conclusion to which Paul comes in his remarkable reflections on the purposes of God in the history of the people of Israel: "O the depth of the riches and wisdom and knowledge of God! How unsearchable are his judgments and how inscrutable his ways!" (Rom. 11:33). The God of Israel is not tethered to our assumptions of the nature of God or what God should and should not do. God does new and surprising things.

Paul shares the bedrock conviction of the biblical witness that God is at work in the world to fulfill his purposes. When Abraham and Isaac journeyed to the land of Moriah to render the sacrifice that God had commanded, Isaac asked his father where the sacrificial lamb was. Abraham replied, "God himself will provide the lamb for a burnt offering, my son" (Gen. 22:8). When Joseph at last met his brothers who had sold him into slavery, he said, "Even though you intended to do harm to me, God intended it for good" (Gen. 50:20). Paul too had experienced the providential working of God. A persecutor of the church, his life was turned around when the risen Christ appeared to him on the road to Damascus and called him to be an apostle to the Gentiles. Throughout his many sufferings, he remained convinced that "in all things God works for good for those who love God, who are called according to his purpose" (Rom. 8:28).

Paul's reference in this passage to the providential activity of God is all the more striking when it is contrasted with the use of the doctrine of providence by defenders of slavery in the antebellum South. Their claim was that divine providence was evident in the evangelization and moral improvement of the slaves that slavery had made possible, as well as in the prosperity that slavery had brought to the South. Paul's doctrine of providence turns this argument on its head. Whereas the American apologists for slavery saw it as a divinely ordained institution and praised its benefits to the slaves and the prosperity that it brought to the South,[1] Paul sees the act of an AWOL slave as a working of divine providence.

FURTHER REFLECTIONS
Providence

Neither for Paul nor for later Christian theologians faithful to his teaching does affirmation of the providential rule of God mean that God is the *direct* cause of every event or that the actions and purposes of God are readily apparent for all to see. Moreover, belief in God's providential rule does not rule out or minimize the freedom and responsibility of human agents. Divine action and human action are not mutually exclusive.

In commenting on this section of Paul's Letter to Philemon, John Calvin, a strong believer in divine providence, notes Paul's effort to underscore the positive results of the flight of Onesimus from his master. An event that seemed to Philemon at first to be simply evil has been used by God to serve a good end. Onesimus has become "a new man," and Philemon has gained a new brother in Christ. Faith can discern in this episode

1. John Patrick Daly, *When Slavery Was Called Freedom: Evangelicalism, Proslavery, and the Causes of the Civil War* (Lexington: University of Kentucky Press, 2002).

recounted by the apostle the "marvelous" providential activity of God.[2]

In his frequent reflections on divine providence, Calvin distinguishes Christian faith in God's providential rule from the belief that everything happens by chance or is the result of an iron decree of fate. According to Calvin, the providence of God is aptly described as the guiding hand of a loving father or mother.[3] He famously summarizes the great benefits of this conviction as "gratitude of mind for the favorable outcome of things, patience in adversity, and also incredible freedom from worry about the future."[4] Emphatically denying that God is the author of evil, Calvin acknowledges that there are "secondary causes" of events, and insists that the often secret purposes of God are fulfilled in and through natural occurrences and human actions. Even if Calvin's critics find his efforts to uphold both the sovereign rule of God and human freedom in a world pervaded by evil to be unpersuasive, the claim that he encouraged an ethos of compliance with unjust conditions goes against the grain of both his teaching and his practice. For Calvin, patience in adversity is not the same as passivity or compliance with evil.[5]

For Karl Barth, who was also deeply influenced by Paul's theology, affirmation of the providential rule of God is altogether different from the idea that the creature is subject to God "like a puppet or tool or dead matter." The providential working of God, far from mechanical or tyrannical, is an ever-surprising drama of a free God with his free creatures. Because the God of providence is none other than the God whose humility in Jesus Christ extends even to death on a cross, we can be confident that God's sovereignty includes God's mercy. In Christ,

> **[God] rules in and over a world of freedom.**
>
> Karl Barth, *CD* III/3:93.

2. John Calvin, *The Second Epistle of Paul to the Corinthians, and the Epistles to Timothy, Titus, and Philemon,* CNTC 10, ed. David W. Torrance and Thomas F. Torrance (1964; repr., Grand Rapids: Eerdmans, 1979), 398.

3. B. A. Gerrish, *Grace and Gratitude: The Eucharistic Theology of John Calvin* (Minneapolis: Fortress, 1993), 27–31, 39–41.

4. John Calvin, *Institutes of the Christian Religion,* ed. John T. McNeill, trans. Ford Lewis Battles, LCC (Philadelphia: Westminster, 1960), 1:219.

5. See Nicholas Wolterstorff, "The Wounds of God: Calvin's Theology of Social Injustice," in *Hearing the Call: Liturgy, Justice, Church, and World* (Grand Rapids: Eerdmans, 2011), 114–32.

God becomes vulnerable, enters into solidarity with us to rescue us from the bondage of sin and death, and calls us to our true human freedom in Christ of faith, prayer, and service.[6]

Belief in divine providence is more than an arcane biblical conviction or a quaint staple of orthodox theology. It continues to influence personal and public life in the modern era. For a nation in the throes of civil war, Abraham Lincoln was not only president and commander in chief but also presiding pastor and theologian. In his magisterial second inaugural address, Lincoln spoke poignantly of the providence of God in a great conflict in which both adversaries read the same Bible and prayed to the same God. If we suppose, Lincoln said, that it was "in the providence of God" that the offense of American slavery came but that

> **The Almighty has his own purposes.**
>
> Abraham Lincoln, second inaugural address.

God now wills to remove it through this terrible war, then all must fervently pray that the war will speedily come to an end. Lincoln continued: "Yet if God wills that it continue, until all the wealth piled by the bond-man's two hundred and fifty years of unrequited toil shall be sunk, and until every drop of blood drawn with the lash, shall be paid by another drawn with the sword, as was said three thousand years ago, so still it must be said 'the judgments of the Lord, are true and righteous altogether.'" Lincoln ended his address with an appeal for reconciliation: "With malice toward none; with charity for all; with firmness in the right, as God gives us to see the right, let us strive on to finish the work we are in; to bind up the nation's wounds; to care for him who shall have borne the battle, and for his widow, and his orphan to do all which may achieve and cherish a just, and a lasting peace, among ourselves, and with all nations."[7]

To declare that God exercises providential care and rule even in events of terrible evil is a daunting claim. In the modern era, faithful

---

6. Barth, *CD* III/3:285. For Barth's description of the "twofold freedom" of God and humanity in the history of their relationship, see his exegesis of the book of Job in *CD* IV/3.1, 383–88, 398–408, 421–34, 453–61.

7. For the full text and insightful interpretation, see Ronald C. White Jr., *Lincoln's Greatest Speech: The Second Inaugural* (New York: Simon & Schuster, 2002).

Jews have wrestled with the credibility of belief in God's providence in relation to the Holocaust. More recently, Americans have had to wrestle with the question of God's goodness and sovereignty in the wake of the terrorist attacks of 9/11. If God is sovereign over the world God has created and redeemed, how do Christians speak of God and how do they respond in practice to such horrendous events?

One of the most thoughtful responses in the aftermath of 9/11 was that of Rowan Williams, archbishop of Canterbury, who was at Trinity Church in New York when the planes crashed into the Twin Towers nearby. Williams acknowledged that the great grief and burning anger occasioned by this terrible event were entirely understandable. He knew that the demand for immediate and massive retaliation would be great. There would be enormous satisfaction in mounting a rapid and devastating counterattack. After the experience of having lost control, a quick response to injuries we receive may make us feel we are in control once again. But Williams counseled that this impulse should be resisted. Not, of course, because he wanted to excuse wanton violence or to encourage resignation and passivity in the face of brutality and injustice. Rather, Williams advised his American friends to take time to think carefully about the origins of violence, about the best use of anger, and about the kind of response to this particular violent event that would most likely contribute to an outcome of justice and peace. He pleaded for "a breathing space," "long enough for some of our demons to walk away."[8] There are, he implied, secret purposes of God that only time discloses.

With his encouragement to Philemon to consider God's providence as the ultimate context of the events that occasioned his letter, Paul can be understood as creating some "breathing space" for Philemon in which the Spirit of Christ, the Spirit of forgiveness, reconciliation, and new life in inclusive community would have a chance to triumph over any thoughts of revenge or retaliation. Christian faith in divine providence is trust that God revealed decisively in Jesus Christ, while not the primary cause of all events, is

---

8. Rowan Williams, *Writing in the Dust* (Grand Rapids: Eerdmans, 2002), 78.

present and active in, with, and over the events of our lives, working
for the good in all things and bending them to the completion of
God's purposes.

Paul advances still another reason for Philemon to respond posi-
tively to Paul's appeal. He contrasts Onesimus's separation from
Philemon, which was only "for a while," with the far greater gain
for Philemon of having Onesimus back "forever." Having Onesimus
back forever means that as a member of Christ's body he is now
bound together with Paul, Philemon, and all the faithful for all eternity. Moreover, Philemon will have Onesimus back "no longer as a
slave but more than a slave, a beloved brother."

Probably more than any other verse of Paul's brief letter, verse 16
constitutes a kind of "hinge text" in its interpretation.[9] The words
"no longer as a slave but more than a slave, a beloved brother" bring
to a head the controversy about the real intent of Paul's intervention
on behalf of Onesimus. What does this much-debated statement
mean?

Peter O'Brien, together with many other scholars, notes that Paul
does not write "no longer a slave" but "no longer as [*hos*] a slave."[10]
The former reading elides an important word in the text and would
be equivalent to an unambiguous declaration of emancipation by
Paul. The proper reading is that Paul is asking Philemon no longer to
regard Onesimus "as a slave but more than a slave."

Does this mean, however, that for Paul the objective status of
Onesimus's bondage to his master is an indifferent matter, that his
participation in the new creation in Christ has no bearing whatever
on his worldly condition as a slave? Such an understanding of the
text seems to assume that, as Lohse puts it, while earthly freedom
is indeed a great good, "In the last analysis it is of no significance
to the Christian whether he is slave or free."[11] Is this not at best a
half-truth? If there are earthly things that are "great goods," can they
really be "of no significance," even "in the last analysis"? When Jesus

---

9. Carolyn Osiek, *Philippians, Philemon* (Nashville: Abingdon, 2000), 139.
10. Peter T. O'Brien, *Colossians, Philemon,* Word Biblical Commentary 44 (Waco, TX: Word
    Books, 1982), 296–97.
11. Eduard Lohse, *Colossians and Philemon* (Philadelphia: Fortress, 1971), 203.

commended those who feed the hungry and give water to the thirsty
(Matt. 25), he surely did not think of these earthly things as of no
significance "in the last analysis." Nor did Paul, who counseled that
"whenever we have an opportunity, let us work for the good of all,
and especially for those of the family of faith" (Gal. 6:10).

Hence when Paul urges Philemon to receive the returning Onesimus "no longer as a slave but more than a slave," when he asks Philemon to call his former slave "a beloved brother"—and not only a
beloved brother but one both "in the flesh" (*en sarki*) and "in the
Lord" (*en kyrio*)—there is far more going on here than the friendly
restoration of old relationships. Paul's emphatic "in the flesh and in
the Lord"—made all the more striking by placing "in the flesh" first—
underscores the earthly, here-and-now side of Paul's appeal alongside
its spiritual dimension. As Douglas Moo observes, "by adding 'in
the flesh'…Paul brings forcefully to Philemon's attention the implications of Onesimus's new status for their existing worldly relationship."[12] Philemon and other readers of the letter are being drawn into
the altogether new world of what Paul calls elsewhere God's "new
creation," where the old has passed and the new has arrived (2 Cor.
5:17). The new world of God inaugurated in Christ interrupts the old
and relegates it to the past (cf. Isa. 43:18–19; Rev. 21:5).

According to many NT scholars, there are several reasons why it
is a mistake to suggest that Paul, either here or elsewhere in the letter, even as much as hints at the idea of manumission to Philemon.[13]

A. One is that such a reading goes against the grain of Paul's theology of the Christian's relation to social and political institutions. In
his Letter to the Romans, Paul declares that the governing authorities have been instituted by God, and they are not to be resisted
(Rom. 13:1–7). Assuming that Paul is consistent, it follows that he
would oppose any effort to alter established institutions, such as slavery, in the name of obedience to Christ. Moreover, if Ephesians and
Colossians are accepted as written by Paul, they provide additional

12. See Douglas J. Moo, *The Letters to Colossians and to Philemon* (Grand Rapids: Eerdmans,
2008), 373; also Ben Witherington III, *The Letters to Philemon, the Colossians, and the
Ephesians: A Socio-Rhetorical Commentary on the Captivity Epistles* (Grand Rapids: Eerdmans,
2007), 80.
13. See the summary of the arguments pro and con in Markus Barth and Helmut Blanke,
The Letter to Philemon (Grand Rapids: Eerdmans, 2000), 412–15.

evidence of his social conservatism. The so-called household codes in these letters declare that slaves are to obey their masters and masters are to treat their slaves fairly (Col. 3:22–4:1; Eph. 6:5–9).

B. Another argument against the idea that Paul requested or even suggested the manumission of Onesimus is Paul's expectation of the coming of Christ in the very near future. The key passage here is 1 Corinthians 7:20–21: "Let each of you remain in the condition in which you were called. Were you a slave when called? Do not be concerned about it." The sentence that follows this verse has been translated in virtually opposite ways: "Even if you can gain your freedom, make use of your present condition now more than ever" (NRSV); "But if you can gain your freedom, avail yourself of the opportunity" (RSV). Obviously, those who dismiss any hints of manumission in the Letter to Philemon favor the first of these translations.

C. Still a third reason for dismissing the idea that Paul wanted Onesimus to be freed is that giving freedom to slaves in the Roman Empire was far from an obvious benefit. Where would they go? What would they do? How would they support themselves? In other words, there was unquestionably a high cost to manumission, and Paul may well have taken this into account in refraining from encouraging Christian slaves to seek their freedom.

A'. In response to the first argument, it must be conceded that Paul does not directly address the institution of slavery as such in this letter. He was no modern social reformer. The primary concern of Paul's letter is for the well-being of Onesimus and for the healing of the wounded relationship between him and Philemon. However, there is no reason Paul could not have appealed to Philemon to let the slave Onesimus go free without taking on the larger question of the theological legitimacy of the widespread practice of slavery.

Regarding the relationship of the Letter to Philemon, widely recognized as written by Paul, to the household codes of Ephesians and Colossians, whose authorship is less certain, the question is complex and controversial. The differences are unmistakable,[14] even if there is some truth in the judgment that the household codes are less about accommodating Christian teachings to surrounding cultural

---

14. See Joseph A. Fitzmyer, *The Letter to Philemon* (New York: Doubleday, 2000), 24.

conventions and more about trying to reform relationships within the Christian household in the direction of mutual love and mutual subordination according to the model of the self-subordination and self-giving of Christ for our sake.[15] Rather than adjusting the message of the Letter to Philemon to the household codes, it makes far more sense to read it in the light of 1 Corinthians 7:21, where, according to respected translations (RSV) of this disputed text, Paul encourages Christian slaves to take advantage of an opportunity to gain their freedom if such should arise.

B'. In regard to Paul's expectation of the imminent return of Christ, this is undoubtedly a strong and pervasive part of Paul's theology and preaching. Such expectation, however, need not be equated with indifference to concern for justice and freedom in the here and now prior to the coming of Christ in glory. True, some forms of eschatological hope lead to passive waiting for the end; others, however, are compatible with or even generative of passion for greater justice, freedom, and peace in the world in preparation for God's renewal of all things.[16]

C'. As for the precarious status of the freed slave in the Roman Empire, the point can be granted; but again, Paul's attention is on Onesimus, and in his letter Paul is clear that he would be pleased to have Onesimus return as his assistant in his imprisonment and in his work on behalf of the gospel. There is absolutely no basis in the letter for thinking that Paul would simply abandon Onesimus should he be freed.

Dietrich Bonhoeffer contended that Christian theology and ethics must distinguish what is ultimate and what is penultimate without separating them.[17] These realities must be properly ordered to each other. That we pray and wait for God's coming kingdom (our ultimate hope) rather than thinking we can ourselves bring it to pass does not mean that we are not called to faithfulness in life and service here and now in preparation for that coming reign (our

15. See Ben Witherington III, *Philemon, Colossians, and Ephesians,* 321: "Paul is trying to model household relationships on the servant-like and self-sacrificial relationship of Christ to his church"; C. Osiek, "The Ephesian Household Code," *The Bible Today* 36 (1998).

16. For a classic statement of such an understanding of Christian hope, see Jürgen Moltmann, *Theology of Hope* (New York: Harper & Row, 1967).

17. Dietrich Bonhoeffer, *Ethics* (New York: Macmillan, 1955), 84-100.

penultimate responsibility). Paul does not confuse the penultimate with the ultimate, but neither does he dismiss the importance of loving the neighbor and working for greater justice and peace when these are properly understood as signs of and preparations for the coming reign of God.

FURTHER REFLECTIONS
Beloved Brother

When Paul calls on Philemon to welcome Onesimus as a "beloved brother," "both in the flesh and in the Lord," and when he declares elsewhere that "for freedom Christ has set us free" (Gal. 5:1) and that in Christ "there is no longer slave or free" (Gal. 3:28), does Paul mean that all are one in Christ spiritually but that this reality has no bearing on the physical and social conditions in which people live? Did Paul feel the contradiction his readers today feel in recognizing a person as, on the one hand, a "beloved brother" in Christ, both "in the flesh" and "in the Lord," and, on the other, owning that person as an object under one's complete control? Exegetical disputes have swirled around these questions for centuries.

Ben Witherington, among other commentators, rightly challenges the strictly spiritual interpretation of Paul's appeal to Philemon. According to Witherington, "Philemon 16 is the only place in the NT that a slave is directly called a brother, and this fact must be allowed to have its full force. . . . Onesimus is now to become a brother to Philemon, not merely in a spiritual sense ('in the Lord') but also 'in the flesh,' that is, in his physical and social condition and location."[18]

Readers should not overlook the power of the word "beloved" (*agapeton*) as used in this passage. Indeed, it deserves special attention. Paul speaks of both Philemon and Onesimus as "beloved" (vv. 2, 16 RSV). Elsewhere he calls Timothy (1 Cor. 4:17), Epaenetus, Ampliatus, Stachys, and Persis (Rom. 16:5, 8, 9, 12) "beloved." The name "beloved" for Paul designates all the saints, all who are

---

18. Witherington, *Philemon, Colossians, and Ephesians*, 80.

in Christ. They are beloved by Paul himself, but even more funda-
mentally they are beloved by God. Jews and Christians in Christ are
God's people, people who were not beloved but whom God has
called beloved (Rom. 9:24–26).

What must it mean to a *slave* to be called a beloved child of God
and a beloved brother or sister of all who confess Christ as Lord?
What must being called a beloved brother or beloved sister mean
to any person's sense of worth, dignity, and self-respect, and especially to one who has experienced living on the outermost margins
of society? By the same token, what kind of conversion is entailed
for a slaveholder, even one who has treated his slaves with civil-
ity and kindness, to come to the realization that former slaves are
beloved of God, persons for whom Christ died, and persons who
have received the gift of God's Spirit and are now beloved brothers
and sisters in Christ? What are the transforming effects of naming
another, or being named by another, "beloved," and what are the
devastating effects of withholding this name from, or being denied
this name by, another?

Can one read Paul's Letter to Philemon and its description of
Onesimus as "beloved brother" with the same eyes after reading
Toni Morrison's novel *Beloved*? Set in the middle 1850s after the passage of the Fugitive Slave Law, the story depicts the unspeakable
and lasting effects of slavery on the mind, soul, and body of Sethe, a
runaway slave mother of four children. When cornered and about to
be captured and returned to her owner, Sethe cuts the throat of her
youngest daughter, an act of desperation to protect her children
from what she considers the even worse fate of being returned to
the horrors of slavery. She later has the name "Beloved" inscribed on
her child's tombstone and remains haunted by her shocking deed.
The deeply unsettling novel ends with the question whether or not
it is "a story to pass on."[19]

"Beloved"—the name that American slave owners would never
have dreamed of calling Sethe and her children, the name that Sethe
has inscribed on the tombstone of her infant daughter whose ghost
haunts her for years—is the very name Paul appeals to Philemon to

19. Toni Morrison, *Beloved* (New York: Plume, 1988).

give freely to Onesimus. Among other reasons, this is why the letter
Paul writes is indeed a story to pass on.

Verse 17. Paul continues his appeal: if you think of yourself as my "partner," then welcome Onesimus as you would welcome me. As he did earlier in speaking of Onesimus as "my own heart" (v. 12), Paul again identifies himself closely with Onesimus. Recall that at the beginning of the letter, Paul has described Philemon as his "beloved fellow worker" (v. 2 RSV). Twice in the letter he calls Philemon "brother" (vv. 7, 20). Now Paul asks Philemon to let their partnership, their sharing in the gospel, become manifest in a love that embraces Onesimus. Treat him as you would treat me, Paul says. "Welcome him as you would welcome me." The appeal is similar to Paul's exhortation in another letter: "Welcome one another, therefore, just as Christ has welcomed you, for the glory of God" (Rom. 15:7).

Verses 18–19. Paul now offers his final reason why his appeal on behalf of Onesimus is both reasonable and fitting. If Philemon has been injured financially by Onesimus, Paul will repay the cost. "I will repay it," Paul assures Philemon. What does Paul have in mind here? Traditional interpretations of the letter often assumed that Onesimus had stolen money or articles from Philemon's home. However, nothing is said in the letter that requires this conclusion. Paul does not say he knows that Onesimus has stolen from Philemon or done anything else to directly injure him. His statement is a hypothetical: "*If* he has wronged you in any way, or owes you anything . . . I will repay." Paul is prepared to make up for whatever loss Philemon has sustained. The most likely meaning of Paul's gesture is that he knows that the absence of Onesimus from Philemon's household would at the very least mean that Philemon had been deprived of the services he had a right to expect of his slave.

Paul's "I will repay" is, as Nordling aptly describes it, "a dramatization of the gospel."[20] Paul is ready to put himself and his resources on the line for a brother in Christ just as Christ put his life on the line, even to death on a cross, for our salvation. Paul not only speaks the gospel, "Welcome him" (v. 17); he also acts out the gospel in his

20. John G. Nordling, *Philemon* (St. Louis: Concordia, 2004), 328; also "The Gospel in Philemon," *Concordia Theological Quarterly* 71 (2007): 71–83.

own life. "Be imitators of me," he exhorts the Corinthians, "as I am of Christ" (1 Cor. 11:1).

After declaring "I will repay," Paul makes a noteworthy parenthetical remark: "to say nothing of your owing me even your own self" (v. 19 RSV). From this aside we may infer that Paul had been responsible for the conversion not only of Onesimus but of Philemon as well. They had both been brought to Christ by Paul and were therefore both "children" of Paul, although Paul never uses that term of Philemon. Is Paul's aside a sly form of pressure on his part, a bit of gentle arm-twisting? Some readers may think so. I would suggest it is more likely another instance of friendly humor, like the earlier play on Onesimus's name, in an otherwise weighty letter. Humor is not out of place in serious theology or earnest pastoral care. It can be a sign that there is a grace at work in our efforts that is not dependent on our intellectual agility or rhetorical skills.

Verse 20. Summing up his appeal, Paul writes: "Yes, brother, let me have this benefit from you in the Lord! Refresh my heart in Christ." The language here reminds the reader of what was said early in the letter. Recall that Paul warmly commended Philemon for the good he had already done by sharing his faith in Christ and showing his love for all the saints (v. 7). To paraphrase Paul: "Let me also be a recipient of your generosity and love. Refresh my heart as you have so often refreshed the hearts—lifted the spirits, encouraged the hopes—of so many of the saints in your community. Your goodness to others is laudable and well known. Include me too among the recipients of your generosity by honoring my appeal for brother Onesimus."

FURTHER REFLECTIONS
Justice in Love

Paul is unquestionably the apostle of the grace of God. "Grace" is the signature word in his theological vocabulary. Yet for Paul the superabounding grace of God is neither cheap nor oblivious to the concerns of justice. Grace includes rather than dismisses the call that justice be done. The love of God is both merciful *and* just.

While Paul does not speak directly of justice in the Letter to Philemon, the issue of justice is not far beneath the surface. Paul's doctrine of God's gracious justification of the ungodly (Rom. 4:5) has a

> **Justice is love correcting that which revolts against love.**
>
> Martin Luther King Jr., speech in Montgomery, Alabama, Dec. 5, 1955.

bearing not only on our standing before God and our hope for the world to come but also on the cause of justice in this world.

Paul is first of all concerned that justice be done to Onesimus as a human being who is a child of God and a brother in Christ. His letter appeals to Philemon to be generous, forgiving, and welcoming to Onesimus, who not only has become a Christian but also has become a useful servant to Paul in his ministry. Also important to emphasize, however, is that welcoming a brother in Christ is not just an act of love but an act of *just* love. It is both the loving and the right thing to do. If God has acted justly in extending reconciling love not to Jews alone but also to all the "ungodly" (Rom. 4:5; 5:6), to both Jew and Gentile, and if Philemon has acted justly in extending his love not only to a favorite few but to "all the saints" (v. 5), Paul is now appealing to Philemon to let his love for all the saints continue to be just by God's standards by also embracing Onesimus as his new brother.[21]

At the same time, Paul does not ignore the fact that Philemon may have sustained unspecified losses because of the absence of Onesimus. The apostle takes this possibility seriously. His promise, "I will repay," is a practical demonstration that his theology of grace is not dismissive of justice claims even for those ensnared in a system of injustice. He does not tell Philemon that if he has been damaged in any way, well, that is his own business, and he will have to deal with it as best he can. On the contrary, Paul couples his appeal to Philemon's generosity with a promise to repay any expenses Philemon may have suffered on Onesimus's account. Throughout the letter, Paul's expression of love for both Onesimus and Philemon has a justice dimension.

Understood in this way, Paul's promise to Philemon, "I will repay," is a striking expression of the inseparability of love, justice, and

---

21. On the harmony of love and justice, see Nicholas Wolterstorff, *Justice in Love* (Grand Rapids: Eerdmans, 2011).

> **[Paul] offers to subsidize the cost of justice, because without justice there is no peace, and without peace between the brethren there can be no ministry.**
>
> Allen Callahan, "The Letter of Paul to Philemon," in *The New Interpreter's Study Bible* (Nashville: Abingdon, 2003), 2148.

peace, both in the redemptive work of Christ and in our participation in the new life in him. Paul's willingness to pay for the expenses that Onesimus has, or at least may have, incurred would be totally misunderstood if it were viewed as a kind of slick bargaining chip to complete a deal. Paul knows that where justice is ignored, gestures of love are superficial and lasting peace is impossible.

Paul thinks and acts here and elsewhere with utmost theological integrity. His doctrines of atonement in Christ, of justification by grace through faith, and of participation in the new life in Christ stand in the background when he promises to repay whatever Onesimus may owe. In his Preface to the Letter to Philemon, Luther famously observes that in the letter Paul is acting in imitation of Christ: "What Christ has done for us with God the Father, that St. Paul does also for Onesimus with Philemon."[22] In other words, Paul fully identifies himself with the slave Onesimus and goes so far as to assume responsibility for his debt to Philemon. Luther's insightful observation about the Christlike character of Paul's promise to Philemon could also be extended to other relationships in the letter. The pattern of imitation of Christ is not limited to what Paul is willing to do. Philemon, too, is given the opportunity of participating in the way of Christ by welcoming both Onesimus and Paul as Christ has welcomed us all. And on at least one occasion in the letter, even Onesimus is described as taking part in the self-giving work of Christ. Recall that according to Paul, the service rendered by Onesimus represents what Philemon himself is unable to do on behalf of the imprisoned Paul and the work of the gospel. This remarkable "triangularity" of the relationship between Paul, Philemon, and Onesimus is marked through and through by the account of the grace of God in Christ

22. Martin Luther, "Preface to the Epistle of St. Paul to Philemon," in *Word and Sacrament* 1, ed. E. Theodore Bachmann, LW 35 (Philadelphia: Fortress, 1960), 390.

Jesus and its exhortation to a corresponding form of life among his followers.[23]

The relationship of God's mercy and God's righteousness, of justification by grace and the call to do justice, remains today among the most neglected and misunderstood aspects of life in Christ. What God has done for us in Christ—justified us by grace through Christ's atoning life and death—calls forth a life in Christ that bears witness to him not only in word but also in corresponding practices of reconciliation, deeds of love, and acts of justice making. The Christian life is to be a reflection of the work of God in Christ. God's generosity to us calls forth a corresponding if always imperfect life of generosity on our part. Justification calls forth justice. Not despite the fact of God's justification of the ungodly but precisely in correspondence with it, the church must stand for justice not only in the way it orders its own life but also in its witness and service in the wider public spheres of life as well.[24]

---

23. Nordling, "Gospel in Philemon," 78–82.
24. See Karl Barth, "The Christian Community and the Civil Community," in *Community, State, and Church* (1960; repr., Eugene, OR: Wipf & Stock, 2004): "The church must stand for social justice in the political sphere" (173).

Paul's Hope to Visit Philemon

Verse 21. As he draws his letter to a close, Paul expresses confidence in Philemon's "obedience" and is certain that he will do "even more" than Paul has asked. To some commentators, the use of the word "obedience" here seems to undercut Paul's earlier claim that, rather than issuing commands, he wants Philemon to respond freely. Did not Paul say that he preferred to do nothing rather than dictate what Philemon should do? What else does "obedience" mean, readers might ask, other than submitting to someone in authority, whether one wants to or not? In the Bible, however, true obedience and true freedom are not viewed as mutually exclusive. Obedience in Christian life is not the same as grudging compliance to a burdensome order or unwilling submission to a superior power. God's grace sets us free, and our freedom takes the shape of free and glad obedience to God's will that Jesus summarizes as love of God and love of neighbor. Just for this reason, Paul can speak of "the obedience of faith" (Rom. 1:5; 16:26) and never considers such obedience to be in conflict with genuine human freedom. Specifically, Paul thinks of the obedience of Jesus Christ recounted in the Christ hymn as paradigmatic. It was not from necessity or obligation or in response to an alien command that Jesus emptied and humbled himself, becoming "obedient to the point of death—even death on a cross" (Phil. 2:5–8). Jesus' act of obedience is a free act. Among the Gospel writers, it is John who underscores the fact that the passion

> Love God, and do what you will.
>
> Augustine, *Homilies on I John* 7.8.

events are not things done to Jesus as an unwilling victim, kicking and screaming on his way to the cross. What he undergoes he freely endures for our sake (cf. John 12:27). Paul and John are in complete agreement that Jesus' obedience and freedom are intertwined.

When Paul says he is confident in Philemon's obedience, it is important to understand on what this confidence ultimately rests. As Paul emphasizes, his confidence is first of all "in the Lord" (v. 20). He expresses the same Christ-based confidence to the Galatians: "I have confidence in the Lord that you will take no other view than mine" (Gal. 5:10 RSV). It is because Paul trusts in Christ and his transforming work that he is confident Philemon will do "even more" than Paul has explicitly asked. What is the "even more"? Is it what Paul has intimated early in the letter, but never spelled out, when he prayed that Philemon would discern "all the good" that is in Christ? Might Paul's "even more" have included the hope that Philemon would send Onesimus back to Paul to assist him in his imprisonment and ongoing ministry? Did the "even more" stretch all the way to giving Onesimus his freedom? As conceded earlier, by the very nature of this letter in which Paul gently leads his readers rather than barking commands like a field general, we cannot say the manumission of Onesimus is more than a strong possibility of Paul's appeal out of love. On the other hand, why should such a possibility, indeed likelihood, be ruled out? Is there not much in Paul's proclamation and practice of the gospel in this letter and elsewhere that bends in this direction?[1]

Verse 22. "One thing more," Paul now adds. He asks Philemon to prepare a guest room for him because he is hopeful that, with the help of the prayers of Philemon and other members of the house church, he will be coming to visit them. This final request may seem mundane and almost trivial, but there is more to it than making a reservation at a bed and breakfast. Paul is alerting Philemon that he will be coming to his home soon and will see for himself how Philemon has responded to the appeal of his letter. Does that put pressure on Philemon? From one perspective, it may seem so. But Paul dispels the idea that the announcement of his coming is a veiled threat by describing

---

1. "While perhaps not the focus of Paul's concern, the emancipation of Onesimus, we feel, is an action indivisible from what Paul hopes Philemon will do." Moo, *Colossians and Philemon*, 436.

it as an answer to the prayers of Philemon and the church in his house. Moreover, given the tenor of the letter, we can surmise that Paul does not want to talk past Philemon. He is eager for an additional opportunity to converse person to person with him, to say more about "all the good" we have in Christ and to listen to Philemon's account of the "more" he may be planning to do on Onesimus's behalf.

Hospitality was commonly extended to fellow Christians in the early church. Paul encourages Christians in Rome to "welcome one another, therefore, just as Christ has welcomed you, for the glory of God" (Rom. 15:7). Furthermore, welcome was extended in the early church not only to apostles and other fellow Christians, but even to strangers. As the writer of the Letter to the Hebrews urges, "Do not neglect to show hospitality to strangers, for by doing that some have entertained angels without knowing it" (Heb. 13:2). Finally, note also that in requesting hospitality and welcome for himself at the end of a letter appealing for a show of hospitality to Onesimus, Paul once again places himself alongside the new brother. Paul thus makes the two acts of hospitality—to Onesimus and to himself—virtually indistinguishable. To the end, Paul remains vigilant in his concern for the well-being and growth in Christ of both brothers, Onesimus and Philemon.

FURTHER REFLECTIONS
Even More

The basis of Paul's confidence that Philemon and indeed every Christian will do "even more" is the inexhaustible reality of God's goodness and mercy in Christ. "Where sin increased," Paul rejoices, "grace abounded all the more" (Rom. 5:20). Because of *this* "even more" of the grace of God, there are fresh and unexpected openings for witness and work in anticipation of the coming reign of God.

In famously declaring that "God is always greater" (*Deus semper maior*) than we think or imagine, Augustine was expressing this "even more" of the goodness and grace of God.[2] Augustine's

---

2. Augustine, *Expositions on the Psalms*, Psalm 63 (*NPNF*[1] 8:262).

declaration echoes the word of the Lord according to Isaiah: "As the heavens are higher than the earth, so are my ways higher than your ways, and my thoughts than your thoughts" (Isa. 55:9). It also reflects the cry of Paul at the conclusion of his meditation on the ways of God with the people of Israel: "O the depth of the riches and wisdom and knowledge of God! How unsearchable are his judgments and inscrutable his ways!" (Rom. 11:33). God is not only always greater than our thoughts of God; God also always does more than we think God is capable of doing. God is not only majestic and strong but can also become weak and lowly in Christ (1 Cor. 1:27). God is not only infinitely rich but can also in Christ become poor for our sake (2 Cor. 8:9). God's "even more" is the power of the "even more" of what Christians may become in and do for Christ.

For a final time we ask: What did Paul precisely intend by speaking of the "even more" he was confident Philemon would do? And if Philemon did in fact do "even more," what was it that he did? As we have noted more than once in our reflection on Paul's brief letter, we cannot answer such questions with certainty. Tradition has it that Onesimus eventually became bishop of Colossae. If this is what happened, the "even more" that Philemon did was to set Onesimus free and to send him back to Paul for missionary service. But there is no way to prove or disprove this possibility. The Letter to Philemon thus leaves us with an open ending. In the final analysis our conjectures and speculations about what Paul *really* intended or what Philemon *really* did must come to an end. What still remains open and unfinished about the "even more" is whether *we* will rise to the challenge to pray and to do "even more" in and for Christ, to do justice, to love mercy, and to walk humbly with our God, the God of superabounding grace, the God of the impossible possibility.

But, it might fairly be asked, are there not limits to the "even more" that we are called to hope, pray, and work for? Must we not consider the circumstances under which we find ourselves? Must we not be realistic in our Christian discipleship? Must we not heed the voices of "Christian realism" that warn of the serious consequences of marching to the drummers of idealistic efforts to bring in the kingdom of God, to conquer evil once and for all, to construct on our own a new and perfect world of justice, freedom, and peace?[3] The warning is important. The powers and principalities of this world are fierce and formidable. Polyannaish attitudes are no boon to the service of Christ. Individual Christians and the church as a whole need to consider well the harsh realities of a world resistant to the reign of God. Moreover, we must never confuse God's promise to make all things new with what is possible for us on this side of Christ's coming in glory. Much zealotry in the name of the good as we perceive it has often been the incubator of a spirit of self-righteousness that is far from what Paul calls "the righteousness from God" (Phil. 3:9).

While all of this is true, we must nevertheless look for the concrete possibilities, however small, that God makes available to us here and now to love others and to lend our support in the cause of greater justice and peace. Confidence in the "even more" of God's grace and glad acceptance of the call to pray and do even more in the service of Christ are indelible marks of the faithful Christian life.

> In a broken and fearful world the Spirit gives us courage to pray without ceasing, to witness among all peoples to Christ as Lord and Savior, to unmask idolatries in Church and culture, to hear the voices of peoples long silenced, and to work with others for justice, freedom, and peace.
>
> A Brief Statement of Faith, in *The Constitution of the Presbyterian Church (U.S.A.)*, Part I, *Book of Confessions*, 10.4.

Are not times like ours of lowering expectations and declining hopes precisely when the church needs to have the confidence to do even more in witness to Christ, in the work for peace, in the struggle for racial, gender, social, and economic justice, in the effort to assist the poor and the forgotten? Is not our time of economic and spiritual recession precisely the time when church leaders should encourage church members and church members should encourage one another to live lives that are not merely socially respectable, or that meet minimal Christian standards of discipleship, but are marked by the call to be and do even more in Christ? We are *in via;* we have not yet arrived at the goal (see Phil. 3:12-14). This side of the Lord's return, we must always be prepared to pray for and do "even more." There

---

3. See Reinhold Niebuhr, *Christian Realism and Political Problems* (New York: Scribner, 1953).

is always more boldness in proclaiming the gospel to be exercised, more forgiveness of enemies to be offered and hospitality to strangers to be shown, more care for the weak and the sick to be provided, more justice and peace for which to struggle. Whether Paul fully grasped the incongruity of the practice of slavery with the gospel of freedom will continue to be debated. One thing is certain, however. Rooted in his own time and place, Paul continues to proclaim the living word of God to the church, and not least in his concluding word of confidence that, empowered by the grace of God, Philemon—and by extension, Christians of every time and place— will do even more than Paul has explicitly asked, even more to discern, take part in, and share with others "*all* the good" that is in Christ.

23–25

Final Greetings and Benediction

Verses 23–24. As in his other letters, Paul concludes this one by conveying greetings from those around him: in this instance, from a fellow prisoner, Epaphras, and from four coworkers: Mark, Aristarchus, Demas, and Luke. Paul never misses an opportunity to strengthen the bonds of friendship and mutual care in the body of Christ. He is never parsimonious in publicly recognizing and thanking those who faithfully serve the Lord.

Verse 25. Just as he began the letter, Paul's final words are a benediction. The start and the end of the letter thus embrace its content in the strong and joyful prayer: "the grace of the Lord Jesus Christ be with your spirit."

Selected Bibliography

Barth, Markus, and Helmut Blanke. *The Letter to Philemon.* Grand
   Rapids: Eerdmans, 2000.

Callahan, Allen Dwight. *Embassy of Onesimus: The Letter of Paul to
   Philemon.* Valley Forge, PA: Trinity, 1997.

Calvin, John. *The Second Epistle of Paul to the Corinthians, and the
   Epistles to Timothy, Titus, and Philemon.* Edited by David W.
   Torrance and Thomas F. Torrance. CNTC 10. Reprint, Grand
   Rapids: Eerdmans, 1979.

Cousar, Charles B. *Philippians and Philemon.* New Testament
   Library. Louisville, KY: Westminster John Knox Press, 2009.

Donfried, Karl P., and I. Howard Marshall. *The Theology of the
   Shorter Pauline Letters.* New York: Cambridge University
   Press, 1993.

Felder, Cain Hope. "Philemon," in *New Interpreter's Bible,* vol. 11
   (Nashville: Abingdon, 2000).

Fitzmyer, Joseph A. *The Letter to Philemon.* Anchor Bible. New
   York: Doubleday, 2000.

Glancy, Jennifer A. *Slavery as Moral Problem in the Early Church and
   Today.* Minneapolis: Fortress, 2011.

Harrill, J. Albert. *Slaves in the New Testament: Literary, Social, and
   Moral Dimensions.* Minneapolis: Fortress, 2006.

Lohse, Eduard. *Colossians and Philemon.* Translated by William P.
   Poehlmann and Robert J. Karris. Hermeneia. Philadephia:
   Fortress, 1971.

Luther, Martin. *Luther's Works.* Edited by Jaroslav Pelikan. 55 vols.
   St. Louis: Concordia; Philadelphia: Muhlenberg/Fortress,
   1958–1986.

Moo, Douglas J. *The Letters to the Colossians and to Philemon.* Grand
     Rapids: Eerdmans, 2008.
Nordling, John G. "The Gospel in Philemon." *Concordia
     Theological Quarterly* 71 (2000): 71–83.
——. *Philemon.* St. Louis: Concordia, 2004.
Osiek, Carolyn. *Philippians, Philemon.* Nashville: Abingdon, 2000.
Witherington, Ben, III. *The Letters to Philemon, the Colossians, and
     the Ephesians: A Socio-Rhetorical Commentary on the Captivity
     Epistles.* Grand Rapids: Eerdmans, 2007.
Wright, N. T. *The Epistles of Paul to the Colossians and to Philemon.*
     Grand Rapids: Eerdmans, 1986.

Afterword

In his little book *Evangelical Theology*, Karl Barth describes the task of biblical exegesis as involving "minute attention" and "bold imagination." Whether my proffered theological interpretation in the preceding commentaries has come anywhere near this high standard, my readers will have to decide. In any case, my intent has been to hold this standard before me as I prepared these commentaries.

One lasting impression that I take away from the study of the Letter to the Philippians is the sheer humanity of the apostle Paul both in his preaching of Christ and in his exercise of pastoral responsibilities. I do not find here either the porcelain saint of his hagiographers or the authoritarian personality of his detractors. Paul is an apostle of Jesus Christ, full of wonder at the grace and humility of God, joyful in the service of his crucified and risen Lord, excoriating those who threaten the purity of the gospel but commending whatever is just and true in the world, thankful for the generosity of friends in Christ but eager to guard his own independence and the freedom of the gospel, a teacher who admits serious mistakes in his past ways of thinking about God and who keeps moving forward in faith because he has not yet reached the fullness of the knowledge of God in Christ or the power of his resurrection.

Although I have long known the great Christ hymn of Philippians 2:5–11, studying it more closely in the context of the letter as a whole was a richly rewarding experience for me. Above all, the seamless bond in the letter between this compact but unforgettable confession and the exhortations of Paul to a life worthy of the gospel made an indelible impression. Were Christians to take the Letter to the Philippians to heart, personally and corporately, were they to indwell it and live out its message, would there not be greater unity of doctrine and life, less division of believing and acting, and far less dreariness and far more joy in Christian witness and service?

A number of surprises awaited me in working on the commentary on Philemon. I had expected that there would be considerable debate in the literature on whether Paul did or did not press for Onesimus's freedom, and this was indeed the case. I had also expected that the historical arguments both pro and con would be inconclusive, and again I was not disappointed. Surprising, however, is the extent to which this question has tended to edge out reflection on the theological and ethical challenges the letter presents to readers today when it is read with minute attention and bold imagination.

There are, of course, many things one might have wished to find in the letter that are not present, at least not explicitly. I trust it is not impious to say I wish that Paul had allowed the voice of Onesimus himself to be heard in the letter in one form or another. Today Christians confess the importance of letting voices long silent be heard both in the church and in the wider society. Paul speaks passionately and eloquently on behalf of Onesimus. What a benefit it would have been if we had also heard the voice of Onesimus speaking for himself, however briefly.

One can also wonder whether the force of Paul's appeal might have been magnified had he drawn explicitly from his theology of baptism and the Lord's Supper in the letter. Given Paul's rich understanding of baptism, how effective it would have been to remind Philemon that Onesimus, by virtue of his baptism, was now "beloved brother" and one with Paul and Philemon in Christ.

The same is true of participation in the Lord's Supper. Since Onesimus was now a Christian and was to be welcomed back into Philemon's household as a brother in Christ, must not that welcome also have included sharing in the common meal of our Lord? This meal, Paul tells us elsewhere, is a common sharing in Christ and his self-giving love. At the Lord's Table, we are all guests, and all invidious classifications, especially that of master and slave, belong to the past. The participation in and practice of union in Christ that occurs at the Lord's Supper, together with the proclamation of the gospel, subverts and transcends all divisions of people based on class, race, ethnicity, gender, or any other wall of separation.

Quite possibly, however, I am tilting at windmills. Paul not only did say many of these things in other letters but may well have said some of them and even more to Philemon, if in God's providence he was able in fact to visit his friend and rejoice with him in the full inclusion of Onesimus in God's household of faith. In any case, the Letter to Philemon continues to encourage Christians today to live up to Paul's confidence that we will do "even more" in witnessing to the gospel of reconciliation in Christ, in extending hospitality in his name to all people, and in praying and working for greater justice, peace, and freedom in anticipation of God's making all things new.

Index of Scripture

Index of Subjects